CHARIOT

CHARIOT

FROM CHARIOT TO TANK,
THE ASTOUNDING RISE AND FALL OF
THE WORLD'S FIRST WAR MACHINE

ARTHUR COTTERELL

THE OVERLOOK PRESS
WOODSTOCK & NEW YORK

First published in the United States in 2005 by
The Overlook Press, Peter Mayer Publishers, Inc.
Woodstock & New York

WOODSTOCK:
One Overlook Drive
Woodstock, NY 12498

NEW YORK:
141 Wooster Street
New York, NY 10012

Manufactured in the United States of America
ISBN 1-58567-667-5

Contents

List of Maps

Preface

This book has been a decade in the making. Its genesis was a suggestion from Professor Robert Drews of Vanderbilt University in Nashville, following publication in 1993 of his *The End of the Bronze Age*, a work which finally blew away the cobwebs of systems collapse, climate change and earthquake activity then obscuring the destruction visited upon the eastern Mediterranean by the Sea Peoples. As its subtitle made clear, *Changes in Warfare and the Catastrophe ca. 1200 BC*, itinerant foot soldiers were the chief cause of breakdown for its palace-centred states. Their overwhelming assaults on chariotries, described by contemporaries as 'swarms', represented a serious setback for what was the mobile arm of ancient armies. When I pointed out a parallel experience in China, and expressed my regret that there was no treatment of the chariot across the Old World, Professor Drews agreed that 'a multi-cultural perspective' was missing and suggested that I might tackle the task.

Our exchange of letters was enough to set me thinking about the chariot: the when, where, how and why of that truly astounding invention, the world's first war machine. Much research later, *Chariot* offers an account of its rise and fall in Europe, West Asia, Egypt, India and China. I remain very grateful for the original suggestion, not least because it led to a fascinating period of investigation. I am also indebted to Professor Drews for the points he raised when he read the manuscript of this book. My thanks are also due to Professor John Brockington of Edinburgh University for his recommendations concerning Indian sources. Without the assistance of Ashley Jones, whose bookshop close to the British Museum was once a veritable treasure trove for the student of ancient history, the illustrations so expertly drawn by Ray Dunning would be less extensive. Closer to home I must express my gratitude to an old friend, Clifford Cope, and my wife, Yong Yap, for invaluable help with translation.

I would also like to express appreciation for the tolerance shown over the years by Lawrence Hardwicke, chairman of Kingston College, as well as other governors, towards my writing. Their positive attitude has permitted me to combine senior management with the pursuit of knowledge across a range of topics, in this instance the chariot. It stands out, I believe, as an example of enlightened governance in further education.

Kingston upon Thames, 2004

Introduction

The first, and most charismatic, war machine ever invented, the chariot altered the face of war throughout the ancient world. Its impact was dramatic as thousands of chariots clashed in fast-moving encounters which determined the outcome of battle. At Kadesh, in 1274 BC, the young pharaoh Ramesses II was surprised by 3,500 chariots in a trap carefully laid by King Muwatalli II of Hatti. Only a series of desperate counter-attacks, led by Ramesses in his own golden chariot, prevented an utter rout. In the swirling chariot battle the Egyptian archers held off their opponents until an allied relief column arrived to distract Muwatalli's chariotry. Then a concerted charge by Ramesses succeeded in breaking its formation, so that the Hittite charioteers and chariot warriors abandoned their vehicles on the bank of the Orontes river, and 'plunged like crocodiles face first into its waters'. Some 5,000 chariots participated in this great battle.

Records of chariot battle are most detailed in West Asia and China, to which this revolutionary method of warfare spread. In chapter 1 the realities of charioteering on the battlefield are examined at Kadesh and Megiddo in West Asia and at Chengpu and Bi in China. In 1918 the English general Allenby copied the tactics of Thutmose III at Megiddo and outflanked two Turkish armies. Cavalry was fed through the same narrow pass which the Egyptian pharaoh had used in 1460 BC to surprise his Canaanite enemies. The Chinese clashes were two of 'the five great battles' of the Spring and Autumn period (770–481 BC), when the chariot was still unchallenged in war. Attention is paid in this chapter to the preparations made before a battle, the tactics employed during the action, and the aftermath of an engagement. Quite remarkable are the different attitudes of Chinese and West Asian war leaders, not only to the violence necessarily involved in fighting but even more to the reasons for committing men to action in the first place. There is nothing like the belligerent assurance of an Egyptian pharaoh or an Assyrian king in ancient China. There a belief prevailed that those who lost a battle deserved to do so through their personal faults.

Chapter 2 looks at the rise of the charioteer. The invention of the war chariot relied on three things: the spoked wheel, the trained horse, and the composite bow. Each is discussed in turn, including the extensive training manual of Kikkuli, 'the master horseman of Mitanni'. Dating from the fourteenth century BC, this is the earliest scheme for the training of horses known in the world. That the manual contains words closely related to Sanskrit, the language of the Indo-Aryan invaders of India, suggests a connection between chariot warfare and successful takeovers of ancient lands. Similarities in chariot design in West Asia and India tend to confirm a western invasion of the subcontinent. Where chariots have come down to us intact, as with those recovered from the tomb of the pharaoh Tutankhamun, we have a rare opportunity to examine at first hand the actual method of construction. Each one of Tutankhamun's six chariots is unique, showing that a standardised approach was never adopted in spite of the arms race that the appearance of this war machine inaugurated. Helpful too in understanding ancient weaponry are the composite bows placed in the boy pharaoh's tomb.

West Asia and Egypt saw the initial military use of the chariot. Though no consensus exists as to the exact origin of the chariot, chapter 3 surveys the historical evidence presently available for its heyday there, the late second millennium BC. During this period chariotries ruled the battlefield. No ruler could afford to be without his 'chief men', his chariot warriors and charioteers. International correspondence took this interdependence for granted. A letter addressed to Tutankhamun, from another ruler, begins with greetings to 'your household, your wives, your sons, your horses, your chariots, your chief men'. Egyptian pharaohs were excellent archers, practising their skills regularly with their chariotries. There is, however, one chariot disaster unmentioned in Egyptian records: it is the loss of the squadrons sent after Moses, when he led the enslaved Hebrews out of Egypt and into the Sinai desert. This is discussed along with the possibility that Ramesses II was the tyrannical pharaoh of biblical tradition.

In chapter 4 the role of the war chariot in Europe is considered. Homer's *Iliad*, the epic account of the Greek expedition against Troy, accords the vehicle high status as a means of transport for Greeks as well as Trojans. But this is its only function: heroes treat the chariot as a battle-taxi from which they dismount to fight on foot. It seems as if the destruction in Greece of palace-strongholds like Mycenae and Tiryns, around 1200 BC, caused a definite break in consciousness that left Homer uncertain when it came to describing chariot battle. The Romans never deployed chariots on the battlefield, even though their successful generals always celebrated triumphs in a chariot drawn by four horses. We have to look to the Celtic peoples for expertise with chariotries. In 55 BC Julius Caesar was met by Britons riding in chariots on a Kent beach, and later he had to rescue legionaries attacked by chariots while on a foraging expedition.

India never forgot the chariot's true purpose as a mobile firing-platform, in all probability because the chariot retained its place for much longer on the battlefield. When in early 326 BC Alexander the Great descended from the mountains of Afghanistan on to the north Indian plain, he found both chariots and elephants in the armies which opposed him. At the battle of Hydaspes river King Porus sent one of his sons with numerous chariots to contest the Macedonian crossing. Chapter 5 argues that one reason for the war chariot's continued use in India was the prestige it enjoyed through the celebration of the exploits of chariot warriors in the *Ramayana* and the *Mahabharata*, the equivalent of Homer's two epics. In them we find the fullest description anywhere of duels between chariot-borne archers; they were conducted with a courtesy that also obtained for centuries on the Chinese battlefield. So traditional in outlook were Indian commanders that chariotries remained on active service after they were effectively overtaken by massed cavalry.

Chapter 6 examines the Chinese experience of chariotry by drawing upon its early chronicles, which are unrivalled as historical documents in the ancient world. The chariot was brought to East Asia by the Tocharians, whose mummified remains have recently excited international interest. The presence of this ancient non-Asian people in the Chinese province of Xinjiang reveals how the steppe once acted as a highway for the chariot. Even though the vehicle arrived in China fully formed and thus saved Chinese craftsmen the tedium of development work, they exploited this advantage through the invention of an efficient method of harnessing and a better wheel. The notorious lightness of chariots elsewhere was unnecessary in China, because protection did not need to be sacrificed for speed. The improved harness permitted a heavier chariot to be pulled, for the good reason that horses pressed against their shoulders and not their necks. Over 10,000 chariots were in regular service before the crossbow outranged the composite bow used by chariot warriors. An abortive attempt to mount a crossbow on a chariot, rather like a machine gun on a modern scout car, indicates the reluctance of the ancient Chinese to abandon it as a war machine.

The decline of the chariot's usefulness in warfare is the subject of chapter 7. A first setback was the destruction suffered in the eastern Mediterranean at the close of the thirteenth century BC, when the Sea Peoples suddenly brought down the Hittite empire. Cities and palaces were razed to the ground in Greece, Asia Minor, Cyprus, Syria and Palestine. Assyria and Egypt alone were spared. On the walls of his memorial temple at Medinet Habu, Ramesses III recorded the savage sea and land battles he had to fight in order to keep the Sea Peoples out of Egypt. Afterwards chariotries still had a mobile function in West Asian and Egyptian armies, but their vulnerability to determined infantry attack was obvious to all. As a consequence, the Assyrians chose to enlarge their chariots as vantage points for archers, and turned to cavalry and light-armed infantry to defend their borders. In China and India the chariot was also obliged to make way for the mounted archer. The Iranians, whom the Romans knew as the Parthians and the Sasanians, had already gone over to cavalry tactics.

Chapter 8 outlines the amazing longevity of the chariot in ancient ritual and racing. At Rome there was the triumph, the ultimate accolade for a general deemed to have won a significant victory over a worthy foe. In 61 BC Pompey rode in a gem-studded chariot, wearing the cloak of Alexander the Great, one of the spoils from his eastern campaigns. When Caesar celebrated his conquest of Gaul almost two decades later, his troops topped the usual ribaldry of a triumphal procession by singing: 'Lock up your wives Romans, we have come home with the bald-headed adulterer.' The strange mixture of admiration and disgust which made the triumph what it was could never have taken place without a chariot drawn by four horses, the favourite mode of travel for Etruscan kings and for Jupiter, head of the Roman pantheon. Even stranger in Rome and Constantinople was the preoccupation of their citizens with chariot races. Hundreds of thousands of spectators cheered on charioteers in a precursor of present-day football crowds. So enthusiastic were they that in AD 67 the Roman emperor Nero could not resist driving his own ten-horse chariot at the Olympic Games: he fell out but still won the prize, a crown made from olive leaves. In Constantinople, however, rivalry between supporters of competing chariot teams reached such a fever pitch that riots became a feature of city life. In AD 532 more than 30,000 people died in three days of violence.

This study of the chariot ends with a discussion of modern misconceptions about its ancient use. For this war machine never functioned as a tank, it was too prone to damage for such a role, even in China where a more robust model evolved because efficient harnessing overcame the problem of weight. The notes and references, immediately following the afterword, expand on the argument in the text, and suggest alternative interpretations where relevant. They are also intended to provide a means of pursuing matters of special interest, since most of the recommended books and articles are readily available.

An Assyrian stele showing an officer and his charioteer

I

Chariot Battle

Then my army came to praise me, looking at what I had done. My
high officers praised my strong arm, and my chariotry likewise
lauded my name, saying, 'What a great warrior who vanquished fear!
You saved the infantry as well as the chariotry.'

Egyptian inscription

Summer heat shimmered along the banks of the Orontes as Ramesses II
directed his chariot horses towards the ford, south of Kadesh. It was early
one afternoon in 1274 BC. Moving well ahead of his army, the young
pharaoh was keen to camp close to the rebellious Syrian city because he
had learned from two local inhabitants that the forces of his chief rival,
King Muwatalli II of Hatti, had retreated northwards on news of his
approach. What Ramesses did not realise, as the few Egyptian chariots
with him in the vanguard splashed through the shallow river, was that the
Hittite king was about to spring a trap which would lead to one of the
greatest battles fought in the eastern Mediterranean. For the Egyptian
record tells us that the two informants had been sent by Muwatalli 'to
speak falsely to His Majesty in order that he might not prepare his troops
for battle'. But the impetuous advance was very much part of Ramesses'
own character. Remembered in Egyptian tradition as a colossus as large as
his own statues, the ideal warrior-king whose sixty-seven-year reign
secured the country's survival as a great power during a period of intense
international rivalry, Ramesses was in fact lucky to avoid defeat at
Kadesh. The twenty-nine-year-old pharaoh had set the pace throughout
the long advance from the Nile delta. 'All the foreign lands trembled
before him,' we are told, 'all their leaders bringing tribute and all rebels
coming in submission through fear of His Majesty's might.' Riding in his
glittering chariot at the head of an army of four divisions, named after the
gods Amun, Re, Ptah and Seth, Ramesses sped past Gaza along the road

next to 'the shore of Amor', as the Egyptians called the Mediterranean. The lions decorating the royal chariot signalled more than the pharaoh's presence, a crucial rallying point in fast-moving, mobile engagements. So drawn to this creature was Ramesses that he took a tame one with him on campaign. It did not, however, use its teeth and claws on his behalf: carved depictions always show the lion, lying with front paws bound, near the pharaoh's tent. Though this old story can thus be discounted, the pairing of Ramesses with a lion is not entirely inappropriate, since the ferocious courage he displayed in the encounter with Muwatalli saved the Egyptians from disaster. 'A strong defence for his army,' one inscription runs, 'His Majesty was like a shield on the day of fighting. Braver than hundreds and thousands combined, he went first into the multitudes, trusting in his strength alone.'

Beneath the walls of Kadesh thousands of chariots were about to clash in a battle whose strange twists and turns are revealed in the account Ramesses later recorded on temple walls at Karnak and other religious centres. The people he claimed to have finally overcome were the Hittites, a name we have derived from the Bible authorised by King James I. Calling themselves, quite simply, 'the people of Hatti', the Hittites had expanded their territories beyond Asia Minor to exercise control over what is today eastern Turkey, Armenia and northern Syria. In 1595 BC a daring raid even sacked the great city of Babylon. Yet rivalry with Egypt, a situation the Hittite kings long sought to avoid, only arose after they conquered Mitanni, once a powerful state centred on the upper Tigris and Euphrates rivers. The Mitannians had recognised Egyptian overlordship of Kadesh and there is evidence to suggest that the Hittites would have tolerated this arrangement had its ruler not proved so difficult. When King Suttarna sent the forces of Kadesh against Hittite troops operating close by, he was soon defeated and led off into captivity, along with his son Aitakkama. Although this put a strain on Hittite-Egyptian relations, there was no immediate reaction from Egypt, but Aitakkama's return to Kadesh as a Hittite ally was less well received. Nothing was done until Ramesses' father, Sety I, decided to restore Egyptian prestige and authority in Syria. He reconquered Kadesh and foiled all attempts by Muwatalli to retake the city. An inscription at Karnak explains how he 'smote the land of Hatti, causing the cowardly rebels to submit'. At the time, the Hittites had little choice but to accept the territorial claims of Sety, and acknowledge that power in Syria was to

Ramesses II, the victor at Kadesh

be shared with the Egyptians. It is possible that this was ratified by treaty, because the one accepted by Ramesses at the end of his Hittite Wars in 1258 BC refers to a previous agreement. The accession of a new pharaoh seems to have been regarded by Muwatalli as a good opportunity for intervention. So it happened that Ramesses found himself suddenly confronted by the whole Hittite army.

While the Egyptians may have exaggerated the numbers they faced at Kadesh, Muwatalli was determined enough to wrest Syria from them by assembling a very substantial force. It was made up of regular Hittite troops, contingents from a wide range of allied states, and large numbers of mercenaries. According to Ramesses, the enemy totalled 47,500 men, including a complement of 3,500 chariots. Against this host he could not deploy so many soldiers, nor were they all available at the start of battle: the Amun division was just behind him, the Re division was crossing the ford, while the Ptah and Seth divisions still remained south of the Orontes. In a concealed position to the east of Kadesh, the Hittites awaited the moment to strike. It came when the Amun division was establishing a camp at a spot chosen by Ramesses on the other side of the city. 'There His Majesty seated himself on a throne of gold', presumably to receive ambassadors from an overawed Kadesh. Instead, Ramesses received a rude shock. Two Hittite scouts sent by Muwatalli to ascertain the exact position of the Egyptian army were captured and, after a beating, revealed the true location of the Hittite army. 'The King of Hatti,' they admitted, 'together with many foreign lands he has brought as allies, is armed and ready to fight behind Kadesh.' Ramesses' senior officers were stunned by the news and abashed at the anger of the pharaoh over their carelessness. After a hasty conference, messengers were dispatched to hurry on the divisions still on the march. By then the Hittite chariotry had 'charged the Re division, cutting through the middle, as it was not drawn up for battle'.

This collapse almost engulfed the Egyptian camp when in panic troops from the broken division rushed there in order to escape pursuing Hittite chariots. A total rout seemed inevitable, until Ramesses asserted his leadership. 'Then His Majesty rose like his father Montu and seized his weapons of war, putting on his coat of mail.' As the Hittite chariotry surrounded his camp in an ever-tightening circle, the pharaoh launched a desperate counter-attack. First, infantrymen were sent to tackle enemy chariots which came too close to the camp, pulling down charioteers and

One of the mounted messengers sent to hurry on the Ptah and Seth divisions

killing them with short swords and spears. Then, taking advantage of this confusion, Ramesses mounted his own chariot and drove into the Hittites with tremendous force. Even though we know how Menna, his shield-bearer, 'saw the vast number of hostile chariots hemming the pharaoh in, and went deadly white with terror', the counter-attack gave the surrounded Egyptians a brief respite, which Ramesses used to rally his troops. He also noticed that the eastern wing of the Hittite chariotry was the weakest part, and next he turned in that direction, a switch in tactics which again disconcerted his opponents. If this move, inspired by another of Ramesses' headlong charges, was meant to convince the Egyptians of their ability to hold out until reinforcements arrived, they were right to trust the judgment of their inexperienced pharaoh.

Not even a new wave of chariots sent by Muwatalli to stop this assault in its tracks could prevent Ramesses from gaining the initiative in the swirling chariot encounter. Time and again the Egyptian chariot warriors got the better of their foes, the pharaoh's bow adding to the growing slaughter. Like all ancient armies, the Hittite one was unable to withstand the impact of such violence for long. Its chariotry was already losing cohesion when a threat developed on the western wing in the form of a column from Amurru. Perhaps its arrival had a similar effect to that on the French of Blücher's Prussians at Waterloo, not least because the distraction may have caused the Hittites to hesitate in driving home their attack on the now hard-pressed Amun and Re divisions. The Amurru, allies from the Mediterranean coast, relieved the Egyptian camp, leaving

Ramesses free to drive the Hittites into the Orontes, where abandoning their chariots 'they plunged like crocodiles face first into its waters'. The Egyptians were thus left in possession of the battlefield: prisoners were rounded up, booty collected, and a grisly count of the dead made by cutting a hand from each corpse. Gathering round the triumphant pharaoh, the Egyptian army 'praised His Majesty, seeing what he had done to the wretched ruler of Hatti', although it was severely scolded by Ramesses for leaving him in such a perilous position at the start of the battle. By this time the Ptah and Seth divisions had arrived and the Hittites were discouraged from further action. Muwatalli's losses were largely confined to his chariotry, but without this striking force he knew his infantry was now vulnerable. So he sent an envoy to propose peace, which Ramesses would only accept as a truce, because he wished to reserve the right to reclaim Kadesh and other cities conquered by his predecessors. That the truce more or less held is an indication of a reluctance on the part of the Egyptians as well as the Hittites over returning so soon to the battlefield.

How great was Ramesses' success is hard to judge. His account plays down the arrival of the Amurru column, as it does the belated appearance of the Ptah and Seth divisions. The Egyptians were certainly mauled until they recovered from their shock and fought off the Hittite chariotry. And they took heavy casualties. Yet Ramesses managed to save his army and his reputation as a commander, quite a surprising outcome in which he could have been helped by another factor than timely reinforcements. The Hittite army was less homogeneous than the one Ramesses led, with the result that allied troops and mercenaries, and possibly even Hittite regulars, may have succumbed to the temptation of plunder on reaching the Egyptian camp. Dismounted charioteers, shown struggling with foot soldiers in several depictions of the battle, might well have been looters caught off-guard. The record does not enlighten us. It concludes by saying

His Majesty turned back in peace to Egypt together with his infantry and his chariotry, strength and power being with him, and the gods and goddesses acting as protectors for his body and his means of dominion over all lands.

Hittite chariots under fire from Egyptian archers

No Hittite account of Kadesh survives, although it is of course mentioned as a victory for Muwatalli.

Ramesses' illustrated record of the battle has led to the suggestion that there was a profound difference between the Hittite and Egyptian deployment of chariotry. Whereas the former are shown using a spear as an offensive weapon, and making a rush at their opponents' vehicles in order to thrust at enemy charioteers, the latter fire arrows at their attackers from a distance. This seems to be confirmed by the apparent absence of bowmen in the Hittite chariots. But it is untrue that the Hittites had failed to acquire archery skills capable of hitting a target from a moving chariot. The battle reliefs of Ramesses' father already indicate this ability, for they depict Hittite chariots equipped with bow cases, while in each chariot a Hittite soldier sports a quiver on his back. There is, then, no reason to imagine that the Hittites fought differently from chariot warriors elsewhere in the ancient world. Only in China were encounters sometimes decided by a specialised development of the spear, the halberd. This multi-headed lance was extended sideways from a speeding chariot so as to disable charioteers charging in the opposite direction. Yet the Chinese still saw the bow as the vital offensive weapon in chariot warfare, at least until it was outranged by the invention of the crossbow. What the Hittite spearmen at Kadesh were concerned to do was protect their chariots from the attentions of the foot soldiers Ramesses sent against them. Horses and charioteers were endangered by determined skirmishers, known to the Egyptians as 'runners', mercenaries skilled in hit-and-run attacks. In brutal fashion they would dispose of stranded chariots. Where the Luxor battle relief, in particular, lays emphasis is on the bowmanship of Ramesses himself, supported by a daring squadron of chariot archers. Such a representation of a triumphant pharaoh is typical of Egyptian royal iconography, for the ruler is usually portrayed as the leader of the chariotry, the striking force of late second millennium BC armies. Egyptian pharaohs, nonetheless, were excellent archers: just over a century earlier Amenhotep II, who also battled in Syria, was renowned for his accuracy. An inscription relates how once from a fast-moving chariot his arrows had hit a series of copper targets spaced at intervals, each of his arrows penetrating the metal by a good few centimetres. To reach this level of skill took a great deal of practice, besides remarkable hand-eye co-ordination. It points to a close relationship between the pharaoh and his charioteers, who would have regularly hunted together.

In international correspondence this is taken for granted by other rulers when they greet not only the pharaoh as their brother, but also his household, his wives, his sons, his chariots, his horses, and his chief men.

Amenhotep II's target practice

A copy of a letter discovered at Amarna, the site of a temporary capital established by the reforming pharaoh Akhenaten in the 1340s BC, underlines the importance of chariotry in the contemporary balance of power. It is addressed to the king of Amurru, who is reminded of his obligations to Egypt and ordered to apprehend certain rebels. The letter signs off with the formula: 'His Majesty is hale like Re, the sun god. For his many troops and chariots, from the Upper Land to the Lower Land, from dawn to sunset, are in perfect order.' The implication is obvious. Either Amurru remains a loyal ally or suffers the damage this mobile host can swiftly inflict upon its people. The military prowess of the pharaoh was always taken for granted, as he was 'more effective than millions of soldiers'. The guarantor of safety, the one who 'made the boundaries of Egypt as far as that which the sun encircles', the pharaoh ruled the world. Sety I understood what was required of him when he described his kingdom as bounded in the north by the sea, in the south by the wind. It enclosed all within the four pillars which held the heavens aloft. Border disputes could thus be dismissed officially as minor irritations, although the Egyptians had experienced invasion and occupation by the Hyksos. These West Asian warriors controlled northern Egypt between 1664 and 1555 BC. Their success had depended upon the chariot, which the Egyptians themselves adopted during the intense struggle to expel these formidable invaders.

Even though Ramesses remained the traditional hero at Kadesh, the divine upholder of the world, the stalemate on the battlefield marked an admission of the permanent coexistence of several major states, despite Egyptian uneasiness about accepting the pharaoh's parity with West Asian kings. Not so the Hittites, whose royal scribes regarded as their master's peers the kings of Egypt, Babylon, Assyria and Ahhiyawa, most probably Greece. Ahhiyawa appears to be the Hittite way of writing the Greek name Achaiwia, an archaic form of Achaia. In Homer's *Iliad*, the ninth-century BC epic account of the siege of Troy, which had taken place several hundred years earlier, the Greeks are often called Achaians. In later times the name of Achaia was applied to areas of the Greek mainland colonised by Achaians, including the northern Peloponnese. There was situated Mycenae, the stronghold of Agamemnon, the leader of the expedition to Troy. Relations between Hatti and Ahhiyawa were generally peaceful, though for some unknown reason in the late thirteenth century BC a ban was imposed on trade between the Achaian

Greeks and the Assyrians, via harbours on the Hittite-dominated Syrian coast. War between Hatti and Assyria may have been the cause. The battle at Kadesh between Ramesses and Muwatalli had left the Hittites in a strong position, having gained considerable territory in Syria at Egypt's expense. Two years after the battle local rulers in Canaan felt confident enough to openly defy Ramesses, who responded by conquering centres of resistance in a rapid campaign. These operations were a prelude to more military efforts against Hittite allies which could have brought about another major confrontation. No second Kadesh occurred; mutual exhaustion and anxiety over the growing power of Assyria held back both Hatti and Egypt from a final showdown. King Hattusili III was convinced of the need to reach a final peace settlement with Egypt. Muwatalli's usurping brother, Hattusili sent in 1258 BC envoys with a large silver tablet on which were inscribed the terms of an alliance between Egypt and Hatti. The anti-Assyrian treaty set the seal on Ramesses' career as a chariot warrior, something the now middle-aged pharaoh was perhaps not unwilling to welcome. Kadesh, even Amurru, was to stay Hittite, but Hattusili swore to come to Egypt's aid in the event of an attack, while 'the good brotherhood' of the kings was eventually strengthened by family ties, for in 1245 BC a fifty-eight-year-old Ramesses wedded a Hittite princess as one of his many queens.

Another Egyptian victory in which we know chariots played a decisive part happened at Megiddo in 1460 BC. Not quite a coincidence was the involvement of the king of Kadesh in the battle. He had sent troops southwards to augment the rebel Canaanite army, because he feared the expansion of Egyptian power into Syria. Following the expulsion of the Hyksos, the Egyptians remained apprehensive about the Canaanites, who might combine together and assist the launch of another West Asian attack on their country. Rather than relying any more on a sphere of influence, reinforced by periodic military activity, the pharaohs' foreign policy became more direct, with close supervision of allies, to the extent of keeping Egyptian officers in loyal courts. Within this buffer zone, local rulers were designated 'His Majesty's tenants', swearing obedience to the will of the pharaoh. Not even succession problems weakened this new approach. In 1504 BC Thutmose III had succeeded his father at the tender age of ten years, and his stepmother Hatshepsut ruled in his stead, first as regent. An inscription unearthed at Thebes relates how Thutmose III's father 'went up to heaven and was united with the gods. His son replaced

A letter from the ruler of Tyre to Akhenaten

him as ruler of the Two Lands . . . His sister, the God's Wife Hatshepsut, handled affairs of state. The Two Lands were subject to her will and taxes were collected in her name.' During the third year of her regency Hatshepsut dropped the pretence of ruling on her young stepson's behalf and had herself crowned as pharaoh. She reigned until 1482 BC, when Thutmose finally gained the throne, ostensibly in the twenty-second year of his own reign. With over thirty years to rule ahead of him, in which he effectively reasserted Egypt's authority in adjacent areas of West Asia, Thutmose had plenty of time to erase the evidence of Hatshepsut's reign by destroying all her monuments. But a challenge he needed to confront was the revolt of Canaan, with the active support of Kadesh. He had to undertake no fewer than seventeen campaigns before the situation was under control, despite his stunning success at Megiddo.

That the king of Kadesh was able to encourage the rebellion of so many local rulers demonstrates his own authority as well as the weakening of Egypt's influence under Hatshepsut. Thutmose could scarcely ignore in 1460 BC news of a large Canaanite army gathered at Megiddo, a fortified city occupying a commanding position midway between the Mediterranean and the Jordan valley. This campaign, which culminated in the capture of the city, was his most successful and, possibly for that reason, the most fully recorded. An Egyptian army of around 20,000 men marched quickly to Gaza in nine or ten days. From this forward base Thutmose pushed straight on to Aruna, a town on the southern slopes of the Carmel mountain range. Megiddo was situated on its northern slopes, and could be approached by three routes: however, a direct, narrow pass, modern Wadi Ara, attracted the pharaoh's attention in spite of warnings from his senior officers. At a conference he was told:

'What is it like to march along this road which becomes so narrow? It is said that the enemy is there, waiting at the other end and daily becoming more numerous. Will not horse have to follow horse, and the army likewise? Will not our vanguard be engaged in battle while there are troops still waiting to start out from Aruna? Now there are two other roads – one, to our right, comes out at Taanach, south of Megiddo, the other, to our left, comes out to its north at Djefty. Let our victorious Lord proceed on one of the easier routes rather than the difficult route in front of us.'

Not for the sake of prestige alone did Thutmose reject their advice, though the campaign account, carved on the walls of Amun's temple in Karnak, suggests otherwise when the pharaoh is supposed to have commented on how the rebels would scoff at him if he chose a roundabout route. 'They will say: "Has His Majesty set out on another road because he has become afraid of us?" This they will say.' For it is clear that Thutmose's choice of the direct route had more to do with tactics than status. Assuming that the Canaanite leaders would think like his own war council, he took the risk and ordered an advance through a pass which shrinks in places to a width of less than ten metres.

A whole day was needed for the Egyptian army to get through Wadi

Ara, whereupon Thutmose pitched camp. Except for a minor skirmish, the passage was as uneventful as it was unexpected. Thutmose was right. The rebels had not anticipated his daring move, and had concentrated their forces at Taanach and Djefty, with only a small force guarding the narrow pass. Like the English general Allenby some 3,400 years later, Thutmose had caught his opponents off-guard. Just as the surprise advance of the Fourth Cavalry Division early one morning through the same pass totally demoralised the Turks, the sudden appearance of the Egyptian chariotry struck such fear into Canaanite hearts that the engagement was almost one-sided. At dawn Thutmose rode forth in his golden chariot, spreading out his army in two great wings. He stationed himself at the centre, 'where Amun was the protection for his body during the fight'. If the 1,000 Egyptian chariots used in the battle were deployed as a single rank, the line would have extended for nearly three kilometres. Once in motion the two wings of the Egyptian army threatened the Canaanites with encirclement, while Thutmose charged straight into their midst. 'When the rebels saw His Majesty prevailing over them,' we are informed, 'they fled straight away to Megiddo with faces of fear. They abandoned their horses and their chariots of gold and silver, so that they could reach safety. Now the people of Megiddo had shut the city gates, but they let down garments in order to hoist them over the walls.'

So swift was the Egyptian attack that it is possible the Canaanite chariotry was prevented from charging at all. Its charioteers and chariot warriors seem to have run away, leaving everything behind. But the chance of booty was too much for Thutmose's men, thus depriving the pharaoh of total victory. A short siege became necessary to reduce Megiddo to submission. Then, all the rebel leaders, with the exception of the king of Kadesh who had rushed home from the battlefield, were made prisoner and compelled to swear eternal allegiance to Egypt. And the impressive list of loot is a reminder of how complete Thutmose's triumph was. Carried off were

> 340 living prisoners and 83 hands; 2,041 horses, 191 foals, 6 stallions and . . . colts; a golden chariot belonging to the enemy; a fine chariot worked with gold belonging to the ruler of Megiddo . . . and 892 chariots of his wretched army – in total 924; a fine bronze coat of mail belonging to the enemy; a fine bronze coat of mail belonging to

the ruler of Megiddo, and 200 leather mail coats belonging to his wretched army; 502 bows; and 7 wooden tent poles, worked with silver, belonging to the enemy.

With the rebellion finally crushed and Kadesh discredited, Thutmose could undertake operations designed to keep the peace in Egyptian territories. He even commanded a sea-borne expedition against Kadesh. Landing at friendly Byblos, he marched directly against the city, laying waste to its land at the time of harvest. The city itself did not fall on this occasion, but later Kadesh was assaulted and taken by the Egyptians for the first time. Thutmose's victories over Mitanni, the other great power in Syria prior to the rise of Hatti, had left the king of Kadesh diplomatically isolated. Egyptian power extended all the way to the Euphrates, which Thutmose crossed in prefabricated assault craft built from cedarwood. 'At the mere sight of an Egyptian,' one victory stele boasts, 'the kings of Canaan flee.' There is no record of Megiddo ever being destroyed, so its ruler must have been pleased 'to kiss the ground to the glory of His Majesty and to beg breath for his nostrils'.

At the battle of Megiddo Thutmose used surprise and mobility as his main weapons for overcoming the Canaanites. These, and his own bravery in driving straight into the opposing chariotry, contributed to the swiftly won victory. They mark him out as a commander who was willing to take chances, though only after calculating the odds carefully. Thutmose believed they were in his favour and the gain was so great that he dared to reject the advice of his closest advisers. Given that the strength of the chariotry on the two sides was about equal, he knew that the concentration of his own forces close to Megiddo would give him the initial advantage, as the Canaanites had divided their army in order to cover both the northern and southern routes of his advance. By the time the latter reunited to face him it was too late to halt the Egyptian attack. The apparent smallness of the Egyptian chariotry should not cause surprise. Each chariot required a team of two steeds to pull it, together with one or two animals in reserve, for replacements. At Megiddo there needed to have been 3,000 to 4,000 horses, which in all probability represented almost all of Egypt's trained stock. The country had no experience of large-scale horse breeding and imported most of its military requirements. Mitanni, and afterwards Hatti, were better placed; they bred horses themselves and had access to neighbouring peoples expert in

Thutmose III, the victor at Megiddo

this difficult art. The logistical problems of moving 1,000 chariots may explain Thutmose's desire for a quick decision on the battlefield. Apart from the maintenance of the chariots, there was the important matter of forage. So far as we are aware, the Egyptians, like other ancient peoples, could only provide their army with a limited supply train. After Gaza Thutmose's men and animals had to live off the land.

Yet the swiftness of the Egyptian chariotry completely dashed Canaanite hopes. General Allenby's cavalry in 1918 had a similar impact on Turkish units guarding its army headquarters at Nazareth. As part of the final Allied offensive in Palestine, the Fourth and Fifth Cavalry Divisions were fed through passes in the Mount Carmel range, while the main Turkish position was turned on the coast. Elaborate measures had been undertaken to persuade the Turks of an attack in the opposite direction, in the Jordan valley. There dummy camps were established, filled with 15,000 canvas horses; infantry daily marched towards them from Jerusalem, only to return by lorry at night; and sleighs drawn by mules raised clouds of dust to make observation difficult and give the impression of activity. This final deception parallels an even more ingenious use of dust on an ancient Chinese battlefield. In 632 BC, at Chengpu, armies belonging to the states of Jin and Chu met in the earliest East Asian battle for which we possess a detailed account. The Jin ruler outmanoeuvred his opponent by luring him into a dangerous advance, and then caught his exposed troops in a pincer movement of infantry and chariots. The successful tactic was executed behind a screen of dust raised by chariots dragging trees. Allenby knew nothing of Chengpu, but ever since the Fourth Cavalry Division advanced through Wadi Ara speculation has centred upon the extent of his knowledge of Thutmose's tactics. The title he chose as a reward for his generalship after the First World War was Viscount of Megiddo and Felixstowe.

In 1919 Allenby told the American Egyptologist James Breasted that 'they had wanted me to add "Armageddon" to the title, but I refused to do that. It was much too sensational and would have given endless opportunity to all the cranks in Christendom. So I merely took Megiddo.' Then he added how curious it was that the cavalry advance should have been 'exactly old Thutmose's experience in meeting an outpost of the enemy and disposing of them at the top of the Pass leading to Megiddo! You see, I had been reading your book and Adam Smith and I knew what had taken place there.' But it should be noted that Allenby did not exactly follow ancient Egyptian tactics with his cavalry. Whereas the pharaoh only used a single pass, Allenby sent cavalry forces through two of them, and also pushed another force behind the Turkish lines near the Mediterranean coast, in places employing the beach itself for rapid movements. But it was the speed of the horse which gave both the Egyptian pharaoh and the English general their incredible victories.

Writing a decade later, Archibald Wavell, a rising officer who was destined to become a British Middle East commander-in-chief during the Second World War, marvelled at Allenby's exploitation of the terrain. He explains how the Fourth Cavalry Division emerged from Wadi Ara

just in time. A small body of Turks was surprised and rounded up
... As the leading troops moved out ... the Turkish force, of
which the captured detachment was the advance guard, was seen
approaching. This was a column in six companies with twelve
machine guns. It received short shrift from the leading regiment of
the Division, the 2nd Lancers. Supported by the fire of armoured
cars, the Indian squadrons were into the enemy infantry with the
lance before they even completed their deployment. Forty-six
Turks were speared, and the remainder, about 500, surrendered.
The whole action had only lasted a few minutes.

The German general Liman von Sanders, commander of the Seventh and
Eighth Turkish Armies, had sent this column to block the pass the day
before. Its slowness in covering the short distance from Nazareth gave
Allenby's cavalry its chance. The Fourth Cavalry Division covered an
astonishing 100 kilometres in less than a day and a half, losing only
twenty-six horses on the way. The unexpected advance beyond Megiddo
amazed Allenby, who wrote to his wife how he was 'almost aghast at the
extent of the victory'. So was Liman von Sanders: he had made a
desperate escape from his quarters in Nazareth, wearing his pyjamas.
Street fighting alone saved him from capture, as mounted troops were not
the best equipped for this kind of combat.

Such a cavalry action, however, would have been impossible in the
ancient Mediterranean world. The chariot was in time supplanted by the
mounted soldier, but two critical items of equipment were wanting in
order to turn him into a lancer. These were the stirrup and the built-up
saddle, two Asian inventions which arrived in the West only after the fall
of the Roman empire. The use of stirrups renders mounting easier,
increases control over the horse, and results in a steadier seat. When
added to an effective saddle, it gave the Franks with their wing-spears and
protective armour the shock of heavy cavalry, and laid the basis for the
era of the medieval knight. In contrast, the unsteadiness of the ancient
rider's seat was legendary when he wielded either a sword or a spear.
Often cited as evidence of this is Xenophon's famous address to the Ten
Thousand, Greek mercenaries who in 401 BC had marched deep into
Persian territory to place Cyrus, the second son of King Darius II, on the
throne. While victorious at the battle of Cunaxa, the would-be usurper
for whom the Ten Thousand had fought so well allowed his impetuosity

to get the better of him and he lost his life. Faced with a long march home without adequate cavalry support, Xenophon sought to raise the morale of his fellow mercenaries by reminding them of their own strength. 'We are on a much more secure footing than cavalry,' he said, 'because they are suspended in the air on their horses, fearing not only us but also falling. We are safely planted on the ground and are able to strike harder blows if anyone approaches. We are also more likely to hit whatever we choose.' Brave though these words were, Xenophon and the other Greek commanders were fortunate in the attitude taken by the Persians, since they were content to harass the withdrawal of the Ten Thousand rather than provoke another engagement.

As the Romans were to discover at Carrhae, in 53 BC, foot soldiers could not long survive a sustained assault by mounted archers. Their opponent was Parthia, the second Iranian power of ancient times. The saying, 'a Parthian shot', recalls exactly the frustration felt by the Romans in northern Mesopotamia. The ill-fated expedition there resulted from Marcus Licinius Crassus' ambition to emulate the eastern successes of Alexander the Great. Though part of the so-called First Triumvirate, a Gang of Three devoted to nothing more than the exercise of power in Rome, Crassus felt himself to be militarily inferior to both Pompey and Julius Caesar, its other members. It still rankled that he was denied a triumph for overcoming the slave revolt of Spartacus in 71 BC; he had had to make do with the minor honour of a procession on foot because of the unworthiness of his foe. The pursuit of glory on the battle-field was a reflection of the militarisation of Roman politics during the late republic, and it was something from which even a successful general like Caesar was never entirely immune. Neither the conquest of Gaul nor his triumph over Pompey in the subsequent civil war quite satisfied the ageing dictator, for Caesar still dreamed of marching his legions in Alexander's footsteps as late as 45 BC, just one year before his assassination.

Hardly surprising, then, was the impatience of sixty-year-old Crassus. He brushed aside concern about the weakness of his cavalry, and advanced on to open plains most suited to its use. This was a fatal mistake, because the Parthian army was essentially a cavalry force. It employed the mobility of the horse to attack where an enemy was weak and to break off contact where strong. Such a tactical withdrawal was misunderstood by the Roman legionaries, with the result that detachments pursued an apparently retreating foe only to become surrounded and beaten in detail. The readiness of the Parthians to flee suggests a nomadic ancestry, which the record seems to confirm when it says that they 'still wore their long hair bunched up over their heads in the Scythian fashion in order to make themselves look more formidable'. But at Carrhae it was their arrows that made them terrifying, not their hairstyles. Surrounding the Romans, the Parthians opened fire from all sides. There was no real need for accurate marksmanship, since the legionaries were so densely packed together that it was impossible to miss the target even if one had wished to do so. The arrival of camel trains loaded with extra arrows sealed Crassus' fate: the head of the would-be Alexander was taken in triumph to Ctesiphon, the Parthian capital, while 10,000 Roman soldiers were captured. Some were settled on Parthia's eastern frontier, where near the Central Asian city of Turfan they may have eventually faced Chinese opponents. A Chinese record tells of the surrender in 36 BC of a Hunnish chieftain, whose followers included a group of mercenaries suspiciously like ex-Roman legionaries from the description of their drill.

Armies older than Roman ones used chariotry to protect infantry against archers, whether riding in chariots or on foot. Muwatalli's unwillingness to fight on at Kadesh was influenced by a crushing weakness in this regard, as his broken chariotry was no longer a match for Ramesses' squadrons of mobile archers. Above all, the Hittite king could not be sure that his foot soldiers would stand their ground when attacked by Egyptian chariots. Chariot horses would never have been prepared to charge into ranks of shouting infantrymen, but at the same time few of these soldiers would have had the courage to remain motionless under a steady fall of arrows, nor would they have calmly awaited the chance of being ridden down. The impact of chariotry, like fully fledged cavalry later on, was moral as much as physical. It served to spread panic on the battlefield, as indeed Muwatalli's chariot assault spectacularly achieved with the Re division, a breakdown in Egyptian morale which required all the leadership and bravery of a pharaoh to reverse.

Regarded with greater embarrassment by the Chinese than Muwatalli's trickery at Kadesh was the ruse already mentioned at Chengpu. The chariot deception was felt to be somehow unworthy of the occasion, notwithstanding the narrative's complete disdain for Tzu Yu, the defeated general. It is as if the ancient account has been unnecessarily diverted from a moral purpose. That the victory was due to the error Tzu Yu committed as a result of the dust thrown up by chariots dragging trees receives little notice. The Chinese chroniclers are more interested in proving that battles are lost by those who deserve to lose. Not even the wayward youth of the victor, Duke Wen of Jin, can detract from his deserved success. Neither drunkenness nor exile was sufficient to thwart Wen's destiny to become an ideal ruler, who recognised the need for counsel and usually accepted it. This emphasis on Wen's essential virtue means that only a few words are spent on the actual engagement at Chengpu in comparison with the exploration of the motives and behaviour of the main participants. Yet a great deal can be deduced about ancient Chinese warfare, as well as the role played by chariotry, in the brief description of the battle. One of the 'five great engagements' fought during the Spring and Autumn period (770–481 BC), Chengpu indicates how far ancient China had fissured into opposing blocs of warring states. In theory the royal house of Zhou held the mandate to rule 'all under Heaven', but the gifts of bows and arrows that successive kings bestowed on leading members of the nobility could not hide a patent lack of strength, for they represented the entitlement to punish any who were disobedient to royal commands. Gradually this devolution of authority left the Zhou kings with only a religious function and an impoverished domain surrounding the northern city of Luoyang. After his victory at Chengpu in 632 BC, Duke Wen was polite enough to present the reigning king with all the booty: it comprised '400 four-house teams of chariot horses and 1,000 foot soldiers'. So pleased was the king with this gift that he 'proclaimed the duke of Jin to be leader of the feudal lords and awarded him a large ceremonial chariot, a war chariot, a red lacquered bow and a set of a hundred red lacquered arrows, ten black lacquered bows and a thousand black lacquered arrows, a jar of fragrant black millet wine, and three hundred tiger-fleet warriors'. Then Duke Wen was sent forth with the instruction to 'bring peace to the states in the four directions, chastise and drive off the king's foes!'

This elevation of Wen to hegemon occurred through a struggle between the older northern states, led by Jin, and the less sinified southern states, led by Chu, a rapidly developing power based in the Yangzi valley. The prelude to the confrontation at Chengpu was the building of alliances with the large number of smaller states that lay in a band between the two blocs. During the winter of 633 BC the Chu army besieged the capital of Song, a state under the protection of Jin, and in the following spring Wen led a relief column made up of contingents from several northern states against the attackers. En route he dealt with two lukewarm allies, Wey and Cao. The latter resisted stoutly and many soldiers died in an abortive attempt to storm its capital.

When the men of Cao took the bodies of the Jin dead and exposed them on the city wall, Duke Wen was greatly distressed, but adopting a plan put forward by some of his advisers, he announced that he was going to encamp on the tombs of the Cao's ancestors and he proceeded to move his forces to the graveyard. The men of Cao, filled with panic and horror, coffined the Jin dead they had taken and had the bodies carried out of the city. The Jin army took advantage of this uncertainty to press their attack, and gained access to the city.

In contrast to the high-mindedness of Wen, the character of the Chu commander is portrayed as contemptible. Driven by the desire to destroy Jin at all costs, Tzu Yu is said to be 'stubborn and lacking in propriety'. Almost the only person who has anything good to say about him is Wen

Hittite chariotry

himself, and he says it only after Tzu Yu's death. So headstrong and
reckless was Tzu Yu that he dared to defy a warning from the deity of the
Yellow river, just before Chengpu. In a dream he was told that success
depended upon his men not sporting elaborate headware or dressing up
their horses with jade-studded straps. As soon as his senior staff heard of
his refusal to accept this divine guidance, one of them commented: 'It
will not be the gods who defeat Tzu Yu. He takes no care for the Chu
people. In truth he will defeat himself!' Quite different was the duke of
Jin's attitude to an omen and a dream, both of which were satisfactorily
interpreted for him. Wen's courtesy is underlined too. As the Chu army
approached, he ordered his own forces to withdraw 'for a distance of
three days' march in order to repay a kindness' shown to him by the duke
of Chu. In spite of unease amongst Wen's senior officers about fulfilling
this obligation, they were convinced of its correctness when it was
explained to them. 'If we withdraw and Chu turns around and goes
home, what more could we ask? And if Chu declines to turn around and
go home, then our duke will have given way and its general will be the
one who is provoking the attack, so the fault of breaking the rules will
not lie with us.' Thus the Jin army withdrew and the Chu troops wanted
to give up the attack, but Tzu Yu would not hear of this. He sent instead
an envoy to Wen with the message: 'We beg to try our strength against
your lordship's men, while you lean upon your chariot-rail and watch. I,
Tzu Yu, will likewise cast my eyes over the encounter.' To which
challenge Wen sent the famous reply:

> The duke heeds your command. He has not ventured to forget the
> kindness he once received from the ruler of Chu and hence has
> withdrawn to this position. And if he will withdraw this far for you,
> an officer of Chu, how would he dare to oppose Chu's duke! But
> since your wishes leave him no choice, he begs to trouble you, sir,
> to tell your commanders: 'Look well to your chariots, reverence
> your lord's orders, and let us meet at the crack of dawn.'

The narrative of the battle itself commences with Wen's instruction for
his men 'to cut down trees and use them to supplement their weapons'.
Meanwhile 'the 700 war chariots of Jin proceeded to tighten the girths
and straps of their horses'. Then fighting began with an advance of both
wings of the Jin army. The Jin left-wing assault on Chu's allies, Chen and

Cai, was powerful enough to rout both of them. Having dispersed the Chu right, the Jin left wing turned and combined with its own centre so as to contain the Chu centre, where the bulk of Tzu Yu's troops were stationed. Tzu Yu had taken command of the Chu left wing, which was now under attack. But when the Jin right wing had closed to the point where it was seen to take some casualties, presumably at bow-shot range, it hesitated, stopped and finally fell back. Behind a cloud of dust raised by a squadron of chariots dragging trees, the commander of the Jin right hoisted two great banners, giving the impression that Duke Wen was himself retreating along with these troops. To Tzu Yu it looked like nothing more than a confused withdrawal, and not the carefully planned manoeuvre it really was. Excited by the prospect of a crushing victory, he permitted his forces to mount a hot pursuit, only for them to discover on the other side of the dust-cloud that the Jin right wing was drawn up in perfect order. Worse still, a sizeable section of the Jin centre detached itself and slammed into the flank of the pursuing Chu soldiers. This blow was delivered by 'Duke Wen's own select troops', an elite force of chariot warriors primed for this moment of action, which 'thereby routed the left wing of the Chu army'. The battle of Chengpu was over. The Chu centre struggled from the field, although it appears to have been spared any serious harassment. As one contemporary commented, 'the ruler of Jin was able to fight successfully because of the power of virtue'.

Allowing for the moral bias of Chinese chroniclers, the victory Duke Wen won in 632 BC took place within a ceremonial context. Possibly meant to exercise a civilising influence over the conduct of war, the emphasis in China on proper behaviour is so unlike the attitudes to battle found in the eastern Mediterranean. There the Egyptian pharaoh is the heroic defender of the divine order, the one who mercilessly smites those outsiders who dare to conspire against Egypt. Spells discovered in Asia Minor conform to the same outlook. Before a campaign the Hittite king would have had his priests pray for his enemies to be deprived of their gods, their weapons, their courage, their lives. Coming from a legalistic culture, he would also have set in train lawsuits against enemy peoples and enemy gods. All who opposed the royal will were rebels. This is very different from the recorded Chinese view, no matter that the state of Chu was thought to be semi-barbarian. At the time, Chengpu was welcomed as the stemming of the previously irresistible tide of Chu advance into the great plain of northern China, but without any suggestion that the people of Chu were considered to be beyond the pale. A profound dislike for military solutions which emerged in the philosophy of Confucius' followers may already have been at work. Confucius (551–479 BC) deeply regretted the growing violence of his own lifetime, and looked back for his inspiration to a past where the state was in effect a collection of families under the care of one leading family. When asked about government, Confucius replied: 'Let the prince be a prince, the minister a minister, the father a father, and the son a son.' The cultivated man accepted the authority of his superiors because he cherished justice, unlike the selfish man who held nothing in respect except himself. When he saw a chance for gain, he stopped to think whether to pursue it would be right; when he saw that his prince was in danger, he was ready to lay down his own life; when he gave his word, no matter how long ago, he always kept it.

The virtuous conduct of Duke Wen, Confucius believed, elicited similar behaviour from his subjects. Tzu Yu's failure at Chengpu could be seen, therefore, as a reflection of the less satisfactory social relations prevalent in the state of Chu. It could indeed be said that Duke Wen counted upon the ungovernable character of his opponents, a shrewd assessment in the light of the disastrous advance of the Chu left wing. Either its own lack of discipline or the inability of Tzu Yu to exercise control once battle was joined spelt disaster. In this analysis the pretended Jin retreat might be excused as a far-sighted strategem aimed at reducing the slaughter, because the counter-attack dispersed the Chu left, leaving its centre with no choice other than quitting the field. And there seems to have been no Jin pursuit.

Such an explanation accords with the reluctance of Chinese chroniclers, especially of the Confucian persuasion, to dwell upon the harsh facts of discipline, weaponry and bloodshed. Thus trickery was passed over in the account of Chengpu for the good reason that the commanders and soldiers of Chu were expected to act without regard to the norms of sensible conduct. They were bound to be rash when apparently offered an easy opportunity to attack. Even in the Warring States period (481–221 BC), when warfare reached levels of violence unparalleled in the rest of the ancient world, the Chinese repugnance for brute force remained strong. Sun Zi's *Art of War*, the oldest surviving military treatise, cautions the eager commander against taking unnecessary risks

with his troops: 'Under fragrant bait there is certain to be a hooked fish.'
Nor should an advantage be pressed too hard: 'Never press an enemy at
bay. Always leave a way of escape, or your foe will be forced to fight to
the death.' Military realism informed Sun Zi's approach to war, but he
was admired as the strategist who held that the greatest victory was the
one gained with the least fighting.

In the warfare of the Spring and Autumn period, however, we
encounter the Chinese equivalent of the epic battles of Greek and Indian
warriors. As well as following set procedures for joining battle, the nobles
relied on divination in order to determine whether or not to fight at all.
Everything was believed to happen within the sight of the ancestors,
without whose aid victory could never be guaranteed. There are records
of ancestral tablets being carried on campaign and it is known that it was
customary before battle to ask 'the spirits of former rulers' for protection
against enemy weapons, which makes the anxiety of the people of Cao
not at all surprising when Duke Wen decided to pitch his camp in the
graveyard containing their ancestors' tombs. Once the decision to fight
had been taken, nobles would mount daring raids and engage in archery

At the battle of Chengpu, the Chinese equivalent of these Egyptian 'runners'
would have accompanied Duke Wen's elite chariot warriors

duels from speeding chariots. Before the battle of Bi in 595 BC three Chu heroes taunted the Jin lines: one drove the chariot, the second loosed arrows, and the third protected the horses from foot soldiers with a halberd. Pursued by a squadron of Jin charioteers, the Chu adventurers were making a daring escape, when a stag leaped up before them and they downed it with their last arrow. As a consequence of this, they halted and presented the beast to their pursuers, who accepted the gift and broke off the chase. In letting the Chu chariot get away, the Jin nobles admitted the prowess and politeness of their foe. The engagement at Bi more than avenged the reverse suffered by Chu at Chengpu. 'Through this defeat,' a Jin counsellor remarked, 'Heaven is perhaps giving a grave warning to our state.' There were so many Jin casualties that the duke of Chu was urged to seriously consider 'piling up the bodies to make an imposing monument'. Another of the 'five great battles', Bi was caused once again by diplomatic wrangles among the smaller allied states. In exasperation the Chu army besieged the capital of Chen, a perpetual waverer between Jin and Chu. To the amazement of his attendants the duke of Chu agreed to a peaceful settlement with Chen, after its lord came to him in submission with 'his chest bared and leading a sheep'. Duke Chuan said: 'This ruler knows how to humble himself before others, and he must therefore know how to employ his own people in good faith. What more can we hope to gain by denying his request?'

Annoyed by Chu's intervention, the duke of Jin sent his army to rescue Chen, only for it to discover that Chen had already made peace with Chu. The Jin commanders were left in a quandary. Should they continue south and confront the Chu army, or abandon the campaign and return home? Without further instructions from their duke, an evenly balanced debate between them ended in a decision not to go on, until, on the initiative of a single commander, the Jin army 'began to cross the Yellow river'. Undoubtedly there was apprehension over intelligence regarding the improved condition of the Chu army. One Jin general wisely observed:

'Since Sunshu Ao became prime minister of Chu, he has selected regulations that are proper to the state of Chu. Thus the whole army is on the move, the men on the right advance in the direction pointed by the chariot poles, while those on the left go in search of fodder, and the forward scouts with their pennants make certain there are no enemy forces ahead. The central column does the planning, the column behind it uses its best troops to guard the rear, and the various officers move in accordance with the directions displayed on flags. Thus the army functions smoothly and efficiently and there is no need to apply punishments, proof that the men of Chu respectfully follow regulations.'

More telling still for battlefield co-ordination was the remark: 'Foot soldiers and charioteers are on close and friendly terms.' In the meantime, Duke Chuan was watering his horses on another stretch of the Yellow river, before ordering his troops back to Chu. When he heard about the Jin move southwards, he was still inclined to withdrawal, a move Sunshu Ao also supported. But another minister advised the duke to seek battle on the grounds that all the Jin generals were 'newly appointed, and do not know how to enforce regulations'; the one who had precipitated the river crossing was 'stubborn and perverse, a heartless man incapable of heeding commands'; and subordinates, who would like to follow orders, 'have no competent officers to lead them'.

Undecided about the wisdom of fighting, Duke Chuan twice tried to reach a peaceful settlement without success. On the day of the battle he need not have worried. While his personal guard of 'thirty chariots, divided into left and right wings' was vigilant in his protection, the entire Chu army 'took to the field' so that the duke might not 'plunge in among the Jin forces'. A false alarm of a Jin advance started the action, sending 'the Chu army forward at full speed, its chariots racing along with its foot soldiers, swooping down on the Jin army'. The Jin ranks immediately broke as soldiers turned to flee to the river bank, where an order to cross in haste only served to increase the panic; for afterwards we are told 'there were so many fingers in the bottoms of boats that one could scoop them up by the handful'. Latecomers, attempting to board, had had their fingers chopped off by comrades fearful of them capsizing the boats. At the Chu encampment 'the din of the Jin crossing was heard throughout the night'. This confused retreat aside, there were still incidents of chivalry witnessed at the close of hostilities.

One of the retreating chariots among the Jin forces fell into a hole and would not move. Chu soldiers told its driver to remove the

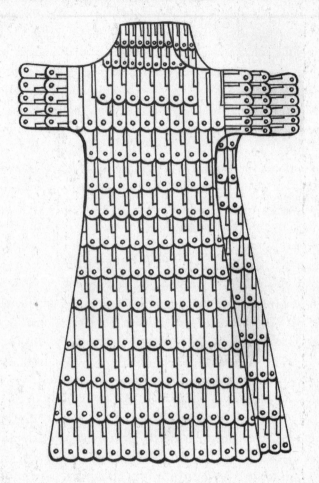

*Egyptian bronze armour, not dissimilar to the corselet which saved
Menelaus' life at Troy*

horizontal bar in front of the vehicle. When this was done, the
chariot moved forward a little, but the horses kept shying to the
side. The soldiers then told the charioteer to remove the pennant
staff and place it on the crosspiece of the yoke. This done, the
chariot finally got out of the hole. Thereupon the released
charioteer turned and said, 'We have not had as much experience in
running away as the men of your great state!'

Into the mouth of the victorious duke of Chu are put words which
totally accord with Confucius' attitude to war. Rejecting the proposal

for a grandiose monument composed of the Jin dead, Duke Chuan said:

> 'The purpose of military action is to prohibit violence, put aside arms, guard the great cause of leadership, establish strength, give peace to the people, bring harmony to the multitude, and gather wealth. If one accomplishes these aims, there is no possibility of sons and grandsons ever forgetting such a glorious achievement. Nothing else is necessary to preserve its memory. You do not understand such things! The character for military affairs is made up of the strokes for "stop" and "halberd". Since I have not succeeded in bringing conflict to an end, how can we think of erecting a monument?'

Even though the mannered skirmishes of charioteers were not to last in China, as battles turned into large-scale infantry actions, with massed armoured columns of foot soldiers supported by crossbowmen, chariotry and cavalry, the chariot itself never lost its appeal to historians. Looking back on struggles between the first ancient states almost as a lost ideal, they tended to give pride of place to the dashing charioteer. Quite typical is their pleasure in retelling the story of the ruler of Chen's lucky escape in his chariot. Pursued after the battle of Yenling, in 575 BC, by the Jin commander Han Chueh, the ruler's chariot was losing the race because his anxious driver kept looking over his shoulder instead of concentrating on the horses. When Han Chueh's own chariot driver pointed this out and suggested they overtake their quarry, the Jin commander demurred, saying, 'I cannot bear to inflict disgrace upon the head of a state a second time!' So the chase was halted.

A similar nostalgia for the heroic days of the chariot is evident in India, long after it ceased to be the decisive weapon of war. Like Egypt, chariotry was introduced into the country around 1500 BC by an invader, whom we know as the Indo-Aryans, but unlike the Egyptian experience with the Hyksos, the conquerors of northern India stayed on and became the dominant group in the culture of the subcontinent. As a consequence of this ancient military success the chariot assumed a key place in the Indian imagination. According to the *Rig Veda*, India's oldest surviving religious work, it was the 'all-outstripping chariot wheel' of Indra which overcame the determined and prolonged resistance of the indigenous population. This great god was then lord of the sky and armed with an irresistible thunderbolt, a weapon the ancient Greeks reserved for their chief deity Zeus. It was Indra who inspired, and actively assisted, the Indo-Aryan charioteers on the battlefield. That the chariots they drove were identical to the models used in West Asia points to an invasion of India from that direction: this now seems more than a possibility because of the discovery that the technical terms used in training horses there are very close to Sanskrit, the language of the *Rig Veda*. The horse-training

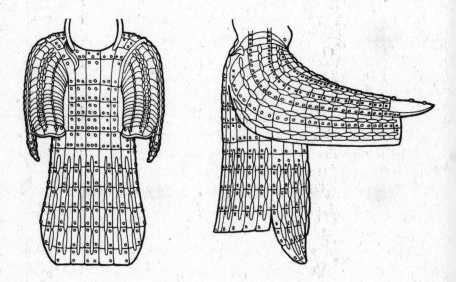

A Chinese charioteer's armour made from iron plates

manual of Kikkuli of Mitanni, which was translated into several ancient languages, is the fundamental text. The fact of its translation shows how great a value was put upon the expertise of this famous trainer, even to the extent of retaining his Sanskrit-like technical terms. Originally composed for the benefit of the Mitannians, in the fourteenth century BC, the manual would have been consulted by trainers responsible for chariotry. It should perhaps be noted, too, how the Mitannians worshipped Indra, Mitra, Varuna and the Asvins, the twin horse-headed gods of ancient India. The association of Indra with chariotry is clear in the *Rig Veda*, numberless verses of which praise the glory of the chariot and mention its various parts. So potent was this divine vehicle that it is said to 'conquer the four quarters of the world'. One commentator could compare prayer itself to a well-made chariot, as 'chanting should be performed in a way that causes it to stand firmly on each syllable, like a chariot stands firmly on each of its wheelspokes in turn'.

Where chariot battle is paid the greatest attention is in two Indian epics, the *Ramayana* and the *Mahabharata*, composed in the fifth to the fourth centuries BC. These two poems recall a time when differences were settled by archery duels between chariot warriors. Despite the importance of his profession, the charioteer still occupied a much lower social position than that of the chariot warrior. King Salya, for instance, lost his temper when requested to act as the charioteer of a fellow monarch by the name of Karna. 'Look at these massive arms of mine,' said the humiliated ruler, 'strong as the thunder. Look at my powerful bow and these arrows that are like the bite of a poisonous snake. Look at my chariot, and at my mace decked with gold and hempen cords. When filled with anger, I can split the earth, scatter mountains, and empty oceans!' This outburst was prompted by Salya's scorn for Karna, who had recently been elevated to kingship. The caste system, a unique feature of Indian society, could not countenance such a change in status. Unaware of Karna's descent from the sun god Surya, Salya was only mollified by a comparison between himself and the great god Brahma, who once acted as a charioteer. As another king reminded him, the driver of the chariot should be better than the warrior, if one desired safety as well as success on the battlefield. Later in the *Mahabharata* Karna was killed in a world-shaking conflict by a crescent-shaped arrow fired from the bow of Arjuna, whose own charioteer was none other than Krishna, an incarnation of the preserver god Vishnu.

The late date for the composition of the epics had no adverse effect on their portrayal of chariot battle, quite probably through the longer survival of chariotry as an attacking force in India. Alexander had to deal with chariots, cavalry and elephants when he met the north Indian ruler Porus at Hydaspes river in 326 BC. Porus employed chariots for scouting and for assaulting the wings of the Macedonian army. The accurate recall in the *Ramayana* and the *Mahabharata* of the methods employed in chariot warfare by the Indo-Aryan invaders is astounding in comparison with Homer's total lack of insight. The *Iliad* reduces chariots to battle-taxis, as they do little more than ferry heroes to and from the fight. Spear throwers are mentioned, chariot-borne archers not at all. For Homer the chariot's function was exactly the same as the horse in his own day: a nobleman rode to the battlefield, where he dismounted and joined his poorer comrades-in-arms as a foot soldier. The ancient Greeks had simply forgotten the original purpose of the chariot, although they sensed the exulted position it once enjoyed in a heroic past.

2

The Rise of the Charioteer

And the gods stood by me, the proud god of the storm, my lord, and the sun goddess of Arinna, my lady . . . and with my chariotry I destroyed the enemy.

Hittite inscription

Chariot warfare relied upon the wheel, the horse and the bow. By looking in turn at the evolution of these three critical components, it is possible to chart the charioteer's amazing rise to prominence.

Wagons as well as carts are known to have been used from the beginning of the third millennium BC, but they were heavy, solid-wheeled vehicles, and were more readily drawn by oxen than horses. For the fast-moving chariot a spoked wheel was essential. So light were the best chariots that their owners could pick them up and raise them above their heads. During the siege of Troy such an idea occurred to Diomedes one night when he raided a Thracian encampment along with Odysseus. The two Greek leaders had already dealt with Dolon, a Trojan spy, before their attack on Troy's sleeping Thracian allies. While Odysseus made off with the Thracian king's best horses, 'Diomedes wondered what was the most outrageous thing he could do, whether to take the chariot in which ornamented armour lay, dragging it by the draught pole or lifting it up and carrying it away.' Because he was slow in making up his mind the goddess Athena advised him to return to the Greek camp, lest other gods arouse the Trojans. As a result of Athena's favour, Diomedes was one of the few Greek leaders to have a safe and speedy voyage home from the Trojan War. There is even a hint at the end of his life, when he was busy founding cities in southern Italy, that this goddess may have assisted in his attainment of immortality. However, in the *Iliad*, Homer's ninth-century BC account of the ten-year struggle between the Greeks and the Trojans, Diomedes is forcefully reminded of the difference between the immortals and the mortals, despite his wounding of the love goddess Aphrodite. 'Take care,' the oracular god Apollo told him, 'and give way! Do not strive to be the equal of the gods. The immortals are not made of the same stuff as men who walk on the ground.' When he heard this he halted his pursuit of the wounded goddess even though he had just driven her husband, the war god Ares, from the battlefield. The point of making clear Diomedes' position as nothing more than an energetic and daring fighter is that ancient Greek representations of warriors holding chariots aloft can then be interpreted for what they are: looters with abandonned chariots, not gods offering special protection to charioteers. Made from light hardwoods, with an interwoven leather platform on which at least two men could stand, an entire chariot weighed less than 30 kilograms.

Confirmation of this deliberate sacrifice of protection for the lightness so necessary to ensure speed came in 1922 from the discovery of the pharaoh Tutankhamun's own chariots, since their fronts and sides were only partly filled with very thin wood, sometimes covered in gold leaf. The sensational find of his tomb by Howard Carter fired the popular imagination, especially when it was realised that magnificent though the treasures were they comprised a collection of personal belongings hastily buried with an ineffectual ruler. At the end of his short reign in 1346 BC, Tutankhamun's young queen Ankhesenamum had begged the Hittite king to send her one of his sons to marry and share the Egyptian throne with her. A Hittite prince named Zannanza was dispatched but he never arrived, leaving the Egyptians and the Hittites to drift into a war which included the engagement at Kadesh, instead of uniting against their common enemy, resurgent Assyria. There is no record of Tutankhamun ever fighting in any of his chariots, despite their heroic decoration: he is usually depicted enjoying the pleasures of the palace gardens in the company of his queen. And the fact that there is room for two persons standing abreast on the thong mesh floor suggests that, like other pharaohs, Tutankhamun did not often drive a chariot himself, notwithstanding a distinct reluctance on the part of artists to give any credit to the charioteer whenever a pharaonic victory was celebrated on a temple wall. But going into battle or hunting alone in a chariot could both be extremely hazardous. To leave the hands free for the use of weapons the reins were tied around the hips. This ostentatious method of driving, not unlike riding a bicycle without holding the handlebars, later became a

The racing accident in the Tomb of the Olympic Games

fashion among the more daring competitors in chariot races. The Romans copied this practice from their northern neighbours the Etruscans, who were supposed to have instituted a festival of chariot racing on the advice of an oracle in order to be rid of the plague. The so-called Tomb of the Olympic Games at Tarquinia, in present-day Tuscany, reveals the fatal consequence of such foolhardiness. One of its wall-paintings depicts a race between four two-horsed chariots. The leading charioteer turns anxiously round to scan his pursuers, two of whom drive on their teams in a frenzy, while the last charioteer hurtles feet first over the top of his distraught horses. One animal has in stumbling broken loose from the yoke and fallen to the ground in a tangle of reins, the other rears up in terror. Between the two horses the hapless charioteer has been shot through the air like a missile fired from a catapult. Had he not had the reins tied around his body he might have retained some control of the chariot, or at least he could have had a chance of throwing himself sideways, out of the way of the wreckage. Other Etruscan tombs show similar accidents with men somersaulting forward out of their chariots.

The ultimate origin of the light, spoked chariot wheel was the solid wooden wheel. Because of the difficulty of finding trees thick enough to provide single-piece wheels, carpenters were obliged to experiment with two or three planks, joining them together with internal mortices. These sturdy but heavy wheels were in use from around 3000 BC on wagons weighing up to half a tonne. Only oxen could pull such heavy loads, for the good reason that harnessing remained a problem. Animals apply

An early Mesopotamian chariot drawn by asses

tractive power by pushing against a harness, which then transmits the force of the pressure to the vehicle in the form of traction. Beneath a yoke attached to a draught pole the oxen were secured by means of thick neck-straps. Although the anatomy of the ox is more suited to this method of traction than the longer-necked horse, the harness was far from efficient. When horses were expected to pull vehicles with heavy wheels, as in the so-called battle-cars depicted on the Standard of Ur, dating from 2500 BC, their tractive power would have been greatly reduced. The four-wheeled vehicles shown on this remarkable discovery, which was recovered in 1926 by Leonard Woolley from a royal cemetery in southern Mesopotamia, were probably the transport of a Sumerian king on his way to the battlefield. As the horses or asses struggle to breathe leaning against braided-rope neck-straps, the men standing on the rear platforms have to steady themselves on the springless battle-cars by holding the shoulders of the drivers.

The patent defect of this ancient harness is that it seriously impaired the breathing of the horses by pressing on the trachea whenever they needed to pull strongly, thus preventing them from taking full advantage of their combined strength and energy. No matter the variations of this kind of harness, the lower ends of which were attached to the yoke, there always remained a degree of suffocation. Outside of China the problem was only solved by reducing the weight of the vehicle itself: hence the incredible lightness of Tutankhamun's chariots. But the Chinese invention of the breast-strap harness, the prototype of the modern collar one, permitted an animal to throw its entire weight against a load because the harness pulled on the shoulders, leaving the throat unaffected. The importance of this advance was first noticed at the beginning of the twentieth century by a French officer, Lefebvre des Noëttes, who asked about the origin of the collar harness. When nobody could answer the question, he proceeded to look at carvings of animals in museums from all civilisations, and at illustrated manuscripts in libraries. What he realised was the general use of the inefficient throat-and-girth harness up to the end of the tenth century AD, with one notable exception, China. There it was obvious that a breast-strap arrangement of harnessing had aided traction from ancient times. A trace on each side of the horse was held by straps, so that the pull came on the shoulders. For the Chinese chariot did not have, like others elsewhere, a straight draught pole but a curved one attached to the breast-strap halfway along its length. In bas-reliefs from Chinese tombs, dating from the second century BC, even single horses between shafts pull with ease two-wheeled vehicles carrying several passengers. The reins are always carried high so as to have a lifting effect and to prevent the horse from lowering its head to the ground, which would cause the vehicle to tilt forward. Apart from this minor detail, traction is identical to the modern system.

Disc-wheeled vehicles appear to have originated in Mesopotamia, the Standard of Ur battle-cars being comparatively late examples. But the swift adoption of this novel form of transport soon spread wagons and carts across large areas of Europe and West Asia. The value of the new transportation aside, an element of prestige and status was involved in the possession of wheeled vehicles, which later became even more evident with the advent of the horse. Yet a certain hesitation lingered over horses in Mesopotamia, despite a desire for their display with a chariot. Some time before 1800 BC Zimri-Lim, the ruler of the city of Mari on the River Euphrates, tried in vain to obtain white horses from fellow rulers. His determined quest was eventually halted on the advice of a palace official, who suggested that it was more dignified for a king to travel by a mule-drawn cart than to use horses, since the training of the latter had probably still to be perfected. 'My lord should honour his position as a king,' the official wrote, 'and not ride with horses.' Neither the ruler of Qatna nor Carchemish, respectively in present-day Syria and Turkey, were able to oblige Zimri-Lim, but he did receive from another monarch some 'red' horses in exchange for a quantity of tin, a crucial

One of the four-wheeled battle-cars depicted on the Standard of Ur

ingredient in the manufacture of bronze, then the dominant metal. Records also survive from the archive at Mari which give instructions about the stabling and feeding of imported horses. These early references to animal welfare, however, bear no comparison to the detail to be found in the great treatise of Kikkuli, who was in charge of the horses belonging to the king of Mitanni in the fourteenth century BC. By this date the horse-drawn chariot had caused a revolution in military tactics as far-reaching as that accomplished by the horseless carriage. Chariot battle was the ancient equivalent of mobile engagements dependent upon the internal combustion engine.

The genesis of the chariot is still disputed. Whereas its development from early solid-wheeled vehicles within West Asia satisfies one school of thought, others would place the invention of such key components as the spoked wheel in Europe. The latter argue for a wider geographical area of experimentation with light, bent-wood, fast horse-drawn carts; an area which includes West Asia, where the final evolution of the cart into the war chariot almost certainly took place, but also extends as far west as Hungary and as far north as Russia. Finds of bone harness strap-dividers there, along with model vehicles possessing both solid and spoked wheels suggest a more extensive interest in wheeled transport than was originally envisaged. Because the archaeological evidence for the spoked-wheeled vehicle is so scanty in Europe though, it is impossible to establish a reliable chronology for its evolution. All that can be recognised now is the excitement of ancient peoples in its potential as well as the effort they put into fully realising it.

Closer to the earliest known use of the chariot for warfare are the striking vehicles unearthed at Lchashen on the southern shore of Lake Sevan in Armenia. The Lchashen barrow graves came to light in the 1950s, when a hydroelectric project significantly lowered the level of the lake and revealed the cemetery. Undisturbed, but waterlogged, the twenty-three vehicles recovered show an amazing range of types, from four-wheeled and two-wheeled wagons and carts with solid wheels to light spoked-wheeled passenger carriages, or chariots. Naturally it was the passenger carriages that were the immediate focus of attention, not least because their dimensions were discovered to be the same as Chinese chariots. The parallel seemed too great to be dismissed as a coincidence, and a case was made for the transfer of this design eastwards by the Tocharians, an Indo-European people who settled in what today is the Chinese province of Xinjiang. That the Lchashen chariots had an open front, and rails at the sides and back, means they were not designed for warfare. They were rather the fast transport of an exulted person. Where their design differs from the standard West Asian chariot is in the placement of the axle, for it is in the middle of the chariot and not at the rear. Stability was given to the light war chariot by a rear axle with a wide wheel base. The long draught pole, which ran all the way under the body, and helped to give support, was attached only at the front. But, like the Lchashen, the West Asian chariot had a floor of interwoven thongs in order to keep the vehicle's weight down and provide some springiness. Bronze models of vehicles with rear axles excavated at Lchashen, however, indicate that the inhabitants of ancient Armenia used chariots in battle too.

Even though the accepted date for the Lchashen finds is rather late, somewhere around 1500 BC, the recovery of wheels each with twenty-eight spokes, morticed at their outer ends into a felloe of two half-circles of bent wood, is testimony to an established tradition of advanced carpentry. The presence of bronze bits as well as models of horses merely serves to underline the great emphasis placed on transport. One of the

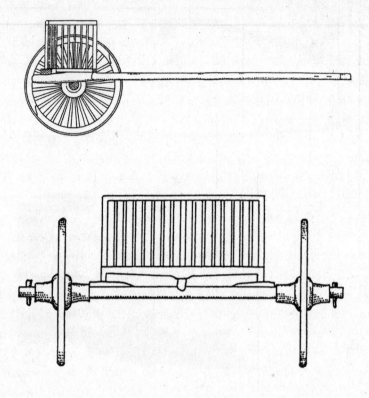

A Lchashen chariot

earliest references to horses is indeed the letter sent by Zimri-Lim acknowledging the receipt of the 'red' horses, which came from the rugged north, 'the mountain of horses', most likely Armenia.

Just as the earliest wheeled vehicles are located in Mesopotamia, so the essential features of the chariot – a light open vehicle with two spoked wheels, drawn by horses yoked on either side of a draught pole – are first evident on Syrian seals dating from the eighteenth century BC. Earlier representations of spoke-wheeled vehicles from Asia Minor, the Hittite heartland, indicate an undoubted advance in transportation, although the yoking of four horses together suggests they were carts rather than chariots. The Syrian seals also reveal the improved construction of the wheel itself, as some of them show eight or nine spokes. It has even been suggested that one of the wheels illustrated on the seals may have been partly metal in construction. Experimentation can be seen, too, in the design of the chariot platform. The use of bent wood to achieve lightness and strength allowed the emergence of the chariot box, the curved front typical of later chariots. In the next chapter the contribution made by various ancient peoples to the rise of the charioteer will be fully discussed. Here it is enough to say that no ethnic or linguistic group seems to have been the sole originator of horse-drawn chariotry. A variety of events conspired to raise the charioteer to supreme status on the battlefield. That he was already adept at archery is made clear by the Syrian seals, no matter that the scenes they record refer as much to hunting as warfare.

After the spoked wheel, the second key component for chariotry is the trained horse. Though most people assume riding and horses are inseparable, the horse was not the first animal to be ridden regularly. In Mesopotamia riding, like driving, started with the slow-moving ox. The wild ass was also adopted as a mount, but because of its small size riding could only be an occasional activity. The same held true for the wild horse, until its domestication on the steppes produced a larger and more robust specimen. Even then the absence of the horseshoe meant that mounted troops were at a disadvantage when compared with charioteers. Asses have harder hooves than horses, whose original habitat was semi-desert or steppe regions. The horse's hoof, like the human fingernail, grows continuously, but the extra weight of a rider will soon wear it down, especially if the ground is hard and dry. The Romans tied a metal sole to the hoof with leather straps, but it was not a very effective shoe. The problem remained insuperable in ancient times wherever horsemen chose to wear armour. Not until the ninth century AD does the nailed horseshoe come into use right across the Old World, reducing in the process wear and tear on cavalry mounts.

It was once argued that the domesticated horse had been brought to West Asia by Indo-European peoples who came there around 2000 BC as charioteers. They were said to have arrived from beyond the Caucasus or the Zagros mountains in present-day Iran. Now the accepted view favours a gradual spread of horses from the Russian steppe, so that the inhabitants of Mesopotamia were familiar with them from the third millennium BC onwards. This does not of course mean that the horse immediately replaced either the mule or the ass: Zimri-Lim appears to have been following a new fashion at Mari with his stable of fine horses. For of all domestic animals the horse remains the most temperamental and nervous. An animal of flight rather than fight, the first reaction of a horse to danger is a gallop to a safer place. Compared to the stubborn ass, it is more difficult to train, not least because so much more is expected from the horse than any other domestic animal. In order to be useful to ancient man, the horse was required to pull wagons, carts and chariots as well as accept bone and metal devices in its mouth and a number of straps on its head and body. The earliest system for the yoke, adapted from that used for oxen, had reins attached to a noseband. When four horses were involved, as in the Standard of Ur battle-cars, only the two central horses were yoked and the two outsiders were controlled by reins or traces alone. Yet as herd animals, horses are easier to manage in such teams than alone, and they are competitive at speed. The outsiders, feeling less pressure against their throats and less yoke pressure on their necks than the inner ones, would have set the pace for the whole team. During the journey they could have been swapped over in order to rest the yoked horses. Possibly the greater willingness of the horse to co-operate in a team helps to explain the reason for the charioteer's initial fame. Putting to one side the absence of horseshoes, stirrups and saddles, it would have been comparatively easier to train chariot horses than cavalry mounts. Ridden horses did not in fact become a regular feature of armies in West Asia until the first millennium BC, and even then charioteers still had a role to play on the battlefield. Shooting arrows while riding and controlling a galloping horse remained far harder than firing a bow from a speeding chariot. Only the mounted bowmen from the steppes, notably the Parthians, were to succeed in mastering this difficult skill in the West.

Another reason why riding became popular long after driving concerns the size of the first domesticated horses. The steppe horse was more like a pony than the modern, selectively bred steed. It was never as large as the medieval horse, which averaged 14 hands as opposed to the modern domestic horse of 15 or 16 hands (a hand equals 10 cm). Today the 14-hand horse is considered suitable for breeding ponies alone. It should be remembered, too, how modern horses left to fend for themselves over a few generations will revert to an average smaller size: witness the mustang in the western states of America. The effort involved in breeding the first domesticated horses, therefore, cannot be overestimated. For during the earliest stage of domestication it is obvious that the horse and the ass remained the same size. As draught animals, they could be employed interchangeably, but neither of them mounted would have been able to sustain galloping for any distance.

A Syrian seal of a chariot

Since wild horses are non-territorial, the nomadic peoples of the steppe had the best opportunity for taming them. These horses would have formed mobile bands, comprising one stallion with half a dozen mares and their young. The stallion guarded and protected his mares and foals, but he would not defend territory. This kind of grouping is a function of migration: it represents a way of dealing with an unpredictable environment and variable conditions for food supply. Mobility was an advantage, since the horse's disgestive system permits survival on large quantities of low-protein fodder. Grazing was possible wherever grass would grow, although larger herds could only linger on stretches of rich pasture before moving to another suitable location. When grass fell into short supply, horses like asses would have eaten bushes or scrub vegetation as well. The special adaptation to the mouth that was necessary for horses to graze on marginal land proved invaluable to ancient man, when it came to harnessing. For there is a gap between the grinding teeth and the incisors at the front of the jaw into which a bit can be readily fitted. In West Asia the bit does not appear in the archaeological record until the sixteenth century BC, about the time the light war chariot made its appearance. But so essential was the bit for directing either ridden or driven horses it is inconceivable that none existed prior to this date. The second physiological adaptation made by the horse which assisted domestication was its digestive system. As it possesses a single stomach, unlike cattle, the horse does not require a period of rest so that it can ruminate after feeding. By skipping these breaks, and being able to feed on many different kinds of grasses, the range and speed of the horse became legendary. For this reason the emphasis placed by Kikkuli on a balanced regime of exercise and feeding is instructive. For the seventy-first day of training, his famous manual recommends:

> When the horses are brought out of the stable in the morning, they are harnessed, and taken out for a short distance. When they come back to be unharnessed and unbridled, they are given water while tethered tightly. At midday they receive hay, but at the time of the evening feed they are brought out of the stable and harnessed. He then drives them, and they gallop over ten fields. When he brings them back, they are unharnessed and unbridled, and given water. In the stable the horses eat hay all night, and their feed is poured out for them.

These orders to grooms and handlers from the master horseman of Mitanni give an indication of the extent of the training that was undertaken for chariot horses. At the end of a seven-month programme, the trained horses were capable of trotting long distances without tiring, and of pulling a chariot at top speed for over a kilometre. No West Asian or Egyptian ruler could afford to risk battle without such a guarantee. At Megiddo in 1460 BC Thutmose III must have got perilously close to the limits of his horses' endurance, a circumstance which may have persuaded him to make an immediate attack on his enemies, from an unexpected direction.

Documentary evidence for horses is sparse before the era of the Mari archives, the late nineteenth or early eighteenth centuries BC. There was indeed surprise among scholars when these records were first published, since it was believed that horses were not common in West Asia until the rise of Mitanni, several centuries afterwards. Chariot warfare was not practised during the reign of Zimri-Lim, who held off both the Assyrians and the Babylonians. For a few years Mari and Babylon were the leading powers in Mesopotamia: then Zimri-Lim fell out with Babylon and Mari was sacked, leaving modern archaeologists to find in its rubble a store of 20,000 clay tablets. They comprise letters, lists of stores, details of palace personnel, legal judgments and tax information. Already we have noticed in one letter Zimri-Lim's desire for imported horses, and the

Grooming a horse

anxiety of his officials over the problems they were likely to cause. Yet the Mari archive implies that there was a good stable of palace horses, which took part in religious processions. References to chariots, indeed swift chariots, cannot be taken to mean that they were pulled by horses, rather than mules. One official reports how 'the king gave me a chariot, but when I went towards the mountains that chariot broke in the middle. Now I travel around without a chariot.' His plea for another vehicle so as to continue his duties again provides no indication of whether it was horse-drawn. During Mari's heyday horses were prized animals, and ownership seems to have been restricted to the royal family. Their source, other than those bred at Mari itself, was the states situated to the north and west. Nowhere is it suggested that breeding or training of horses was the exclusive preserve of the hill peoples who were soon to found Mitanni and place the charioteer centre-stage. Peoples from diverse ethnic and linguistic groups, including the nomads of the Syrian desert, were involved with the horse and its evolving role in ancient society.

Among nomadic peoples the horse was to become indispensable. To walk was nothing less than misery. Life without a mount would have

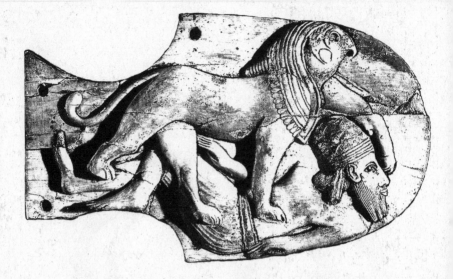

A blinker showing a griffin treading on a fallen warrior

been impossible when whole peoples were on the move. Thus the Mongols despised the Turkic peoples of Central Asia as 'utterly exhausted, without horses and without clothes'. We know how the nomadic Xiongnu supplied the ancient Chinese with horses, although the latter were interested in getting better ones from Ferghana, which were famous all over the ancient world. The Han dynasty emperor Wu Di sent in 115 BC an envoy named Zhang Qian to Central Asia in order to obtain breeding stock. As a result, one of the chieftains living near Lake Balkhash, in modern Kazakhstan, asked for the hand of a Chinese princess and dispatched 1,000 horses as a betrothal present. The chieftain was given Liu Xijun, a princess of the imperial blood, who set off in 110 BC with a large retinue for the distant land. Ever since, the homesickness of the princess has proved a fascinating subject for both painters and poets: she who yearned 'to be the yellow swan that returns home'. But the emperor was soon dissatisfied with indirect contacts and in 101 BC, after a three-year campaign, a Chinese general succeeded in conquering the Ferghana basin, beyond the Pamir mountains, and securing enough horses for stud purposes. These large horses were used as cavalry mounts for heavily armed men against the Xiongnu archers who rode the smaller Mongolian pony. Chariotry was never an option against the nomads roaming the steppe beyond the line of the Great Wall. Success depended upon matching their cavalry tactics, something Huo Quling did before his early death at the age of twenty-four years. He conducted a series of brilliant campaigns against the Xiongnu, thereby securing China's route to Central Asia. In recognition of this achievement, a grateful Wu Di accorded the young general the honour of a state funeral adjacent to the imperial tombs, north of Chang'an, the Chinese capital. On an artificial hill raised above the grave were placed a variety of stone carvings, executed by the imperial workshops. The purpose of these fabulous beasts, monsters and horses trampling nomads was the perpetuation of Huo Quling's victories through the attraction of benevolent spirits.

Neither the statuary, which spiritual advisers assured the emperor was effective, nor the crossbow, then a standard infantry weapon for Chinese soldiers, was adequate against the Xiongnu, whose cousins appear to have been the Huns, the scourge of the western provinces of the Roman empire under Attila's leadership. By 91 BC Emperor Han Wu Di had to admit that there was no possibility of further campaigning, and an uneasy peace was agreed between China and the northern nomads led by the Xiongnu. That the outcome of the struggle was determined by cavalry indicates how important the horse had become across the Old World. Where peoples, like the Persians, had ceased to be nomadic and settled as farmers, the horse never lost its mystique. According to the Greek historian Herodotus, Darius I succeeded to the throne because his horse neighed first after the sun rose. When it was agreed among the contenders for power that this auspicious sign would determine the succession,

Darius went to see his clever groom called Oebares. He told him of the arrangement they had come to, whereby they should sit on their horses' backs and the throne should be given to the one whose horse neighed first. 'Can you find a way,' Darius asked, 'for me to win this contest?' Oebares answered: 'Well, master, if your chance of winning depends upon nothing else, you may be confident that you will be king. I know a charm which will just suit your purpose.' So Oebares, as soon as it was dark, took from the stables a mare which Darius' horse was particularly fond of, and tethered her on the outskirts of the city. Then he brought the stallion and led him round and round the mare, getting closer and closer in narrowing

An Assyrian groom holding a pair of richly caparisoned horses

circles, and finally allowed him to mount her. Next morning just
before dawn the six contenders, as was agreed, came riding their
horses through the city, until they reached the spot where the mare
had been tethered the previous night. At once Darius' horse started
forward and neighed. At the same time, though the sky was clear,
there was a flash of lightning and a clap of thunder. It was a
sign from heaven, and the election of Darius was thus assured. His
five rivals leapt from their horses and bowed to the ground at his
feet.

So Herodotus says Oebares ensured Darius' elevation to the throne. Only
the esteem in which the horse was still held by these ex-nomads can
really explain how this arrangement was ever agreed.

In West Asia there was not the same level of worship accorded to the
horse, notwithstanding the Persian conquest. Babylon fell in 538 BC and
Egypt a decade afterwards. Following his enthronement in 522 BC as the
Great King, Darius I annexed northwestern India, campaigned in
Europe, and commenced building at Persepolis in modern Iran his

monumental capital. By this date West Asian armies had largely abandoned the chariot as a war machine. Almost in desperation the last Persian king, Darius III, used in 331 BC a special type of scythed chariot at the battle of Gaugamela, near the modern Iraqi city of Erbil. Drawn by heavily blinkered horses and driven by a single charioteer, the chariots carried razor-sharp blades on their axles and on the front and sides of the yoke pole. The intention was that these chariots, launched at full speed, would break up the formation of Alexander the Great's infantry and that the Persian cavalry would gallop into any gap or attack disordered enemy units. But as chariots need a level surface, Darius prepared three avenues of advance and, in so doing, alerted the Macedonians to the threat they posed. Regular chariots, along with elephants, were added to the cavalry stationed on the Persian left in order to oppose Alexander's best horsemen and offer an opportunity of envelopment. By adopting an oblique line of advance, the Macedonians thwarted Darius' special chariot charge. Some of the scythed chariots were disabled by javelin throwers, while the rest passed harmlessly through openings in the infantry line, a piece of drill Alexander must have made his men practise before the action started. Spears would have been thrust at the passing chariot horses too. It is worth noting how Alexander commanded on horseback, and sealed the fate of the Persian empire by leading his cavalry directly towards Darius, who in panic turned his chariot and fled. Darius' hasty departure ended any hope of further resistance to Alexander: his pursuit of the fugitive Persian king came to a halt when Darius was killed by his personal attendants.

The gratitude Alexander felt for his war-horse surprised his army when in northwestern India he named a city after it, Bucephala. There the faithful stallion had died of exhaustion and old age. It had been named Bucephalus, or 'ox-header', after the ox-head shaped brand-mark of a famous Thessalian stable. King Philip of Macedon, Alexander's father, was taken by the horse, but it proved unmanageable and was being rejected as a royal mount when Alexander said he could ride the powerful thoroughbred himself. Turning the horse's head towards the sun, so that he would no longer be startled by his own shadow, Alexander calmed Bucephalus, then mounted him, to Philip's delight. The king is supposed to have commented on the suitability of such a war-horse for conquest beyond the shores of Europe. In fact Bucephalus

An Egyptian horse possibly wearing a protective covering

died an immense distance eastwards in late 326 BC, almost a decade after
Alexander commenced his long campaign in Asia.

One ancient practice, the slitting of horses' nostrils, was not favoured
by nomadic peoples. A stone relief from Amarna in Egypt, which is dated
to 1350 BC, shows the extent of the operation: its purpose was helping
the animal to breathe more freely. The practice seems to have begun in an
effort to compensate for impaired breathing caused by pressure from the
noseband that preceded the bit. This method of control was employed on
the Standard of Ur battle-cars, since its horses were steered by means of
nosebands, the reins from which passed back to the driver through a
double ring set on the yoke. Surviving metal rings indicate that they were
attached to a pole. There is no real necessity for slitting horses' nostrils,
but the practice died hard, and it can still be found in odd corners of the
world today, especially where donkeys are used to tackle very heavy
loads. Directional control remained poor before the introduction of the

bit, essentially a straight or jointed bar: it developed complicated forms, to which were sometimes added cruelly spiked metal cheekplates. These were required to turn a galloping team quickly: manoeuvrability was always the prized quality of a chariot during high-speed engagements, a skill in which Ramesses' charioteer obviously excelled at Kadesh. The pharaoh's quick changes in direction as he led successive counter-attacks against the Hittite chariotry did much to save the Egyptian army there.

Early Egyptian use of the bit can be deduced from recent excavations in northern Sudan. There the Egyptians had built trading posts and strongholds from the beginning of the second millennium BC. In the remains of one of these fortified outposts at Buhen, which was destroyed by fire in 1675 BC, archaeologists unearthed the skeleton of a nineteen-year-old horse. Not only is it the earliest known Egyptian horse, but it also proves beyond doubt that the bit was in service at the time. This is clear from the excessive wear on the grinding teeth, caused by the horse champing on a bronze or bone bit. The Buhen horse measured around 150 cm at the shoulder. Such a strong and large horse would have been an asset in any chariot team. For the light, horse-drawn chariot was never used to charge into dense infantry formations. Above all it was a high-speed firing platform: the charioteer's task was to rapidly find suitable positions for the archer with him to harass and demoralise enemy infantry with his arrows.

The weapon that the chariot archer wielded so effectively was the composite bow. It was far more deadly than the so-called self, or ordinary, bow. What gave the composite bow increased velocity for its shot was the extra strength derived from adding strips of horn and sinew to wood. Power in a bow depends upon whether it is made of a simple stave, a combination of wood and bone, or of wood, horn, sinew, and glue. All these react differently to heat and moisture, so that a composite bow loses strength in damp conditions while the wooden stave suffers a similar loss of power in very hot weather. Either on horseback or in a chariot, a short bow is the desirable weapon. Surviving Indian, Iranian, Turkish and Chinese bows bear witness to this fact. One Turkish bow measures 96 cm when strung, the bow string being 89 cm in length. With a thickness for the bow of under 5 cm, the total weight is well under a kilogram, a lightness that would have pleased both the archer and his mount. The bow is constructed of buffalo horn and ox sinew, glued

An Egyptian horse with slit nostrils

to a thin piece of wood that forms its core. The projecting ends of this wooden strip are enlarged so as to become the solid ends of the bow where the bow string can be attached. The bow's leather outer covering is lacquered bright red and elaborately decorated with gold tracery. A skein of some sixty lengths of strong silk comprises the bow string: to prevent it fraying the bow string is joined at each of its ends to a separate loop, made of tightly twisted sinew. By means of this simple device the silk of the bow string is kept away from the body of the bow itself, thereby avoiding unnecessary damage. Stringing such a short bow requires great effort, and can only be achieved by using the legs. The archer needs to bend the bow between his legs and, at the same time, stoop down to fit the bow string.

Arrows fired from a bow like this would have been around 63 cm in length, and made to a standard pattern. Where the Turkish archer had an advantage over his opponents was in his use of the horn groove, which he wore on the thumb of his left hand. In resting the arrow in this groove, he could draw the point back some 5 cm within the inner surface of his bent bow. Thus he was able to shoot a short and light arrow that would fly much further than the longer and heavier one he would have had to use if he had shot without the grooved horn. Experiments conducted early last century showed that another 90 metres in range resulted from adopting this technique. The other piece of finger equipment that enhanced the Turkish archer's performance was the thumb-ring. Made from ivory or stone, the thumb-ring allowed him to release the bow string with the slightest movement, like pressing the trigger of a cocked gun. Again experiment revealed that an arrow shot by means of a thumb-ring always went beyond that of an arrow shot with three fingers holding the end of an arrow in the European fashion. The strength of the Turkish bow described above, or the weight that was required on the centre of the bow string to pull it down from the bow to the full length of the arrow, is 60 kilograms.

Only the ancient Chinese seem to have bothered to classify bows according to weight. Detailed records of the bowyer's craft allow us an insight into the construction of the composite bow. One Chinese text dating from Warring States period (481–221 BC) speaks of the 'six materials essential to a first-rate bow'. The first is 'the stave to let the bow have distance', the second 'the horn to give it speed', the third 'the sinew to afford penetration', the fourth 'the glue to bind it', the fifth 'silk to provide strength', and the sixth 'lacquer to proof it against moisture'. The text goes on to discuss the qualities required in these materials. Bow-staves are best made from 'dark brown' wood with a 'ringing sound' and 'straight grain, lest a twisted grain makes the bow warp'. Only white ox horn should be used for 'its resilience', although 'blackness is an indication of elasticity'. Above all it must not come from the pointed end of a horn, for this is 'hard but brittle'. An 'aged glue' is best for it 'can seep deep into cracks and fill them, so that when the bow is stretched tight, it will not break under pressure'. With sinews the bowyer needs 'long, narrow strips with sturdy ligaments'. The careful workmanship involved is brought home by the remark that 'all bows are made-to-measure to their owner's stature'. They also have to take account of temperament: that is to say, 'the owner's character and aggressiveness'. Whereas those with a 'slow disposition require a swift bow', archers known for their violence and vigour need 'a slow bow' to fire 'fast arrows'. The emphasis on balance and rhythm derives of course from a profound awareness of the control an archer had to have in order to hit and penetrate a target.

As with the chariot, the invention of the composite bow remains a mystery. There can be no doubt though that this advanced weapon pre-

Assyrians checking composite bows and arrows

dated the chariot, and its antecedents are most likely to be found among nomadic peoples. We are aware, for instance, how the Persians esteemed families with large numbers of children, the king sending gifts to the parents of these future warriors. And how from the age of five to twenty years, when military service began, boys were required to practise archery, a skill in which the Persians had been specially instructed by the Scythians. This name was given by the ancient Greeks to Central Asian peoples living to the north of the Black Sea. They traded with the Greek coastal cities founded there, exchanging wheat and fur for pottery, wine and jewellery. Expert mounted archers, the Scythians pushed southwards in the late sixth century BC until Persian arms drove them from what today is Turkey, and in Europe back across the Danube. The Persian king had already decisively beaten the Sakas, the name given in India to the Scythians still inhabiting Central Asia. These Scythians were to invade northwestern India in the first century BC and briefly rule there as the first wave of a series of invaders. Their military edge came from the composite bow, which was revered because of its accuracy and the number of years it took to make. That this weapon was common among nomadic, and semi-nomadic, peoples like the Scythians suggests an ancestry for it on the steppe far older than in the cities of West Asia and Egypt.

Friendly Scythian tribes always contributed cavalry to the Persian army, and in 490 BC they distinguished themselves against the Greeks by forcing the Athenian centre to retreat at Marathon. Although Darius I's punitive expedition against Athens failed, obliging his son Xerxes I to lead personally a great army into Europe ten years later, the Scythians had acquitted themselves well. Greek ambivalence towards them is evident in comedies, where they are always portrayed as drunks, and in the reception given earlier by the Athenians in 590 BC to the Scythian philosopher Anarcharis. This man became so celebrated that he was regarded as one of the seven sages. But in Athens, too, Scythian archers were employed as guardians of law and order. In Greek vase-painting they are depicted taking careful aim and shooting horizontally, quite unlike English longbowmen who shot their arrows high above a mass of advancing enemy soldiers. The fall of arrows could be devastating on the battlefield, as the French found during the Hundred Years War, but it meant that archery then resembled artillery fire, since the English archer did not aim at an individual target. Where the close relations of the Scythians with the Persians is perhaps most illustrative is in the easy communication, not to say co-operation, it signals between city dwellers and semi-nomads. In this connection, it is helpful to recall the fact that the Scythians and the Persians spoke closely related languages and understood each other without translators. Something similar may well have happened when the first composite bows were imported from the steppe.

In Egypt they were in use from an early date. Over thirty composite bows have been recovered intact from the tomb of Tutankhamun. He was the last surviving son of Akhenaten, the heterodox pharaoh Amenhotep IV. In reaction to his late father's excessive worship of the sun god Re, he had changed his own name from Tutankhaten, 'the living image of the solar disc Aten', to Tutankhamun, 'the living image of Amun'. A ram-headed god, sometimes shown as a bearded man wearing a cap with two feathers, Amun enjoyed a period of ascendancy in the Egyptian pantheon during the sixteenth century BC when the Hyksos invaders were expelled and Egypt's borders advanced into Canaan. Rivalry with Re was eliminated by the association of Amun with Re as Amun-Re, except in the notorious reign of Akhenaten. As a dynastic guardian, Amun-Re would have suggested through his priests the idea of Tutankhamun's new name. The young pharaoh issued an edict restoring the traditional cults, which had been outlawed by his father, and described at great length the wretched state to which Egypt had been reduced by this repressive religious policy. The measures he announced amounted to a return to the situation before Akhenaten came to the throne. Tutankhamun was guided by others in both religious and military matters. General Horemheb took him on a 'flag-flying' campaign in Palestine, but there is no record of any battle having taken place. Dying childless in 1346 BC, Tutankhamun left the way to power open to others, and even Horemheb was pharaoh from 1343 to 1315 BC. The ex-general was succeeded by another ruler without royal blood, Ramesses I, the grandfather of Ramesses II, the victor at Kadesh.

How Tutankhamun came to die so unexpectedly remains a subject of speculation. Early examination of the nineteen-year-old pharaoh's mummy revealed a wound on the left cheek, over the jawbone near the ear, suggesting that he may have died of a cerebral haemorrhage. This discovery encouraged the idea of his assassination in a palace intrigue hatched by his immediate successor, the courtier Ay, or the next-in-line, Horemheb. But an x-ray has now shown that Tutankhamun suffered additional physical damage, since the mummy lacks a breastbone and the frontal ribcage. This recent revelation has led to the suggestion that the boy pharaoh sustained fatal injuries in a chariot accident. It is argued that during a hunt he was either rash enough to drive alone, as is shown in the ostrich hunting scene found in his tomb, or he was involved in a collision

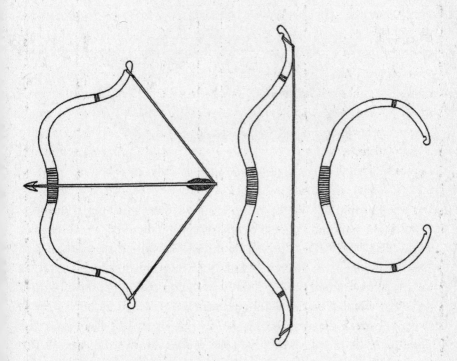

A composite bow, strung and unstrung

along with his charioteer. Afterwards the injured pharaoh would have been carried back to the palace where he could have lingered long enough in a coma for the facial wound to start to heal: there are signs that this process was actually underway when he died. The silence of the historical record has lent support to those who prefer the assassination theory, but the present evidence does not rule out the possibility that Tutankhamun was the victim of a chariot accident. His tomb and his burial have all the signs of haste following a death that took the Egyptian court by surprise.

A Scythian archer stringing his composite bow

Tutankhamun's bows, like much else in his diminutive burial chamber, were found amongst a jumble of objects apparently of daily and religious usage. They had been disturbed by thieves on more than one occasion, before the tomb was finally resealed. Near dismantled chariots, the bows lay casually on a bed of wood and woven cord, although most of them were still wrapped in linen. Inscriptions on the composite bows refer to Tutankhamun's divinity and his strength as an archer. One reads 'the good god, strong of bow, vigorous in drawing it, the son of Re, Tutankhamun', while another calls the pharaoh 'the crusher of foreign lands'. The bows themselves are quite varied in manufacture, for two are made from double staves of ash. Typically they consist of a wooden core, with a layer of sinew applied to the back and a layer of horn on the face, the whole bow being covered by a protective bark sheath. Only one bow is entirely covered with gold: its inscription speaks of the pharaoh as 'king of Upper and Lower Egypt, lord of the Two Lands'. Though trees have always been scarce in Egypt, it does not mean that Tutankhamun's weapons were imported. Foreign wood, including bark, would have been available to Egyptian craftsmen, and so there is no reason to suppose the absence of an arms industry in Egypt. Confirmation of this capability comes from wall-paintings discovered in tombs at Thebes. They clearly establish that composite bows were made there in the workshops of Amun's temple during the reign of Thutmose III, who triumphed at the

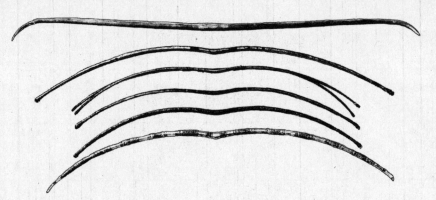

Bows from Tutankhamum's tomb

battle of Megiddo in 1460 BC. As pharaohs like Thutmose sought renown as archers, with the new and powerful composite bow, they could never have tolerated dependence on a foreign manufacturer.

Much of Egypt's military success, which enabled it to push its frontier as far as modern Lebanon, and on occasions further north still, must be attributed to chariotry. For the combination of highly trained horses, light chariots and composite bows worked nothing less than a revolution in ancient West Asian warfare. Previous battles had been decided by foot soldiers alone. Now opposing infantry faced scores of archers mounted on chariots and armed with composite bows, the archers shooting arrows with impunity until an infantry formation was so disheartened that it became vulnerable to attack by other infantrymen. The only answer to such harassment was of course the development of chariotry on both sides, with the result that military organisation changed as well as each society supporting it. That such a revolution alters the capacity of states to create and project military power is obvious, once the initial steps have been taken. Quite possibly the chariot only became militarily significant when it was first combined with the composite bow, which had long been a luxury item reserved for rulers and their closest friends. Hunting in chariots would have been the activity that inspired someone to consider what might happen on the battlefield, if a number of chariots carrying bowmen fought together. The earliest chariot warfare seems to have occurred in Asia Minor, where Troy may have been founded by chariot warriors. Yet there is evidence that by 1650 BC chariots were used by the Hittites, and by the Hyksos who took over northern Egypt around the same time.

Egyptian wheelwrights

The Hyksos (which is the Greek rendering of an Egyptian word meaning 'rulers of foreign lands') set up at Avaris in the Nile delta a dynasty which had six recorded pharaohs in just over a century. 'This city of Avaris,' we are told, 'was fortified with massive walls and guarded by a very strong garrison.' Its eventual surrender to the resurgent Egyptians in 1555 BC, after a prolonged siege, was sealed with a peace treaty which allowed the Hyksos, 'with all their possessions and households complete' to leave Egypt and 'journey over the desert to Syria'. The Hyksos, an assortment of West Asian adventurers, failed to secure their grip on Egypt, but they left behind a legacy of chariotry associated with the composite bow. It was always assumed that the initial success of the Hyksos derived from their skill as charioteers, but excavations at Tell el-Dab'a, the site of ancient Avaris, have turned up no traces of chariots, and little of horses. This apparent gap in the archaeological record could be connected with the terms of the final surrender, or the partial nature of the excavation. It does not, however, invalidate the view of the chariot's arrival in Egypt during Hyksos rule, since in the 1990s wall-paintings were located at Abydos showing the use of the light horse-drawn chariot under Ahmose, who died in 1545 BC. This pharaoh not only expelled the Hyksos, but he also undertook the reconquest of Nubia, where at his orders Buhen was rebuilt as the administrative centre of a province. It became the seat of the viceroy of Kush, the name by which the Egyptians knew the far south. And the dynasty Ahmose founded, the so-called Thutmosids, included Thutmose III, Akhenaten as well as Tutankhamun.

Military revolutions have profound effects on and off the battlefield. We have seen how by the reign of Akhenaten in the late fourteenth century BC the standard greeting in correspondence between up-to-date states always included reference to the ruler's chariots, horses and chief men. They were the basis of state power and the means of dynastic survival. Only countries that had developed this new military strength themselves could hope to sustain their positions internationally. It was impossible to leap-frog to success in chariot warfare by simply acquiring horses, chariots and composite bows. Without pre-existing skills in all three, and without a society that esteemed those who had already mastered them, there was no chance of meeting in battle the Hittites, the Egyptians, or the Assyrians. In our time oil bought Saddam Hussein vast quantities of Russian, French and American arms, but these sophisticated weapons could not on their own confer battlefield effectiveness on forces conscripted from a society that was neither modern nor united. So in ancient times the application of bent-wood technology to chariot construction, the improvement in manufacture of the composite bow, the evolving methods of training chariot horses, and the developing tactics of manoeuvring the chariot to best advantage had to be transmitted at first hand. Initially they were limited to a few specific places since they needed to be practised first. Once Hatti and Mitanni had demonstrated their effectiveness by the start of the sixteenth century BC, the spread of chariotry became general in West Asia and Egypt, so that a new social group arose, the chief men, whose status derived from prowess in chariots on the battlefield.

In Mitanni the chief men were called maryannu, foreign experts in chariotry upon whom the Mitannian kings relied. Although the language of Mitanni was Hurrian, a non-Indo-European tongue, there is no doubt of the presence of an Indo-European vocabulary in Mitannian documents. The Hurrian plural maryannu, meaning 'warriors', is marya when singular and identical to the Sanskrit marya, which meant 'young warrior'. Also words used to describe the colour of horses, for instance, parallel the language of the *Rig Veda*, India's oldest surviving text. How non-Hurrians came to occupy such a prestigious position in Mitanni is a matter of debate. There is no dispute, however, about the fact that these Indo-European speakers were outstandingly competent charioteers, who assisted the Mitannian kings in expanding their territories from the upper Euphrates and Tigris rivers to the shores of the Mediterranean and the Zagros mountains, in present-day Iran, and brought them into conflict with both the Hittites and the Egyptians. The maryannu prided themselves on the management of light war chariots and the training of horses to pull them. It is more than likely that the famous horse trainer Kikkuli was a marya. What is unusual about the maryannu, apart from

Assyrian chariots with bowmen

their Indo-European ancestry, is the position they acquired in Mitannian society. For they enjoyed a superior status through really understanding how to exploit the wheel, the horse and the bow. That their fame as charioteers survived in ancient documents goes some way to explain the attention the maryannu receive today. But this interest, especially when it is entwined with attempts to locate the homeland of the Indo-European speakers, should not be allowed to obscure the efforts of similar groups in Hatti, Egypt, Syria and Mesopotamia: all these chief men contributed to the rise of the charioteer.

The chariotry dispersed by Ramesses II at Kadesh thus constituted the elite force of the Hittite army. Originally the Hittite chariot had a crew of two – a driver and an archer armed with a composite bow. By the time of the battle of Kadesh in 1274 BC, this number had been increased to three by the addition of a spearman, who also carried a shield. Whether the Hittite king personally led the chariot assault on the Egyptians there is uncertain, although he was the commander-in-chief and always went with his troops on major campaigns. It seems from Egyptian reliefs of the battle that Muwatalli II remained with his infantry, concealed behind the city of Kadesh itself. Presumably he intended to advance with this large body of men as soon as his chariotry had thrown the Egyptians into disorder. The failure of Hittite charioteers to get the better of their opponents, who followed the young pharaoh in a series of daring counter-attacks, gave the Egyptians a chance to recover from the surprise Hittite assault and await the arrival of reinforcements. If Muwatalli had given command of the chariotry to a deputy, he must have regretted the decision when it became obvious that the battlefield remained firmly in Egyptian hands. As Ramesses could not help pointing out afterwards, the Hittite king had stripped his land of silver in order to swell his infantry with hired troops. It represented a great outlay for very little purpose. With his chief men defeated, Muwatalli had no choice but to call off the action, once the rest of the Egyptian army and its allies arrived.

Hittite kings were battle-hardened, making Muwatalli's tactical error at Kadesh all the more remarkable. Unlike Ramesses, he was not conspicuously in the thick of the fighting where his presence would have counted to wavering Hittite charioteers. Their headlong flight into the Orontes river would have caused dismay among the rest of Muwatalli's men. Although foot soldiers always provided the bulk of the Hittite army, and at Kadesh comprised well over 90 per cent of the troops under his command, the immediate offer of peace made by Muwatalli is an indication of how seriously he took the repulse of his own chariotry. He was not prepared to commit to action a force of infantry which still outnumbered the Egyptians. For the Hittite king realised the danger facing his kingdom if he suffered a major reverse on the battlefield. Until he rebuilt his chariot corps, his military capability was limited to the pace of the foot soldier – that was not enough when dealing with opponents like Egypt and Assyria. Engagements against them invariably occurred near cities on fertile plains, country easily dominated and defended by chariotry. Even Egypt's open borders could be easily protected, since depictions on its temples show invaders retreating across the desert pursued by charioteers firing composite bows. Where infantry came into its own was in mountainous or hilly terrain; otherwise it took the leading role in siege warfare. If a defeated enemy refused to surrender and had a strongly fortified city in which to take refuge, their conqueror in the field might be faced with the prospect of a long siege, without any certainty that the city would eventually fall. Thutmose III only managed to avoid this problem at Megiddo by luck as much as judgment. So swift and decisive had been his chariot-led charge that the defeated Canaanites had no stomach left for prolonged resistance and quickly came to terms.

3

West Asia and Egypt

And the waters returned, and covered the chariots, and the horsemen, and all the host of Pharaoh that came into the sea after them; there remained not as much as one of them.

Exodus

Prior to the rise of Babylon in the late nineteenth century BC as the great power in Mesopotamia, the kingdom of Mari fell under Assyrian influence and was governed by Yasmah-Addu. This listless son of King Shamshi-Adad I of Assyria caused his father great anxiety. He feared for the safety of the Assyrian forces stationed at Mari and warned Yasmah-Addu against taking unnecessary risks. Correspondence found in the Mari archive tells of Yasmah-Addu's incompetence as well as his liking for wine. 'If you have no good wine to drink,' wrote the ruler of neighbouring Carchemish, 'write to me, that I may send you what you need.' The success of his elder brother on the battlefield irked Yasmah-Addu even more than his father's constant criticism. Drink obviously helped with the humiliation he felt, and allowed Yasmah-Addu to live a quiet life as governor. After Shamshi-Adad's death, however, a great upheaval occurred in northern Mesopotamia, so that Assyria suffered assault from several directions and Ashur, its capital, was captured by the Babylonians. Zimri-Lim managed to rule an independent Mari during these troubled years. A member of the original royal family, Zimri-Lim drove the Assyrians out of Mari and, for a time, he succeeded in maintaining peaceful relations with Babylon.

We have already noticed Zimri-Lim's excitement over horses. But it would appear from Assyrian records that Mari had a stable during Yasmah-Addu's governorship. In a letter from Shamshi-Adad to Yasmah-Addu, the Assyrian king says that he wishes to have a team of horses and a chariot for a religious festival at Ashur; Yasmah-Addu is ordered to send the animals and the vehicle at once. That the Assyrian capital lacked horses and a chariot is quite startling, and reveals the novelty of this mode of transport. Considering the reign of Shamshi-Adad marks the first attempt to bring the whole of northern Mesopotamia under one authority and, at the height of his power, he controlled an area stretching from Assyria to Babylon in the south and Mari in the west, there can be no doubt that the charioteer had yet to make his decisive appearance on the battlefield. Following the fall of Ashur, northern Mesopotamia entered a long period of obscurity during which it came under the control of Mitanni.

The kingdom of Mitanni was completely forgotten for 3,000 years until archaeological discoveries proved its existence. The product of two ethnic groups who thoroughly fused, the Hurrians and the Indo-Aryans, Mitanni pushed into northern Mesopotamia and eastern Syria by force in the early sixteenth century BC. The effectiveness of the Mitannian army was founded upon the light war chariot, then coming into use in Asia Minor as well. Although the evidence for the presence of Indo-Aryans in Mitanni is exclusively linguistic, it seems reasonable to assume a close tie between them and horsemanship. A small but significant portion of personal names is Indo-Aryan, often derived from gods mentioned in the *Rig Veda*, while others actually refer to horses or chariots. Biridaswa means 'possessing many horses' and Sattawaza, meaning 'winner of seven prizes', celebrates success in horse racing, while King Tushratta's name probably meant 'having a terrifying chariot'. The key text is of course the horse-training manual written by Kikkuli. The text, which was recovered from Hattusha, the Hittite capital, is written on four clay tablets in the Hittite language. Yet the technical terms, and some of the numerals, are not Hittite. Instead they are related to the Indo-Aryan family of languages. This special vocabulary of horsemanship, preserved in a Hittite translation from the Hurrian, must indicate how influential the Indo-Aryan element of the population had been in developing chariotry in Mitanni. It has led some scholars to suppose that Indo-Aryan chariot warriors superimposed themselves on a Hurrian-speaking population to form a ruling dynasty that lasted for several centuries. More likely is the welcome integration of a small but skilled Indo-Aryan group into Hurrian society. Records from Nuzi, an Assyrian site near modern Kirkuk in northern Iraq, indicate peaceful relations, involving inter-marriage and a general mixing of the Indo-Aryans and the Hurrians.

Another insight provided by the Nuzi texts is the fact that carpenters enjoyed a status not much below that of a charioteer. A less plausible suggestion is that there were no Indo-Aryan speakers in Mitanni during Kikkuli's lifetime. The few Indo-Aryan names and words present in the

A letter from King Tushratta of Mitanni

Hurrian language are explained as the result of contact made when the Indo-Aryans, on their way to India, passed along the Hurrians' borders. It was then that the Indo-Aryans were supposed to have learned about chariots from the Hurrians, and the latter borrowed a small part of the Indo-Aryan vocabulary and pantheon.

The respect accorded to the 'words of Kikkuli, master horseman from the land of Mitanni' cannot be gainsaid. The other early chariot warriors, the Hittites, followed his instructions for the training of their own horses, as the translation of his manual into Hittite makes apparent. Another version of Kikkuli found in the Hattusha archive is in Akkadian, the language of the Assyrians and the Babylonians, which again shows how important this text became for ancient kings right across West Asia. What all these rulers needed was a foolproof method of preparing their chariotry for war. They could not afford to commit such a valuable asset to battle unless they were certain of its quality and especially the readiness of the chariot horses for the swiftness of such encounters. This is why Kikkuli emphasises continuous training, day and night.

> When midnight comes the charioteer brings the horses out of the stable and harnesses them. He drives them for over a kilometre, and then gallops for more than seven fields ... When they return, he unbridles the horses and rubs them dry. In the stable they receive two handfuls of hay, one of wheat, and four handfuls of barley. When they have finished this feed, he lets them eat hay for the rest of the night.

Exercise and nutrition, practice and reward – these were the methods by which a charioteer developed a close and trusting relationship with his team of horses. We are told that at dawn

> he takes them from the stable and puts on harnesses. The horses are driven for a kilometre and gallop for seven fields. After three more kilometres of driving, they return to the stable, are unharnessed and rubbed down. Their feed is hay and barley mixed with wheat. When they have eaten this, hay is given to them the whole night.

How conscious the grooms and stablehands have to be of the horses' welfare is stressed by Kikkuli when he writes:

> After a long gallop a stable gets very warm. If the horses are restless, and start to sweat, their halter is removed as well as their blankets, and a snaffle-bit put on them. Salt is dissolved on a fire, and after

wholemeal barley has been mixed in a pitcher, they are given a bucketful, and hay to eat.

The regime of training gradually extends the range of gallops to ten, twenty, ninety fields, and even longer distances. Feeds are also varied. Sometimes little is offered to the horses, presumably because on campaign supplies could well be erratic, and at other times extensive feeding is provided to build up their stamina. Attention to hygiene runs throughout Kikkuli's training manual. Horses have to be washed with warm water five times a day, or bathed in a river, when necessary. They always have to be rubbed down. Periods of rest are recommended too. These are usually followed by bursts of intense activity for a number of days, when the horses receive 'the grain ration twice'. Despite the incompleteness of the manual, the sections we have almost reach the final stages of training. Typically, the last surviving lines of the text are about animal care, for we are told that

the horses are brought down to the river and bathed there four times. Each time they are given a handful of hay and a scoop of water. Afterwards they come back to the stable, and are given a scoop of flour, before having their grain ration poured out for them.

It goes without saying that the comprehensiveness of Kikkuli's scheme impressed his contemporaries. The details of exercise and feeding were seen as a guarantee of success in the training of chariot horses. Like racehorses, they had to perform at their peak when the moment came.

The Hurrians (in the authorised version of the Bible they are the Horites) spoke a language which has no relation to Indo-European or Semitic linguistic families. It was first recognised at the end of the nineteenth century, when scholars began translating the Amarna archive from Egypt. They discovered letters in a hitherto unknown language, written by Tushratta, king of Mitanni. In one letter addressed to Amenhotep III (1410–1372 BC) there is a report of a Hittite defeat. 'There was not one of them,' wrote Tushratta, 'who returned to his country.' As a token of his continued affection, he tells Amenhotep he has sent him 'a chariot, two horses, and attendants, from the booty from the land of Hatti'. At this period the rulers of Egypt and Mitanni were bound by a

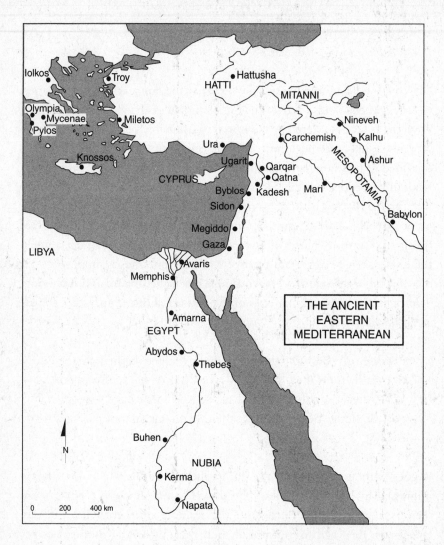

Iolkos
Troy
Hattusha
HATTI
MITANNI
Olympia
Mycenae
Miletos
Nineveh
Kalhu
Pylos
Carchemish
Ashur
MESOPOTAMIA
Knossos
Ura
Ugarit
CYPRUS
Qarqar
Qatna
Byblos Kadesh   Mari
Sidon
Babylon
LIBYA
Megiddo
Gaza
Avaris
Memphis
THE ANCIENT
EASTERN
MEDITERRANEAN
Amarna
EGYPT
Abydos
Thebes
N
Buhen
NUBIA
Kerma
0   200   400 km
Napata

peace treaty, which had been sealed through marriage. The Amarna
archive makes mention of at least four marriages between Amenhotep
and West Asian princesses – two of whom were Babylonian, two
Mitannian. For one of the latter, Kelu-Heba, Tushratta's own sister, his
letter mentions a present of gold jewellery and sweet oil. These
diplomatic marriages between an Egyptian monarch and the daughters or
sisters of foreign potentates were a one-way arrangement: Amenhotep
bluntly said that no Egyptian princess ever married a foreigner. Both
Mitanni and Babylon acquiesced, but showed concern that their prestige
in Egyptian eyes was affected by giving and not receiving wives. Later

Tushratta tried to insist that his own daughter should become 'mistress of Egypt'. He got nowhere, because Amenhotep's enthusiasm for marriage alliances was not without its problems in Egypt, where a wife had well-established property rights. His foreign unions did not allow the imported wives, once widowed, to claim a third of his wealth, but rather required their marriage to the next pharaoh. Just how strong the position of Egyptian women was can be gauged from Hatshepsut's usurpation of the throne. Her regency to Thutmose III, following the death of her husband Thutmose II, rested on her entitlement to a large share of the royal fortune: Hatshepsut's lineage in the absence of a grown heir left most of the wealth in her hands. It took the future victor of Megiddo more than twenty years to come into his inheritance.

Egyptian policy towards Mitanni changed near the very end of Amenhotep's reign. One temple text at Luxor declares how the pharaoh 'made a great name in every foreign country, his battle cry having resounded in Mitanni, when he put fear in their hearts, as their bellies split open'. Another carved on his memorial temple, beneath a representation of Amenhotep in his chariot attacking Asians, says 'he broke Mitanni with his strong arm'. This change of attitude, after half a century of cordial relations between Egypt and Mitanni, may possibly be explained by Amenhotep's intimation of the coming eclipse of the Hurrians. Already he had worked out an alliance with Ugarit, present-day Ras Shamra on the Syrian coast. This trading city was later drawn into the Hittite sphere of influence, although it still maintained extensive overseas contacts, including close links with the Minoan cities on the island of Crete and Mycenaean ones on the Greek mainland. It was Mitanni's misfortune to act as a buffer between the Hittites and the Assyrians. Under King Ashur-uballit I (1363–1328 BC) Assyria regained its independence and began a long series of campaigns against Mitanni. With Egypt's friendly attitude having cooled and the pharaoh entertaining Assyrian ambassadors at his court, the Hurrians were hard pressed. To make matters worse, the Hittites determined to avenge their defeat by Tushratta. King Suppiluliuma I concentrated the forces of Hatti for an attack on Mitanni as well as its allies in Syria. In order to establish Hittite supremacy he launched an all-out invasion of Mitanni, because as long as Syrian states could call upon the support of their Mitannian overlord, there was no chance of the Hittites dominating the entire region.

The war opened with an appeal to Suppiluliuma from a Syrian ruler,

A stele, dedicated by the charioteer Tjay to his ex-master, the royal scribe of Egypt

who was in dispute with Mitanni. It also coincided with an anti-Hittite move in Isuwa, a territory to the north of Mitanni. Dispatching an expeditionary force southwards to relieve the beleaguered Syrian king, Suppiluliuma led the main Hittite army across the Euphrates and conquered Isuwa, before striking south into the heart of Mitanni. Unprepared for the speed of the Hittite advance, Tushratta could offer no effective resistance to Suppiluliuma, who took the Mitannian capital, Washukanni. It was then that Tushratta was murdered in a civil war and his son, Mattiwaza, fled to the Hittites for asylum. Suppiluliuma married the crown prince to one of his daughters, and set him on the Mitannian throne. Having reduced Mitanni to the status of a puppet state, the Hittite king conducted a lightning campaign in Syria, reducing to obedience all former Mitannian allies, except the stronghold of Carchemish. The rulers of the conquered states were deposed and transported along with their families to Hattusha. A state which fell victim to the Hittites was one Suppiluliuma had intended to leave alone. It was Kadesh. Formerly an ally of Mitanni, this city on the Orontes river had been forced to acknowledge Egyptian overlordship during the Syrian campaigns of Thutmose III. A coalition of Canaanite states led by the kings of Kadesh and Megiddo had been decisively defeated by Thutmose, and later on Kadesh itself fell to the Egyptians. Mitanni accepted the Egyptian gain without complaint, and Suppiluliuma was ready to accept the situation as it stood, until local events prevented this from happening and Kadesh became a Hittite dependency. The loss eventually led the Egyptians to meet the Hittites in the famous chariot battle of Kadesh, which was claimed by Ramesses II as a great victory.

No detailed account of the chariot battles in which Mitanni fell now survives. But the swift disappearance of this once formidable state from West Asia meant the remaining great powers were Hatti, Assyria and Babylon. The immediate beneficiaries were the Hittites, whose military might lay, as had the Hurrians', in chariotry. Their capital, Hattusha, east of modern Ankara, was effectively established by King Hattusili I (1650–1620 BC): his adopted title means 'a man of Hattusha'. Hatti itself, the name by which his kingdom became known, seems to have been in origin a very ancient word connected with the district around Hattusha. The Hittites in fact took over this name and much of the previous state, which the Egyptians called Kheta. The swamping of central Asia Minor with Indo-European-speaking Hittite settlers resulted in the original Hattian language dying out. Where it survived at all was in the cults of certain deities, like the fierce earth god Wurunkatte, the centre of whose worship was near the Taurus mountains, in southeastern Turkey. Otherwise the Hittites absorbed into their language Hattian words, declining them by means of Indo-European grammar.

The foundation of Hattusha, a natural stronghold dominating the northern valleys, gave the Hittites a secure base from which to expand their influence in Asia Minor, and beyond. Even petty kingdoms in Cyprus came to acknowledge Hittite overlordship. The Hittite empire consisted largely of a network of vassal states, whose rulers enjoyed considerable local autonomy but were committed by oath to the Hittite king, their obligations being spelt out through personal treaties. Of these obligations the key one involved the military assistance the Hittite king could call upon in time of war. Like other ancient peoples, the Hittites

were surrounded by enemies or potential enemies. Hardly a year passed
without a call to arms against a rebellious vassal, a troublesome neighbour,
or a sudden invasion. Yet fighting was never regarded as unusual: for the
Hittites it was a natural activity in which they excelled until the twelfth
century BC, when Hattusha was destroyed by fire during a catastrophe
which engulfed many kingdoms in the eastern Mediterranean. In this
dramatic reshaping of the political landscape a notable casualty was to be
the charioteer.

Vigilance was, however, always a Hittite concern. Watch-towers were
planted along borders, and the gates of fortified cities were closed at
night. Seals were then affixed over the lock of each city gate in a
ceremony overseen by the chief inhabitants. In times of trouble the rural
population and their animals sought refuge inside city walls. Hittite
intelligence was also well developed and often used to hoodwink enemy
states. At Kadesh the Egyptian army was lured into a trap by two local
men who falsely claimed the Hittite king had withdrawn on hearing of
Ramesses II's arrival. This clever piece of disinformation nearly cost
Egypt dear. Letters from provincial officials, found in the Hattusha
archive, give warning of enemy incursions and the extent of the damage
done. 'The enemy,' one states, 'has entered our territory under the cover
of darkness. Over a thousand of them have begun harvesting our grain. If
the crops are ripe in other areas, the grain should be quickly harvested
before any more is lost.' Besides receiving news from outposts and spies,
the Hittite king could enquire of the gods concerning the plans of the
enemy. 'Will the king of Assyria advance this year?' asks a ruler worried
about his supply of tin. Assyrian merchants resident in Hatti traded in this
vital ingredient of bronze tools and weapons, but there was no certainty
the supply would not dry up. This may have been one of the reasons for
King Hattusili I's regular campaigns in Syria – to protect the eastern trade
route to Hatti. How dangerous overland commerce was can be seen in
correspondence from the Amarna archive. Pharaoh Akhenaten is at pains
to urge foreign kings to avenge the murder of Egyptian merchants, while
having to admit that a caravan with an armed escort is still likely to be
robbed, even by his own subjects. Merchants seem to have been
especially prone to trouble in northern Syria, where banditry was rife.
Yet Syrian states themselves could put the squeeze on trade passing
through their territories by means of excessive tolls and taxes. A

complaint laid before the Hittite governor of Carchemish refers to a levy of 400 donkeys made on a single caravan by a greedy local ruler.

As commander-in-chief, the Hittite king determined the course of campaigns, appointed and removed senior officers, mobilised his subjects for war, corresponded with allies, and regularly took the field himself. He

A letter addressed to Queen Tiy of Egypt

could indeed expect to go to war most summers. Unless there was fighting on several fronts, or a great religious festival required his presence, the king was active on the battlefield. His senior officers were drawn from the ranks of the aristocracy and the royal house itself. The most reliable of the Hittite princes ruled in Carchemish as a kind of viceroy over the allied states of Syria. The next level below these senior officers comprised a group of divisional commanders: in order of seniority they were Chief of the Chariot Warriors of the Right, Chief of the Chariot Warriors of the Left, Chief of the Infantry of the Right, Chief of the Infantry of the Left, Chief of the Shepherds of the Right and Chief of the Shepherds of the Left. Here the distinction between infantrymen and shepherds refers to the standing army, the regular foot soldiers, and the extra men recruited from the countryside during a prolonged campaign. When the situation did not warrant a large number of troops, or when a rapid response was necessary, the king would rely on his full-time chariotry and infantry. Their needs were supplied throughout the year, unlike the shepherds who were sent home at the end of the campaign season. Additional forces for wars against other great powers were raised from allied states and the hire of mercenaries. Prior to the opening of hostilities an oath-taking ceremony was used to induct junior officers and the rank-and-file troops into the army. A serious consequence of breaking this oath, according to the surviving ritual, was the likelihood of men literally turning into women. Should they so transgress, then 'let them break the bows, arrows and clubs in their hands and let them put in their hands spindles and mirrors!' The troops also swore to hand over to the king any of their officers who were disloyal.

The chariotry was the most prized part of the Hittite army, a position it kept in royal esteem from the earliest days of the empire down to the end. At first each chariot carried a crew of two men: a chariot driver

The Egyptian attitude to subject peoples

and a fighter armed with a composite bow and a plentiful supply of arrows. During the reign of Muwatalli II (1295–1272 BC) a third man was added to the crew: he sported a shield and a spear. The archer wore a quiver on his back, and his bow case, along with more arrows, was attached to the outside of the chariot box. Egyptian temple reliefs show the characteristic shape of the Hittite shield – rectangular, with convex edges on the top and bottom and concave edges on the sides. Other shields, round in shape, were carried by Hittite allies or mercenaries. Over 2 metres long, the spears were intended to give the chariot a degree of protection from enemy infantrymen, who were apt to attack whenever there was a lull in a chariot battle. The chariots were pulled by two horses whose flanks, backs and necks were protected by scale armour. En route to the battlefield the chariots would not have been driven, since they were built for speed and manoeuvrability to such an extent that they would have broken down over rough roads. Only when the enemy were in striking distance would all the chariots have been readied for action. As the king and senior officers always fought from chariots, they would have had at their service extra vehicles – both for transport and battle. The Hittites possessed a small cavalry, as horsemen are depicted on Egyptian reliefs, but they seem to have acted only as scouts and messengers.

As already noted, it was the great eastern drive of Suppiluliuma I (1344–1322 BC) which overcame Mitanni and converted Syria into a Hittite sphere of influence. This war took place near the end of his reign because first he had to deal with three pressing enemies, Kashka, Armatana and Isuwa. Another reason perhaps for Suppiluliuma's long preparation against Mitanni was his usurpation of the Hittite throne: with a brother slain in the seizure of power, he needed to be sure of his own position at home before risking a major contest abroad. A constant worry for Hittite kings were the Kashka, a barbarous people whose mountainous homeland to the north of Hattusha provided a perfect base for raids. First the Kashka in the north, then the kingdom of Armatana in the south east, were forced back and order was restored to Hittite lands in Asia Minor. At last Suppiluliuma could turn his attention to Isuwa, and even Mitanni. During the struggle against Armatana the Hurrians had dared to intervene, for King Tushratta of Mitanni reported to Egypt, as we have seen in the Amarna archive, a victory then over the Hittites. Suppiluliuma may have been encouraged to settle accounts with the Hurrians at

A guardian, a sculpture on the King's Gate at Hattusha

this time by reports of renewed unrest in Mitanni. The assassination of the Mitannian king by an officer named Utkhi had caused Tushratta's enthronement. But his elevation did not go unchallenged and for several years a rival claimant who styled himself 'king' posed a serious threat to the stability of the country. Possibly the initial stirrings of the civil war that broke out in Mitanni on the Hittite invasion, and cost Tushratta his life, was all the encouragement Suppiluliuma required to attack Isuwa and Mitanni together. For the Hittite king had been careful to minimise the risk of Egyptian involvement in his conflict with Mitanni by assuring the pharaoh that he had no designs on his subject territory in southern Syria and Palestine.

After taking the Mitannian capital, and bringing Hurrian chariot power to an end, Suppiluliuma conducted a series of lightning conquests in northern Syria, before returning home laden with booty. In his account of the war, the Hittite king makes it quite plain that the troops were directed solely against Tushratta's dependencies. As yet he had no quarrel with Egypt. He did not attack Ugarit or Amurru, two Egyptian allies, and maintained the Orontes river frontier intact, with the exception of troublesome Kadesh. Egypt's reluctance to aid Mitanni sealed its fate. It must have been shortly afterwards, when for the first time Egypt and Hatti had a common border, that a treaty was drawn up between Suppiluliuma and Akhenaten regularising relations between the two states. Akhenaten's preoccupation with religious reform could have been construed by Suppiluliuma as lack of interest in an Asiatic empire, and there were rumours that Egypt would not march to defend the Syrian frontier. Yet the Hittites were restrained, at least until the recently acquired Syrian states plotted their independence. These rebels even attempted to force Ugarit to join them against Hatti, on pain of invasion. Its king, Niqmaddu II, refused and appealed to Suppiluliuma, although he had an Egyptian wife and cultivated close relations with Egypt. The unexpected switch from Egypt signalled the immense prestige that Hatti now enjoyed. Suppiluliuma was not slow to grasp the opportunity. Troops were dispatched to drive the rebels from Ugaritian territory, and after the Syrian rebellion was crushed Ugarit seceded from Egypt.

An alliance with Ugarit had much to offer the Hittites. Though it was never a major power, neither was Ugarit a mere city state. Its territory on the headland of Ras Shamra, south of modern Lattakia, was far from small and backed by thickly wooded mountains. Rich in timber, grain, wine, oil and livestock, Ugarit was renowned for its metalwork and cloth. As a trading port, it acted as an intermediary between the islands and shores of the Mediterranean and the lands stretching to the Euphrates. The substantial tribute payable by Ugarit, as recorded in treaties with Hatti, is testimony of its wealth and the valuable source of revenue the Hittites gained through Niqmaddu's appeal. A letter from Suppiluliuma marks the closer relationship, when it states 'as previously your forebears were friends and not foes of Hatti, now you, Niqmaddu, are in the same manner a foe of my foes and a friend of my friends!' Later a Hittite chamber of commerce was established at Ugarit, but without the right of buying property in the city. While the Hittite viceroy at Carchemish kept a close eye on Ugaritian affairs, the Canaanite state remained essentially autonomous until its eventual destruction about 1190 BC. Ugarit's own military forces, though smaller, were like those of Hatti. Able-bodied men were subject to call-up in emergencies to supplement regular troops. One legend even tells of the blind and infirm being pressed into the ranks. Chariotry was of course the key weapon in the Ugaritian armoury, and surviving texts from the city archive record the high status of the Chief of Chariotry. The Indo-European loan word maryannu is frequently used to denote chariot warriors, who seem to have been awarded grants of land by the king. Of interest for chariot warfare is the description of a unit comprising infantry and chariots. This highly mobile strike force is a parallel of the Amun division which Ramesses II led into the Hittite trap at Kadesh, since the Egyptian chariotry with him was accompanied by foot soldiers known as 'runners'. Ugaritian charioteers were under the charge of the Chief of Grooms, who would have been responsible for the training of chariot drivers and their teams. Equipment carried by the chariot warrior included a bow and arrows, a sling and stones, a javelin, a club and a shield.

Upon these forces the Hittite king could call whenever he felt his own army needed reinforcement. Available as well were the ships belonging to the Ugaritian fleet. But except during the last, desperate struggle against the so-called Sea Peoples in the twelfth century BC, Ugarit was obliged to render military service only in Syria, and not least against the Egyptians at Kadesh. Relations remained amicable between Ugarit and Hatti to their common bitter end. Not knowing the amount of tribute previously paid to Egypt, it is impossible to tell whether the amount levied by Hatti represented an increase. If the new tribute was more, it was no doubt compensated by land taken from the defeated Syrian rebels. Ugarit's economy does not seem to have suffered by the change of allegiance, nor did the supervision from Carchemish in any way inhibit the expansion of trade. For once a permanent peace was agreed between Ramesses II and Hattusili III an even greater volume of exchange occurred as Ugarit renewed its commercial ties with Egypt. An Egyptian corporation soon transacted business in Ugarit, entering into financial deals, the purchase of large quantities of oil, and contracts with its king for products from the extensive royal estate.

Though war was almost a business for the Hittites, and an important source of revenue in terms of plunder and the annual tribute paid by subject peoples as well as allies like Ugarit, success on the battlefield was believed to come neither from superior logistics nor clever tactics, but solely through the will of the gods. The king was believed to act on earth as the deputy of the storm god, the dominant deity in the Hittite pantheon. Natural disasters were due to the storm god's wrath, and upon his goodwill the security of Hatti was said to depend. Rather like his Indo-Aryan cousin Indra, the champion of the chariot warriors, this Hittite god of mountains and the sky protected his favourite people, the

A seal with the name of King Hattusili on it

inhabitants of Hatti. He shared in the spoils of their victories just as he endured the consequences of their defeats. Other West Asian storm gods, such as the Ugaritian Balu and the Mesopotamian Adad, fulfilled a similar function, but for the Hittites a deity responsible for the elemental forces – thunder, lightning and rain – seems to have been a fundamental necessity. They and their kings were devoted to his worship, in the shrines dedicated to him at Hattusha and those set up in response to his local manifestations throughout Asia Minor. Before the commencement of a campaign the Hittite king always sought divine approval. Sometimes this might be given by way of omens, a flash of lightning or an eclipse; at other times a message arrived in the form of a dream. In the latter case the

The Hittite king and queen worshipping a deity

dreamer would have spent a night at a holy place. Whichever method was used, and there were many ways of taking oracles, an expert in divination was expected to pronounce on the action most favoured by the gods. Only then would orders be given for an assembly of troops. After the taking of oaths, priests or priestesses would say prayers for victory and anoint military leaders, plus their horses, chariots and weapons, with sacred oil. Thus ready to confront the enemy, the Hittite army set forth under the command of the king or a deputy.

Morale on campaign was likewise dependent upon the appearance of divine favour. When the king of Armatana's capital was struck by lightning, the morale of his army sank while Hittite confidence rose, much to the satisfaction of Suppiluliuma I. If things went badly and the Hittite army suffered a reverse, the reason for the withdrawal of divine support had to be ascertained and appropriate measures taken to appease the gods. It was the only occasion on which human sacrifice was practised. A man, a goat, a dog and a pig were cut in half, and placed each side of a gate of hawthorn, through which all the soldiers had to pass. Afterwards they sprinkled themselves with water, close to a fire. By this grisly ritual the Hittites hoped to put their military failure behind them, and with morale restored, go on to victory. Since all depended on divine help, it was usual to share booty with priests and priestesses after the end of hostilities. Often it took the form of precious objects looted from conquered cities, or captured craftsmen skilled in their manufacture. The rest of the spoils, including prisoners and livestock, were distributed among the army, after the king had received the lion's share. The pleasure Hittite rulers derived from their chariot exploits both in war and the hunt is evident in the layout of the royal palace, which occupied a rocky plateau overlooking the city of Hattusha. They did not need to use the main gate of this fortified citadel, because a special gate was built to allow them easy entrance and exit. It led through the city's outer defences via a ramp with a width and gradient suitable for chariots.

Somewhat less warlike than the Hittites, the Egyptians also reckoned that military success or failure was the result of the gods' will. According to the Egyptian priest Manetho, who compiled in the third century BC a dynastic history from early times, the Hyksos occupation of 1664–1555 BC was some kind of divine punishment. 'In the reign of Tutimaius, for what reason I know not,' wrote Manetho, 'a blast from Heaven smote us, and unexpectedly, from the eastern lands, unknown invaders marched in confidence of victory against our land. By force they easily defeated our rulers, set fire to our cities, razed our temples to the ground, and enslaved the people.' The founder of the Hyksos dynasty was Salitis, an Asian pharaoh whose allies against continued Egyptian resistance at Thebes were the Nubians, a southern people frequently subject to interference from Egypt. At Kerma, on the upper Nile, the Nubians established a kingdom largely based on the pharaonic model which lasted for more than a century. But once the Hyksos were expelled from Egypt, the end was in sight for Nubian independence. Salitis' successors failed to conquer the whole country and, possibly through adopting the Hyksos war chariot, the Egyptians finally drove the invaders out. Again the record notes divine approval of the expulsion, for even donkey-like Seth, an Egyptian deity treated well by the Hyksos, was heard to roar in his temple. Not to be outdone, the birthday of the goddess Isis, the wife and sister of the underworld god Osiris, was marked by a downpour.

The Hyksos had retained power in Egypt for a period slightly shorter than that in which the Nubians enjoyed their freedom. Many questions relating to their occupation, which was a turning point in the country's history, cannot be answered. In the same way, the Hyksos seizure of power is little understood. Manetho asserts an invasion, but it is equally possible that the takeover of the Nile delta was by and large peaceful and the inevitable outcome of an increasing foreign presence there coupled with the declining authority of the ruling Egyptian dynasty. Ancient

West Asian states were ethnically mixed, although the isolated position of
Egypt, surrounded by wide deserts, made it the most homogeneous of all
until the Hyksos assumed control. The Hyksos, unlike the Hebrews later
on, were unable to resist the allure of Egypt: their leaders adopted the
paraphernalia of Egyptian royalty and left little behind them that is
culturally distinct. They are credited with having introduced the
Egyptians to the chariot as well as the horse, even though the skeleton
excavated at Buhen, a fortress destroyed in ancient Nubia about 1675 BC,
makes their introduction of the horse unlikely. Credit could only be
given to the Hyksos for both if it can be shown how they served in the
Egyptian army as a foreign chariotry prior to the takeover of 1664 BC.
Since there is no evidence for this military assistance at present, it must be
assumed that the Hyksos' contribution in new weaponry was the chariot,
which they brought to Egypt with them.

The final upsurge of the Egyptians against the Hyksos is eloquently
demonstrated in the marks of violent death on the mummy of Sekenenre
Ta'o. Recovered in 1881 by the French Egyptologist Gaston Maspero
from a cache of royal mummies saved from pillaging 3,000 years earlier,
the pharaoh's corpse has multiple wounds to the head from a spear, an
axe and a dagger. The defeat of this Theban patriot, so savagely cut down
on the battlefield, did not deter the Egyptians, who under his sons
Kamose and Ahmose rallied and expelled the Hyksos. It was during
Ahmose's reign (c. 1569–1545 BC) that Egypt was finally reunited. After
defeating the Hyksos, Ahmose also re-established Egyptian authority in
Palestine and reconquered the Nubians. According to an inscription:

> When His Majesty had slain the nomads of Asia, he sailed south
> along the Nile in order to destroy the Nubian bowmen. His
> Majesty made a great slaughter among them.

Ahmose, Kamose's younger brother, then founded the most famous
dynasty in Egyptian history – the Thutmosids, whose last pharaoh was
Tutankhamun. The first direct reference to a chariot in Egypt is found in
the tomb biography of Ahmose Si Abena, who claims to have followed
on foot the chariot of Pharaoh Ahmose in the attack on Avaris, the
Hyksos capital. Confirmation of this fact was discovered in the 1990s
when painted fragments from the pharaoh's memorial temple at Abydos
came to light, showing Egyptian chariots in action. These fragments

make clear that horses and chariots were in regular use: whether they had been introduced into the Egyptian army by serving Asian mercenaries before the Hyksos occupation or simply copied by the disconcerted Egyptians afterwards, however, remains a mystery.

The Egyptian word for chariot, wrrt, which occurs in the Ahmose Si Abena text, does not derive from a Semitic root, and so it cannot be tied the speech of the Hyksos. Though an Indo-European root cannot be ruled out, it looks like a native Egyptian word. Not until the fifteenth century BC does the Semitic term for chariot, mrkbt, make an appearance in Egyptian texts, but it never supersedes wrrt. From the start of its deployment for war, the Egyptian chariot was equipped with a bow case. Another case for javelins had been added by the reign of Ramesses II (1279–1213 BC), although the composite bow remained the chief offensive weapon on this fast-moving platform. Egyptian pharaohs took great interest in archery, a skill they honed through hunting wild animals. Some of the gods were believed to have gone hunting as well: falcon-headed Horus, the dutiful son of Isis, was a keen hunter, an attribute that encouraged his identification with the Egyptian ruler. In the underworld

Nubian prisoners roped together

a pharaoh was thought to become Osiris, and his successor on earth Horus. In his fight with Seth, the murderer of his own father Osiris, Horus lost an eye and replaced it with the divine serpent, which henceforth acted as an emblem of royalty. Without a specific deity for the hunt, the Egyptians tended to leave the chase to the lioness-goddess Sekhmet. Also known as the eye of the sun god Re, Sekhmet was once so intoxicated by the smell of blood that the earth had to be flooded with beer containing red ochre to make it look like blood. Otherwise she would have forgotten Re's order to thin out troublesome humanity, and killed everyone instead.

Details of the Egyptian chariot can be gathered from paintings and reliefs, plus a number of chariots that have miraculously survived, including six from the tomb of Tutankhamun. The latter are of singular importance because this incredible find offers the possibility of comparing complete vehicles, not only with each other, but with chariot evidence from elsewhere. In Egypt, chariots were placed in tombs belonging to pharaohs and high officials, but horses were never buried with them. This was not the case in Mesopotamia, nor China where chariots and teams of horses were interred together from the Shang dynasty onwards. Remains of seven Chinese chariots, dating from the period before 1027 BC, are now available for study and reconstruction. Like Egyptian chariots, each is composed of five major parts: wheels, axle, body mounted on the axle, pole and yoke for two horses. The sole difference is that the Chinese draught pole had a marked upward curve, which when combined with the efficient harness developed in China gave the vehicle greater stability and speed. Four of the six chariots recovered from Tutankhamun's tomb were placed in the antechamber and two in the treasury. These chariots are in different states of preservation for a variety of reasons. Because the entrance passage to the tomb is narrow, wheels were removed and axles shortened. Manoeuvring the two chariots into the treasury, beyond the burial chamber, must have been particularly difficult and necessitated their complete dismantlement. Further damage was done to the vehicles by tomb robbers who tore off their gold decoration and carried away portable metal parts such as linch pins. After the looting, officials responsible for the royal necropolis tidied the tomb, leaving the chariots in the antechamber piled haphazardly together. Resealing the tomb, perhaps on more than one occasion, they could not avoid shutting in moisture that caused the glue and leather employed in the construction of the chariots to deteriorate.

Tutankhamun's chariots would have had different functions. Three of them, all richly decorated with gold, were probably reserved for ceremonial use, while the less ornate models had more practical purposes. The latter were built for rougher conditions than the parade ground or journeys along carefully prepared routes to the great temples. Two of the more robust chariots have wooden tyres, composed of four pieces of wood bound to the felloe by bands of bark-covered leather as well as bronze wire that passed through holes near the tyres and was then wound around the felloe. At the same time the wire held the butt ends of the tyre together. That irregularly worn segments of a wooden tyre could be easily replaced can be seen from one of the wheels, since a new segment was added before its placement in the tomb. Ornate bow cases left close to the non-ceremonial chariots suggest these vehicles were intended for active service – in warfare or for hunting expeditions. A case containing three composite bows has metal loops on its side for attaching it to a chariot. No victories are credited to Tutankhamun, but we know that Horemheb, his general and one of his successors, took him on a tour of Egypt's tributary states in Palestine, so that it is possible the young pharaoh rode from city to city there in the sturdier chariots left in his tomb. Tutankhamun's early death, without a son and heir, caused a power vacuum. It was filled by the military after the brief reign of Ay (1346–1343 BC), a high court official. Perhaps Ankhesenamum, the widow of Tutankhamun, willingly married Ay, when she realised that the Hittite prince she had sought as a replacement pharaoh was not going to arrive in Egypt. Ay can be observed in a wall-painting in Tutankhamun's tomb administering the rite of opening the mouth, a duty performed by an heir. Arguably the most important ancient Egyptian ritual, its believed effect was the reanimation of the dead. It was sometimes accompanied by secondary ritual gestures supposed to open the eyes. One of the ornamental chariots carries an inscription which refers to Ankhesenamun, 'the great royal wife, the beloved one who lives'.

Analysis of surviving Egyptian chariots show that the body, yoke, wheel hub and felloe were cut from elm, which would have been imported from Ugarit. The draught pole was made of willow, and the wheel spokes of plum. Neither of these trees grew in Egypt, while the nearest source of the birch bark used for coverings was Asia Minor. These

Tutankhamun hunting in his chariot

different woods reveal an extensive system of international trade, largely directed by the pharaoh in order to supply his own needs. How hazardous trading could be for Egyptian merchants, even those travelling in the comparative safety of a ship, is evident in Wenamun's account of a journey he undertook to Syria around 1130 BC. Robbed by a fellow traveller, Wenamun was forced to recover his silver by going ashore at Sidon and committing robbery himself. Yet at Byblos the harbour-master would not let him purchase timber, presumably because news of his activities as a robber had arrived before him. For twenty-nine days Wenamun loitered in spite of the refusal of the harbour-master to let him trade. Finally the local ruler granted the Egyptian merchant an interview, and Wenamun found himself up against a very hard negotiator. Since the stolen money fell short of covering the cost of the timber he wished to buy, he was told in no uncertain terms to send back to Egypt for a cargo of goods to make up the difference. It took nearly a year for the shipment to arrive and the timber to be cut and got ready for export. At this point, warships arrived from Sidon to demand justice for Wenamun's robbery, since word must have got out about the arrival of his Egyptian goods. He tells us how he sat down on the beach and cried. But frightened of offending Egypt, the harbour-master let Wenamun slip away with the Sidonese ships in close pursuit. Though a storm saved his ship from capture, it was driven towards Cyprus, where Wenamun was seized once the captain put in for repairs. The loss of his timber, even his own life, now stared him in the face until he was lucky enough to encounter the local ruler, a queen who spoke Egyptian. So it happened that Wenamun finally got home and sold his precious cargo, the profits offering some compensation for the anxieties he had endured.

Such difficulties did not curtail international trade, but they made the items purchased abroad by the Egyptians costly, and in particular wood. That is why carpenters in Egypt had to make the most of the limited supply. It turned them into craftsmen renowned for the quality of their products, whether chariots, ships or furniture. They artificially bent wood, shaping it as required and then joining the separate pieces by means of glued joints. Gypsum, a hydrated form of calcium sulphate which occurs naturally in Egypt, was prepared as a thick plaster which could be applied to timber to disguise the grain. Gilding was another popular means of finishing or decorating wood. Gypsum was also used as an adhesive for holding the gold leaf to timber, as can be seen on Tutankhamun's gilded ceremonial chariots. Glue and rawhide were the usual binders in chariot construction, bronze wire was only added to the wooden tyres. Despite their basic similarity, none of the chariots buried with Tutankhamun are identical. Hardly a single component of one chariot actually duplicates that of another. The vehicles were not the product of any standardised method of manufacture, although we know that chariots were built in workshops employing woodworkers, metal-workers, gilders and those skilled in leatherwork. But this integration of crafts failed to evolve into anything resembling an assembly line. Each craftsman contributed to the overall construction of a chariot, which on completion was a unique product. Carpenters, for instance, made more than the basic frame, as Tutankhamun's chariot horses wore wooden blinkers.

One of the things we can learn from the chariots of Tutankhamun, which could not be deduced from pictorial representations alone, is their relative proportions. These vehicles are wide, rather than deep-bodied like the Roman racing chariot, and the lightness of their materials, essentially bent wood and leather, plus a sophisticated wheel construction, gave them a mobility which must have been very hard to match. It is hardly surprising that Egypt, in spite of its shortage of suitable timber, became a major exporter of chariots, the rulers of its Asian tributary states welcoming the opportunity to exchange such high quality models for products needed by the Egyptians. King Solomon of Israel, a kingdom whose formation Egypt later welcomed as a counter-balance to the Philistines, would have received chariots along with the pharaoh's daughter he married in the late eleventh or early tenth century BC. Solomon was famous for his horses, and is reputed to have maintained 4,000 chariot teams and 12,000 horsemen. Though these inflated figures have to be discounted for a king who never went to war, the Old Testament records the high prices Solomon was prepared to pay for his chariot horses and his chariots. Whereas his father David had paid 50 shekels for a team of oxen and a threshing floor, Solomon paid 150 shekels for each horse and 600 shekels for each chariot – prices in line with those charged in Egypt. No prices are recorded for the composite bows he bought for his chariot warriors: their slow process of manufacture would have made each one very expensive indeed. Solomon may have financed his chariotry through trade, because he acted as a middleman in the export of Egyptian chariots to Syria.

Horses were also involved in Solomon's transactions, because Egypt always struggled to become a horse-breeding country. No Egyptian deity was associated with horses, the only example of such an association being the Syrian goddess Astarte, who was a popular import in the fourteenth century BC. Worshipped as a mother goddess in Ugarit, where she was the wife and sister of Baal, the most active Canaanite god, she was in Egyptian painting and relief portrayed as a mounted war goddess. Feared for her aggressiveness by the Ugaritians, who believed Astarte enjoyed wading through the blood of her human victims, her accomplishment as a divine horsewoman seems to have filled a gap in the Egyptian pantheon. Introduced by the Hyksos, Astarte borrowed the horns of Hathor, the far from docile Egyptian cow goddess, and became a favourite of charioteers. Where her mount came from was probably the same source as Egypt's imported horses – the northern borderlands of West Asia. The horse was native to the Zagros mountains, in present-day Iran, and the hill country of what today is Turkey and Armenia. Further north on the steppelands of Russia the first domestication and breeding of horses may well have taken place. The shortage of horses in Egypt caused the donkey to be the principal beast of burden in ancient times, and ensured that its chariotry was never as large as that of the other great West Asian powers, a circumstance which spurred Egyptian craftsmen to perfect their design of the war chariot. Each division of the army was usually accompanied by a chariot force, sometimes 200 vehicles strong. At Megiddo, in 1460 BC, Thutmose III is supposed to have attacked the Canaanites with 1,000 chariots, a rather high number considering the logistics of his swift advance. After the battle the Egyptians found that the booty included 2,138 horses and 924 chariots, virtually the combined chariotry of half-a-dozen states. In spite of the obvious pleasure the Egyptians took in accurate bookkeeping – a relief at Abu Simbel actually shows a scribe on a battlefield noting down the number of severed hands another is counting – it would have been out of character for an ancient West Asian ruler to minimise any aspect of victory, and so these recorded figures should not be taken at face value. The immense cost entailed in the maintenance of chariotry would have been a major limiting factor on the size a state could afford. For all its fabulous wealth derived from gold mining, Egypt was unable to field a big chariot force.

Infantry stayed throughout Egypt's long history as the backbone of its army. Possibly its ability to repulse the invaders who brought down Hatti, Ugarit and other West Asian powers in the twelfth century BC has something to do with this traditional strength. Pictorial representations of uniformly clad and equipped foot soldiers marching in ordered ranks survive from very early times. Reliefs of Ramesses II's victory at Kadesh indicate a similar discipline among the Hittites, notwithstanding Hatti's greater reliance on mercenary troops. But it seems probable that the Egyptian army had the advantage of more cohesion and resilience as a fighting force, which may have been a factor in its recovery from the initial shock of the surprise Hittite attack there. Egypt adopted the chariot when other West Asian peoples demonstrated its effectiveness on the battlefield, but there was no reliance on this new weapon to the exclusion of the infantry: Egyptian foot soldiers were feared for the punch of their attack. Having advanced slowly in formation towards the enemy, they would progressively increase the momentum of an attack until the signal was given for a concerted charge. Then, with shields and spears ready, they crashed into an enemy whose ranks were already disrupted by arrows fired from chariots. Rigorous training for such encounters was as important as the co-ordination practised by the chariotry, since tactics had to be adapted to the situation on the battlefield. An early text complains about the unpredictable movements of Asian opponents, when it compares them to crocodiles. 'The vile Asian,' it says, 'never announces the day of combat ... He lays on the river bank like the crocodile, snatching at whatever passes by.' This complaint reflects not only the frustration of pharaohs, but also the dismay their troops so often felt about campaigning abroad. Motives behind all this military activity must have had a commercial basis, as Egypt tried to protect its trading and mining operations abroad, even though royal prestige cannot be ignored in any ancient conflict. The meticulous portrayal of victories on temple walls, pylons and stelae underlines the sense of fulfilment pharaohs clearly derived from battlefield successes. To the pharaoh alone is victory due, for he 'is the raging one, who enters the fray slaying thousands of the

The goddess Astarte on horseback

enemy as if they were no more than grass-hoppers'. They come 'straight on to a fire'.

A quite different voice is heard in a description of an Egyptian foot soldier's lot. Called up for service in Syria, he is obliged to march through mountains and live on salted food. 'His body is ravaged by illness and yet he faces the enemy, assailed on all sides by missiles . . . His body is weak, and his legs fail him.' After the battle is won, there is the long march home. 'If he deserts, all his relations will be imprisoned. He expires on the edge of the desert with nobody to perpetuate his name. In life as in death the poor soldier suffers.' This passage appears in a book of exercises for scribes, who would have been pleased to copy out a story which contrasts their safe and sheltered existence with an infantryman's fate.

Satirical though the exercise is in its treatment of warfare, the arduous nature of foreign campaigns for the rank-and-file was overlooked in pharaonic records. Not untypical is the campaign against Tunip conducted by Ramesses III (1198–1166 BC). Emphasis is placed on the daring aspects of the assault, with scaling ladders and battle-axes breaking down the city gate, while everywhere the enemy is cut down by brave Egyptian soldiers. The stylised relief is nothing more than a prelude to the plundering of Tunip, which failed to recover from the experience. Here the metaphor most favoured to describe the Egyptian army as a 'full flame' became reality when the plundered city was fired. The wrath of pharaoh and his troops were indivisible at this moment of destruction.

The most spectacular failure of the Egyptian army occurred at the time of the Exodus. According to the Bible, the Hebrews were then led from slavery in Egypt by Moses, an Egyptianised Hebrew. Their growing numbers, and the Hyksos-like threat this growth implied, persuaded one pharaoh to oppress the Hebrews with the making of bricks for building projects and 'all kinds of work in the field'. When this strategy failed to bring about any reduction, he ordered Hebrew midwives to kill all male babies. But they refused to comply with this cruel order, and so the pharaoh decreed that Egyptians should throw them into the Nile instead. After three months of hiding her baby boy, Moses' mother made a basket of rushes, and placed it with the baby near the bank in the hope that he might escape death. In an amazing reversal of fortune, an Egyptian princess discovered the infant and decided to adopt him as her own, at which time the name Moses was given. A parallel of the birth legend of the Akkadian king Sargon the Great (2340–2315 BC), whose priestess mother had to hide the loss of her chastity, this folk-lore beginning to Moses' stay in the Egyptian court should not be allowed to cast doubt on the possibility of his presence there. Thutmose III had initiated the practice of bringing princes of subject West Asian kings to Egypt in the mid-fifteenth century BC. They were trained in Egyptian ways so as to prepare them to replace their fathers. 'Now the children of rulers,' a text tells us, 'are brought to the court as hostages. When any of these rulers die, His Majesty will send his son to mount the throne.' Thus foreign princes were no strangers to the Egyptian court, and some of them are known to have been appointed to high positions in the government. It is not impossible, therefore, that Moses enjoyed such a privileged life until, that is, he killed an Egyptian overseer for abusing Hebrew slaves and fled

An Assyrian chariot pursues fleeing enemies
while a bird of prey contemplates its dinner

into the desert, where he learned of his own Hebrew heritage. God revealed himself to Moses shortly afterwards, charging him with leading his people out of Egypt.

Denied this request, Moses warned his stepbrother the pharaoh of dire calamities – 'on the gods of Egypt . . . judgments' – until it was granted. The series of plagues seemed to bear out this threat: the blood-red waters of the Nile signalled Osiris' death rather than his resurrection; the innumerable frogs embarrassed Heket, the frog goddess; sickening cattle was an open affront to the cow goddess Hathor; but, most of all, a violent storm darkened the sky, overshadowing mighty Amun-Re, the great Theban god who protected the pharaohs themselves. In the Exodus story, the shaken pharaoh's response to the thunderstorm is to confess that he and his people were wrong, and he implored Moses to intercede with his god on their behalf. When the last plague, the ninth, carried off the pharaoh's eldest son, Moses was given to understand that he could lead the Hebrews away. But the pharaoh sent the Egyptian army after them in revenge. At this point the Hebrews were saved by a miracle, the drowning of the Egyptians in the Red Sea, after they had safely crossed under Moses' direction.

And Moses stretched out his hand over the sea; and the Lord caused the sea to go back by a strong east wind all that night, and made the sea dry land, and the waters were divided. And the children of Israel went into the midst of the sea upon the dry ground; and the waters were a wall unto them on their right hand, and on their left. And the Egyptians pursued, and went after them to the midst of the sea . . . And the Lord said unto Moses, Stretch out thine hand over the sea, that the waters may come again upon the Egyptians, upon their chariots, and upon their horsemen. And Moses stretched forth his hand over the sea, and the sea returned to his strength when the morning appeared; and the Egyptians fled against it; and the Lord overthrew the Egyptians in the midst of the sea.

Whether the 'Red Sea' or the 'Sea of Reeds' is to be located among the lakes and marshes stretching northwards from the Gulf of Suez is still a matter of scholarly debate. That an actual setback suffered by the Egyptian chariotry is recalled in the Exodus story may not be at all unlikely. The Egyptians would never have recorded this dramatic reverse, nor would a pharaoh like Ramesses II admit any fault on his own part. There is little question that the character of Ramesses fits the picture of the arrogant ruler who rejects divine commands. His engagement with the Hittites at Kadesh was another near disaster, caused by an elementary failure of military intelligence, and prevented mainly by the last-minute arrival of allied reinforcements. And we know Ramesses, 'beloved of Amun, great in victories', employed thousands of prisoners-of-war and imported slaves on his massive building projects. Though the lush Nile delta would have first attracted them as a place of residence like other pastoral nomads, the Hebrews could have been coerced as labourers on large-scale projects when the Egyptians discovered how Ramesses' plans outran the supply of manpower. Wadi Tumilat, a narrow fertile piece of land that extends east from the delta and runs to modern Ismailya, was settled by peoples from the Negev and Sinai before the Hyksos occupation of Egypt, and archaeological finds from campsites or villages indicate continued Semitic settlement down to the reign of Ramesses II. Whilst the Hebrews' departure from Egypt cannot be verified from Egyptian records, the Exodus narrative is still plausible, even though it may have been revised to take into account the dubious reputation of the supreme monument-building pharaoh, Ramesses II. This merely turned the pharaoh of oppression into the pharaoh of building.

Egypt's relations with other great powers fluctuated according to their relative strengths and ambitions in West Asia. After King Ashur-uballit I's death in 1328 BC, Assyria waged a prolonged war against Babylon. This hard-fought conflict was part and parcel of the antagonistic relations that prevailed throughout the history of these two ancient states. Yet the war with Babylon was only one of the military efforts of Assyria, for successive kings were slowly building up the size and might of its army through campaigns against hostile tribesmen along its northern and eastern borders. The reign of Tukulti-Ninurta I (1243–1207 BC) brought the Assyrian empire to unprecedented power. A vigorous campaigner, Tukulti-Ninurta styled himself 'king of the world, the mighty king, favourite and priest of the god Ashur, rightful ruler, beloved of the goddess Ishtar', but he never claimed divinity like the pharaohs. He defeated the Hittites and the Babylonians in great chariot battles, plundering the city of Babylon itself and carrying off much booty to Assyria. Yet Tukulti-Ninurta died not on the battlefield but in his own palace, the victim of his son's impatience for power. Following a period of confusion, the Assyrian throne was occupied by Tiglath-pileser I (1114–1076 BC), who even surpassed the military achievements of Tukulti-Ninurta.

Assyria escaped the worst of the catastrophe that overwhelmed other West Asian states in the twelfth century BC, although it was not entirely free from the attention of invaders. The most pressing were the Mushku, probably the Phrygians who settled in western Asia Minor. The Greeks knew the Mushku king Mita as Midas, a ruler famed for his wealth. So greedy did he become that the god Dionysus granted Midas his wish that all he touched might become gold. Soon after, he found that this applied to his food as well and he beseeched the god to take back the gift, which Dionysus did. The myth alludes to the natural wealth of Phrygia: it also recalls the vast spoils the Mushku gathered through the collapse of Hittite authority in northern Syria and Asia Minor. The Assyrians maintained a strong chariot corps, allocating land for the livelihood of these professional fighters. The practice survived down to Persian times, as records from Babylon dating from the fifth century BC mention 'chariot lands' and 'horse lands'. Land was set aside, too, for bowmen, the elite of the Persian army. At first the Assyrian chariot was similar to the models used by the Hittites and the Egyptians; later it increased in size and was capable of carrying a crew of four men: a driver, a bowman, a shield bearer and a spearman. The composite bow remained the chief weapon for chariot warriors, in both battle and the hunt, although spears came into increasing use during hand-to-hand engagements. Eight-spoked wheels gave the Assyrian chariot a greater robustness, and larger horses were bred in order to pull the extra load. Of all the West Asian great powers, however, Assyria relied the least on chariotry. Because it so frequently fought against barbarous enemies on its northern and eastern borders, where the terrain comprised rugged mountains, the Assyrians developed a formidable and sizeable infantry. Where the battlefield suited the deployment of chariots, they came into play; elsewhere, the Assyrian kings used their foot soldiers, armed with bows, spears, swords and shields. 'The widespread armies of Mushku,' says Tiglath-pileser, 'I easily brought down. I subjugated them, and took away their possessions.'

Assyria, Babylon and Egypt survived the foreign invasions of the twelfth century BC. In particular, Egypt and Assyria fought off determined

Foot soldiers, the backbone of the Assyrian army

invaders, some of whom were called the Sea Peoples. In 1190 BC, the eighth year of Ramesses III's reign, the Egyptians repulsed an onslaught by these northerners. Further attacks by them, as well as the Lybians, sorely tested the morale of the Egyptian army, not least its infantrymen who bore the brunt of the fighting in the Nile delta. Equally challenged was the Assyrian army, which won a great victory for Tiglath-pileser I over 20,000 Mushku tribesmen in the mountains of Kurdistan. Other migrating peoples were likewise kept from the Assyrian heartland by force of arms. Again these victories were secured by foot soldiers, not charioteers. Determined foreign infantrymen had shown how chariot forces could be overwhelmed by sheer numbers, if they were equipped with javelins, long swords and rudimentary defensive armour. Chariotry would not disappear from the battlefields of West Asia for another millennium, but military and political power in future would belong to those states in which warfare was a common concern, with all adult males liable to serve in the ranks of its armies. The days of supremacy for a chariot-owning aristocracy were well and truly over.

4

Europe

Hector was stung by Sarpedon's rebuke. Swiftly he jumped down
from his chariot in full armour, and swinging a pair of sharp spears in
his hand went everywhere among his men, driving them into battle
and rousing their fighting spirit.

Iliad

Inseparable though the chariot is from Homer's account of the Trojan
War, no massed chariotry engagements are described in the *Iliad*. The
epic poem accords the vehicle a very high status in that its possession
marks out the owner as an important person, a leader of men like the
Trojan hero Hector, but the use to which it is put has no parallel in West
Asia and Egypt. For on the plain of Troy the chariot functions as a means
of transport to and from the actual fighting, which occurs on foot,
although there are ideas preserved in parts of the text which suggest
alternative possibilities of deployment on the battlefield. Since there is no
direct mention of mounted riders, the large number of chariots
introduced by the poet are condemned to the wasteful and ineffectual
role of battle-taxis. Yet the critical importance of a good team of chariot
horses is still emphasised. 'For many swift horses,' Homer tells us,
'snapped their draught poles at the head of the shaft and left chariot and
charioteer behind.' Even the Greek hero Achilles appears to take for
granted his good luck in having fine steeds. When he accused them of
letting down his close companion Patroclus, whom Hector slew, the
horse Xanthus rebuked Achilles for his lack of trust, and then warned of
his approaching death. In anger at this prophecy, the Erinyes, the furious
spirits of justice and vengeance, at once struck the immortal horse dumb.
Their intervention was probably caused by a desire to see that events ran
a normal course and were not disrupted by any warning of a future event.
Not that 'Achilles of the nimble feet' cared a hoot: he told Xanthus he

was doomed to die at Troy. Though Achilles' horses lacked wings, the usual feature of such marvellous creatures as the flying horse Pegasus, their speed was 'as swift as the pace of Zephyrus', the god of the west wind. It seems likely that the divine horses of Achilles were imported into Greek mythology from West Asia, where they are known to have been worshipped at Ugarit, an ancient port of call for Greek merchants. What did not arrive with them, however, was any awareness of the devastating effect they had when leading hundreds of chariots together, hurtling into an attack.

The closest we come in the *Iliad* to a realistic use of chariotry is in the instructions Nestor gives to his charioteers. This respected elder statesman of the Greeks, 'the clear-voiced orator from Pylos', carefully placed his chariots at the front of the line of battle, keeping back as a rearguard 'a mass of first-rate foot soldiers'. Then Nestor told his charioteers to control the horses lest their chariots become entangled in the confusion of the fight. He said:

'Do not think that bravery and skill entitles a charioteer to break ranks and fight the Trojans on his own. And don't let anybody drop behind and weaken the whole force. When a man in his own chariot comes within range of an enemy vehicle, it is time for him to try a spear-thrust. Those are the best tactics. This is the way our forefathers took walled cities by storm.'

Even here the impact of a massed chariot attack is diminished by the expectation of its climax as no more than a thrusting match between opposing vehicles. Rather like the modern misunderstanding about Hittite dependence on the spear, Homer fails to appreciate the advantage a composite bow added to a chariot's effectiveness. Both the Hittites and the Egyptians put its killing power to good use, against each other as well as enemies who separately dared to challenge them. They knew, too, that most victories derived from combined operations – the mutual support of chariotry and infantry.

Homer is of course a poet, not a military historian. He dwells on the prowess of individual fighters locked in single combat, or on the struggle of a lone hero pitting his strength against several assailants, rather than analysing the movements of armies. Unaware of the true nature of warfare during the Trojan War, which is dated to around 1300 BC, Homer celebrates the glory of dismounted warriors. This is really his heroic theme in what is a very circumscribed poem. The whole story told in the *Iliad* unfolds in less than two months, with armed conflict measured in days, not weeks. When the Greeks and the Trojans clash on the plain between the city of Troy and the Greek camp, the various engagements are at locations within a few kilometres of each other. Attack and counter-attack continue without result until Achilles' feud is ended with

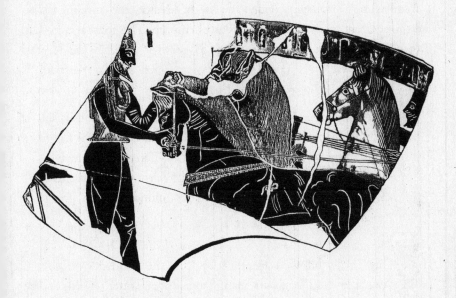

Achilles harnesses his chariot team

Agamemnon, the commander-in-chief of the Greek expedition against Troy. Only then does the decisive encounter take place. For after slaughtering many Trojans, and driving others in panic back to their city, Achilles discovered that Hector waited to fight him outside its walls.

Swept into their city like a herd of frightened deer, the Trojans wiped the sweat from their shaking bodies and quenched their thirst within the safety of massive defensive walls, while the Greeks advanced outside with their shields at the slope. Fate, for her own evil purposes, kept Hector in front of the Scaean Gate.

But when Hector saw Achilles face to face, he 'began to tremble . . . and no longer with the heart to stand his ground . . . he left the gate, and ran away in terror'. What follows is a nightmarish pursuit on foot in which 'the pursuer cannot overtake nor the pursued escape'. As the gods alone could end this impasse, Zeus held up 'his golden scales, putting death sentences in each pan, one side for Achilles, on the other for horse-taming Hector. When the balance began to tilt towards Hector, his fate was decided. Apollo immediately abandoned him, while the goddess Athena let Achilles know of his forthcoming success.'

Achilles' powerful spear ended the life of Hector, the only man who had the courage to challenge the Greek champion. The combat over, the Trojans should have been permitted to recover Hector's body, but Achilles subjected

> the fallen prince to a dreadful humiliation. He slit the tendons at the back of both his feet, inserted leather straps, and made them fast to his chariot, leaving the head to drag . . . Then he whipped his horses, who galloped off. Behind a naked Hector raised a cloud of dust, his once handsome head dragged ignominiously through the Trojan soil.

Though he finally allowed Hector's body to be handed over to the Trojans, Achilles had behaved in an appalling manner. Without the divine assistance of Aphrodite, who among other things rubbed on 'ambrosial oil' to slow down decomposition, the corpse would have been in a terrible state. For it should be noted that Achilles chose to add insult to injury by riding in a chariot, while Hector twisted and turned in the dust behind. Homer thus makes the Trojan hero's degradation all the greater through this startling contrast: the boast Hector had made to the dying Patroclus about how his 'fast horses' were a guarantee of protection for the Trojans has been turned on its head. The remains of Hector were now lower than the hooves of Xanthus and Balius, Achilles' chariot horses. Thus the chariot's ancient importance as a war machine is superimposed on an anti-heroic outrage. Homer's avoidance of a mounted horseman in favour of the heroising charioteer could not be more obvious.

The abduction of Persephone by Hades in his flying chariot

Before his death, Hector had approached the wide ditch which the Greeks dug in order to protect their encampment, along with their beached ships, and confidently predicted that 'our horses will easily jump it with one bound'. As this feat was beyond the capability of a yoked team, it implies that Hector's 'fast horses' were ridden into battle. Proof is perhaps to be found in the capture of Trojan horses by Diomedes' squire Sthenelus; at the suggestion of his master, he leaped on the back of one horse and drove others to the Greek lines. In vain, therefore, do we look to Homer for information on either Greek or Trojan chariotry. Despite his best efforts to give the chariot a triumphal position in the fighting at Troy, he could not entirely eliminate references to mounted warriors, however oblique cavalry was to the main action. Like horses in his own lifetime, the ninth century BC, Homer saw them as the easiest means of transport for noblemen, who dismounted to fight on foot.

Missing from the Greek epics as well is the composite bow. The bow of Pandarus, an ally of the Trojans from the neighbouring city of Zelia, is a poetic fiction. Its description indicates that Homer lacked any real knowledge of the composite bow. Goat horn on its own would have been far too stiff and unyielding a material, no matter the expertise of its maker, 'a craftsman in horn, who fitted the two horns of an ibex together, made all smooth, and put a golden tip at the end'. So out of character with heroic warfare indeed is the action of Pandarus in wounding Menelaus with an arrow, and thereby breaking a truce between the Greeks and the Trojans, that Homer is at pains to explain this unusual man. Leaving eleven brand-new chariots at home, Pandarus had decided to walk to Troy against his father's advice because he feared there might not be available enough fodder to feed his well-nourished chariot horses. Nowhere is it suggested that he ever fired his bow from any of these vehicles. The sheer unexpectedness of an arrow breaking a solemnly agreed truce left Agamemnon aghast. He told his wounded brother that Zeus 'may postpone the penalty, but he imposes it in the end, and the transgressors pay a heavy price . . . Troy will be destroyed'. But this end may be a long way off, Agamemnon admitted, should Menelaus now die and the Greeks give up their attempt recover Helen, his runaway wife. Menelaus was able to reassure him, saying 'the arrow did not reach a vital spot. Before it could do so, it was halted by my belt and the armour beneath, with the bronze they put on it.'

Not only is Homer concerned to convey disdain for Pandarus' archery skills, so impersonal are they as a method of fighting in contrast to hand-to-hand combat, but even more he reveals their abject failure to affect the course of battle. As Pandarus tells Aeneas,

'I have already shot a couple of their best men, Diomedes and Menelaus, and in each case I certainly drew blood, but I only roused these Greeks to greater efforts . . . If I ever get home again and set my eyes on my own country and my wife and the high roof of my great house, I shall be ready to let anybody cut off my head there and then, if I don't smash this utterly useless bow and throw it into the fire.'

In reply, Aeneas invites Pandarus to join him as his charioteer: 'You take the reins and whip, and when the time comes I will dismount and do the fighting. Or let me take care of the horses, leaving you to fight the man.' Together they encountered Diomedes, who was on foot, but instead of following Aeneas' plan by dismounting from the chariot, Pandarus threw

Achilles binding Patroclus' wounds

at speed a javelin which pierced Diomedes' shield. Elated by what he imagined to be a hit, Pandarus claimed a victory until Diomedes' return throw struck him fully in the face. 'He crashed from the chariot,' Homer says. 'That was the end of Pandarus.'

This section of the *Iliad* has been cited as evidence for two things. The first is proof that the ancient Greeks never associated archery with chariot warfare. It is argued that Aeneas' invitation to Pandarus was made to an ally who had decided to abandon the bow for the spear: the implication is that the archer was always a foot soldier. The second piece of evidence the section is supposed to provide concerns the spear as the offensive weapon in chariots. The armoured chariot-fighting spearman is, therefore, seen as the supreme warrior on the ancient Greek battlefield. It has even been suggested that the bronze sheet-armour excavated at Dendra in the Argolid could have belonged to such a fighter. One of the most surprising discoveries made in Greece, archaeologists found in 1960 the burial of a warrior wearing a complete bronze cuirass, surrounded by other military gear. It remains today the only such armour known from

The bronze suit of armour found at Dendra

ancient times in Europe and was buried around 1450 BC. Constructed as two shells which fastened at the side with twisted thongs, this protection for the chest and back was supplemented by a high collar, shoulder guards, three bands below the hips, rather like a skirt, and greaves. The rest of the warrior's equipment consisted of a boar's-tusk helmet with metal cheekpieces, plus the remains of a shield, little more than leather stretched over a wooden frame. His sword and spear were absent from the tomb, which had been disturbed by robbers. Because the Dendra equipment is far too heavy and unwieldy for a foot soldier, some scholars believe its wearer would have stood in a chariot. But again the weight and cumbersomeness of the armour could not but have been a serious liability in a fast-moving chariot. Unlike the armoured medieval knight, the Dendra warrior was not seated on a high saddle with his legs gripping the sides of a horse, and his feet placed safely in stirrups: instead, if an archer never accompanied the charioteer, he was trying to maintain his balance while thrusting sideways with a two-handed spear.

The argument for the Dendra armour belonging to a chariot warrior is unconvincing. Apart from the weight problem, there are records of lighter corselets more suited to this purpose, similar to the protection Menelaus was lucky enough to be wearing at Troy. Most telling of all, however, is the narrative of the *Iliad*, for Pandarus did not fight from Aeneas' chariot as a thrusting spearman. On the contrary, he threw a javelin at Diomedes, a weapon used in addition to the bow by the Egyptians in their chariots. Pandarus' sudden death after the failure of this throw may well have seemed just to Homer, since the javelin as well as the arrow harmed heroes at an unfair distance, especially when launched from a speeding chariot. It was a fitting end to a man who left eleven chariots at home. From the *Iliad* we might be tempted to conclude that chariots never played an active role in Greek battles, with warriors firing arrows from them as they did in West Asia and Egypt. But Homer's ignorance of the composite bow should not be taken to mean that it was unknown in ancient Greece. It may simply be that by Homer's time its role was forgotten, not least because warfare had completely changed. Infantry engagements now took the place of chariot battle as Greek communities moved from citadels to city states. Chariot-riding aristocrats no longer ruled from fortified palaces, but fought alongside their fellow citizens as foot soldiers.

Another reason for the lack of archery in the *Iliad* could well be a disdain on the part of Homer towards the bow. That both the Greeks and the Trojans used bows with little effect does not necessarily mean that the poet considered there was nothing to condemn in the archer, nor that he regarded the bow as a legitimate weapon for a hero. The truce Pandarus broke with his arrow had been agreed between the Trojan king Priam and Agamemnon so that Menelaus and Paris could meet in single combat to decide Helen's future. Their inconclusive duel let Helen stay with Paris, to the ultimate grief of the Trojans. But Priam dismissed her own guilt and sorrow at causing the Trojan War: 'I bear you no ill will,' he told Helen. 'I blame the gods.' Nothing could be done about their interference, except continue with the conflict. Had not Paris, the most

famous archer on the Trojan side, discarded his bow in order to fight
Menelaus in heroic fashion? Had not Hector ignored the attentions of
archers and slingers when, standing in no-man's-land, he proposed he
truce? 'The long-haired Achaeans,' Homer tells us, 'kept up their
archery, making Hector the target for their arrows and stones', until
Agamemnon ordered them to cease shooting. Paris is presented in this
episode as the archer-turned-hero, while his elder brother Hector
displayed a heroic indifference to the attentions of unworthy opponents,
archers and slingers. At the battle of Gaugamela, in 331 BC, Alexander
endeavoured to inspire his troops with contempt for their Persian foe by
reminding them that many were armed only with javelins and stones
thrown from slings. His soldiers understood the insult perfectly: in
classical Greece the slingers were the lowest of all combatants, just below
the position occupied by archers.

Ironic, then, is the news that the dying Hector gave Achilles, when he
told his hard-hearted opponent to pause before exacting further revenge
on his corpse. 'Take thought before you act,' said Hector, 'in case the
angry gods remember how you treated me, when your turn comes and
you are laid low at the Scaean Gate in all your splendour by Paris and
Apollo.' Aided by 'the archer god Apollo, son of Zeus', none other than
Helen's lover was destined to slay with a single arrow 'the swift and
excellent Achilles', terror of the battlefield. In heroic character, Achilles
remarked to what was by then Hector's corpse: 'As for my own death, let
it come when Zeus and the other immortals determine.' Often though
Apollo's support for the Trojans is mentioned in the *Iliad*, his most critical
intervention was the help he gave Paris in securing the death of Achilles.
Apollo's partiality for the Trojans stands in contrast to the allegiances of
the other gods and goddesses, because it cannot be explained in terms of
the so-called judgment of Paris, the reason for the Trojan War. Chosen
by Zeus to decide among bickering Hera, Athena and Aphrodite as to
who was the most beautiful goddess of all, Paris selected the love goddess
Aphrodite in return for the promise of Helen, wife of King Menelaus of
Sparta. Her elopement with him was the ostensible cause of the ten-year
Greek assault on Troy. During this long struggle the efforts Apollo made
on their behalf were not fully appreciated by the Trojans, who remained
loyal worshippers of Athena, one of the goddesses whom Paris had so
badly offended. Like Apollo, Athena possessed a temple on the acropolis
at Troy, from which Odysseus and Diomedes rescued her statue in the

final days of the war. And Homer even has Hector, on the advice of the seer Helenos, encourage his mother to make an offering to Athena, the goddess responsible for his fateful encounter with Achilles.

A shadowy figure, Helenos' function in the *Iliad* is prophecy. But on one occasion he produced a bow from nowhere and fired an arrow into the chest of Menelaus, a sudden attack that the Spartan king survived only through the strength of his body-armour. Thought to be a later addition to the poem, this episode combines nonetheless two of the attributes of Apollo, namely prophecy and archery. Along with his twin sister Artemis, the virgin huntress, Apollo was feared as an immensely powerful deity, whose cult was associated with Asia Minor. The importance of his worship in the vicinity of Troy can be seen at the very start of the *Iliad*, when Agamemnon slighted Chryses, the god's priest from a town close to the city. In his prayer to Apollo, Chryses mentioned Chryses, Killa and Tenedos as places dedicated to 'the archer god', and asked that the Greeks 'pay with your arrows for my tears'. These were no ordinary arrows because Apollo had control of the plague, the curse of an armed encampment. The Greeks suffered such a visitation: they felt the plague-infected shafts of West Asian deities like Reseph, who terrorised Cyprus

The archer god Apollo trying to recover his tripod from the hero Herakles

with his deadly aim. Since this island was an early meeting-place for West Asian and Greek religious ideas, it would have been the source of the most terrible arrows in Apollo's quiver. By the time the *Iliad* assumed its final form Apollo was a thoroughly Greek god, the owner of the greatest oracle of all at Delphi, but not every aspect of his older character was lost. He still remained the mainstay of the chariot-riding Trojans, the deity who guided the arrows fired from composite bows. The inability of Homer to envisage chariot battle pushed Apollo's favourite archers to the margins of the epic action, with the notable exception of Achilles' death. Then the effect of a well-aimed shot had to be acknowledged, even though the archer was not then standing in a chariot.

The other bow Homer is obliged to mention is the one which Odysseus left on Ithaca, his mountainous island home. Quite apart from the climax its stringing represents in the *Odyssey* when, after years of wandering, Odysseus arrived at his palace and slaughtered the suitors who had pestered his wife Penelope and lived at her expense, the tone of Homer throughout this epic poem is far from unfavourable to the non-heroic weapon. There can be no doubt that the great bow of Odysseus is composite. For the first thing the returned hero did when it came into his hands was to see whether 'worms might have eaten into the horn in the long absence of the owner'. Even more the weapon is described as 'incurved', the shape of an unstrung composite bow, while the whole business of stringing makes no sense at all for an ordinary, or self, bow. Like the composite bows recovered from Tutankhamun's tomb, the weapon was carefully protected from damage when not in use. Homer tells us how Penelope went to fetch Odysseus' bow for the suitors to string and shoot an arrow through the holes of twelve targets.

> She quickly undid the thong attached to the door-knob, inserted the key into the lock, and then thrust back the bolt. The key did its work . . . the doors flew open before her . . . Then Penelope, standing on tiptoe, pulled the bow from its peg in the shining case that covered it. And there she sat down with the case on her knees and burst into tears as she drew out her husband's bow.

That the contest was to take place on a day sacred to Apollo is yet another indication of how central archery always was to the *Odyssey* story. As one of the suitors pointedly asks: 'Is this holiday in honour of the archer god the right time for bending bows? . . . Better in the morning . . . that we sacrifice to the great Apollo and then try the bow and see who wins.' The contest never occurred because once Odysseus got hold of the great bow and gave it a final inspection,

> he strung it without effort or haste and with his right hand proved the string, which gave a lovely sound in answer like a swallow's cry. Confounded, the suitors turned pale, while to mark the critical moment there was a roll of thunder from Zeus. Then the heart of long-suffering Odysseus leapt for joy at the sign of divine favour – from the son of Kronos of the crooked ways.

The king of the gods had acknowledged how the time for Odysseus' vengeance was come. With the help of Apollo, the archer god, he was about to slay those who arrogantly occupied his home.

It would seem that originally Apollo, the champion of Troy in the *Iliad*, was the divine protector and helper of Odysseus in the *Odyssey*, a role usurped by the goddess Athena in Homer's rendition of the heroic tale. Otherwise it is difficult to see the poetic purpose behind the slaughter on Apollo's holiday. Put simply, the different attitude of Homer to archery in the *Odyssey* was dictated by the essential part played by Odysseus' great bow: it was too important in the epic to be ignored. Though Athena is given credit for prompting Penelope to issue to the suitors the challenge of the bow, the goddess disappears from the scene as soon as Odysseus is within reach of his trusty weapon, not least because its effective use is Apollo's preserve. In the earliest versions of the tale there would have been no need for Athena to offer any assistance to Odysseus at all. While in the *Iliad*, therefore, Homer reinterpreted fighting on the battlefield in terms of his own times, downgrading the bow yet keeping the chariot without understanding its real purpose as a fast-moving platform for an archer, in the *Odyssey* he had no need to concentrate on warfare since the latter is fundamentally an adventure story. The heroic ideal was not compromised by Odysseus' renown as an archer, although the killing of the unarmed suitors remains a ferocious event, no matter how outnumbered Odysseus and his son Telemachus were in the hall.

'You dogs,' Odysseus shouted aloud. 'You never expected me to return from Troy. So you devoured my wealth, raped my maids, and wooed my wife though I was still alive. All this was done with no more fear of the gods than the human vengeance that is about to happen. I tell you, one and all, your doom is sealed.'

Apollo and Artemis, with a quiver and a composite bow

'With Apollo's help' he had already ended the life of Antinous, a suitor who 'nursed a secret hope that he would be the one to string the bow and shoot through all the marks'. An arrow 'passed clean through the soft skin of his neck' as Antinous balanced a two-handled cup of wine in his hands.

The heroic ideals embodied in the *Iliad* and the *Odyssey* descend from Mycenaean times, an era dated to between 1600 BC and 1100 or 1050 BC and named after its chief site, Agamemnon's stronghold in the Argolid. Artefacts unearthed by archaeologists, and early linguistic forms of Greek deciphered from tablets inscribed with the Linear B text, show that the roots of Homer's poetic inheritance run back into the rule of the great palaces at Mycenae, Tiryns, Pylos, Iolkos, Orchomenus and Gla. Then, in parallel with the disaster which overwhelmed the Hittites and the Ugaritians, this ancient phase of Greek civilisation went into steep decline to the extent that the art of writing was lost, and not recovered until the adoption of the Phoenician alphabet early in the eighth century BC. But the tradition of a heroic past was preserved in the prodigious memories of those bards who sang or recited the epic tales during the dark years in which Homer was born. As Homer's final shaping of them in his two epics could not be expected to accurately recall every aspect of the vanished Mycenaean world, it is worth reviewing what survives now from this ancient period, which was first revealed in 1876 by the German enthusiast Heinrich Schliemann. That year he uncovered just inside the Lion Gate at Mycenae a circular enclosure, some twenty-four metres in diameter, containing six shaft-graves whose stone markers were decorated with scenes of chariots at full gallop. Because the classical Greek travel writer Pausanias claimed that 'in the ruins there . . . lie Agamemnon and those murdered with him', and because the grave goods included impressive gold breast plates, necklaces and face masks, Schliemann believed he had found the resting place of Homeric heroes. Modern archaeology has fixed the last interment at about 1500 BC, two centuries before the Trojan War. The epoch-making find established beyond doubt the existence of a mature culture on the mainland of Greece, but the name used for it must not be taken to imply any centralised political authority. Mycenae was one of several palace-strongholds; it never ruled a Mycenaean empire.

Argument over what is sometimes termed the shaft-grave dynasty at Mycenae turns on whether its rulers were native chieftains who gathered sufficient power to have themselves recognised as local kings, or foreign immigrants similar to the Hyksos occupiers of Egypt. The appearance of an indigenous ruling class, in the various parts of mainland Greece where palaces were built, could have led to the import of chariots from either West Asia or Egypt. Purchasing chariots abroad would have been fraught with problems, however. Unless Mycenaean dynasts acquired the men who knew how to repair the vehicles, to care for the horses, to drive them into battle, and to fight from a fast-moving chariot, then there was no point in buying such expensive military equipment. At most a ruler's chariot would have been restricted to a ceremonial role, whose occupant was marked out from ordinary men by his exceptional means of transport, an interpretation invalidated by the scenes carved on the shaft-grave markers. These portray scenes of chariot combat and not, as was once thought, chariot racing. Though by no means accepted as the only possibility, the arrival of the chariot in mainland Greece may have resulted from a takeover of its fertile plains by invaders, princes who belonged to an international elite of charioteers.

There is no reason why they should not have come from the lands south of the Caucasus by sea; unassembled chariots and teams of horses were capable of transport along the southern shore of the Black Sea. Homer's audience had no difficulty imagining the Greek expeditionary force sailing with its chariotry to Troy, and we know from the palace archive at Knossos that the Mycenaean Greeks brought the horse and chariot to the island of Crete no later than 1400 BC. A sea-borne invasion of Greece 200 years before this date is suggested by four coastal sites destroyed at this time – Kirrha on the Corinthian Gulf, Eleusis on the Saronic Gulf, Argos on the Aegean Sea, and Pylos on the Ionian Sea. Only Crete and the Aegean islands were spared, presumably through the strength of Minos' navy. Greek legend is notably ambivalent about Minos, the ruler of Knossos appearing as a just lawgiver as well as a cruel oppressor. Since Minos seems to be a title rather than a personal name, the ancient Greeks remembered the great days of Cretan civilisation by a single nameless king. The source of Minos' reputation as a wise ruler and a great judge was the meeting he had with Zeus, or the Cretan equivalent of this deity, once every nine years. On the other hand, the second aspect of his legendary character, autocracy, in all probability refers to an actual king, the last Mycenaean ruler at Knossos, whose harsh rule over the island was a means of financing an attempt to extend his power beyond the shores of Crete. Nonetheless, Greek tradition names Minos as the first king to exercise control of the Aegean waters, a scourge of pirates and a protector of traders.

From the imports found in the shaft-graves at Mycenae it is evident that the newly arrived mainland Greek dynasts engaged seriously in overseas trade. Some kind of arrangement had to be made with the Cretans, otherwise the sea routes out of the Aegean to Cyprus and the Syrian coast would have been blocked, prior to a collapse of Cretan strength which gave unrestricted access to eastern Mediterranean waters. This sudden end is attributed to both the Thera eruption of 1500 BC and the Mycenaean attack of 1450 BC. Four times greater than the Krakatoa eruption of 1883 off the Indonesian island of Sumatra, an event heard in Australia over 3,000 miles away, the eruption of Thera, modern Santorini, caused sea floods and spread ash among the Aegean islands and southwestern Asia Minor. Deep-sea sediment cores establish an ash-fall five centimetres thick, half the amount required on Iceland to cause the abandonment of present-day farms. If this fall proved too severe for ancient agriculture, then famine and unrest would have prepared conditions on Crete for a Mycenaean invasion. In the event, the invaders spared only Knossos, because the city and the palace were converted into the capital of a Mycenaean dynasty, which depended on chariots for the defence of its rule on the island.

The building of monumental tombs on half a dozen plains in mainland Greece would support the argument for some kind of takeover by outsiders – the coming of the Greeks. Before 1600 BC there was nothing like the tholos tomb, a circular beehive of stone constructed below ground level, nor were shaft-graves used for burial. Well over 100 tholoi have been excavated. Although they are widespread, a special concentration exists in Messenia, where the earliest known example is near modern Koryphasion. Nearby Laconia, later Sparta, was certainly under the

An Assyrian chariot being rowed across a river

control of the Vaphio kings by 1500 BC. Their palace has yet to be located, but in 1888 their royal tholos was discovered at Vaphio, unusually built on top of a hill and then covered by a mound. Amongst the grave goods were two gold cups of exquisite workmanship. On these vessels are narrated, in repoussé work, the ensnaring of a wild bull by means of a decoy, the tethering of one of its hind legs, and the drawing tight of a strong net. The early collapse of the tomb may account for the preservation of these splendid drinking cups. The tholos at Dendra, the burial place of the rulers of Midea, also suffered a cave-in of the vault, but it did not prevent modern looters removing its precious objects: fortunately, bronze sheet-armour did not interest them. The palaces these wealthy rulers inhabited were fortified, with the very notable exception of Pylos, traditionally Nestor's home. Their development into the great palace-fortresses we recognise in the impressive ruins of today happened around 1300 BC.

How far the writs of these rulers ran outside the plains their palaces dominated is a matter of conjecture. Some of the least accessible mountainous valleys must have retained a degree of independence, their inhabitants supplying sturdy men for service as foot soldiers instead of agricultural produce as taxes. Unfortified Pylos, situated close to the sea on the Navarino bay, is one of the most difficult palaces to assess as regards its area of influence. Initial decipherment of the palace archive led to claims that Nestor's ancestors controlled most of the western coastline of the Peloponnese. Now it is believed that they had authority over a much smaller area, around seventy kilometres square: and in the middle of this tiny kingdom there are hills which in a few places reach 1,000 metres, thereby reducing the amount of land suited for settlement. Yet the kingdom of Pylos was well populated and excavation of the palace site has confirmed its agricultural wealth. The rooms surrounding the throne room were either stores or pantries, where some 3,000 drinking cups and 6,000 jars were unearthed. As Homer always insisted, the generosity of Pylos ensured that guests 'ever found their golden cups brimming full of wine'. From baked tablets recovered there, it can be inferred that a person's status was measured by amounts of grain. Most went to the king, the wanax, one of the two words Homer uses for a ruler. Basileus, the second, which occurs in Linear B inscriptions in a slightly different form of guasileus, had a less exulted meaning for the Mycenaean Greeks, who employed the word generally as 'leader' of a group. Despite the same use in the *Iliad*, basileus survived in later times as the word for king, along with a military connotation.

In Athenian legend the two sons of one early king are credited with a division of the monarchy. To Erechtheus went the basileia, and to his brother Butes, the hierosyne or priesthood. As a chariot-riding war leader, Erechtheus was successful in fighting an early war against Eleusis, a city state later absorbed by the Athenians. But it was Erichthonius, and not Erechtheus, who was associated with the introduction of the chariot. In the *Georgics*, which Virgil composed during the reign of the first Roman emperor Augustus (31 BC–AD 14), we are told that Erichthonius was born with snaky lower limbs or feet, and that he devised the chariot in order to cover them up. Why Erichthonius, rather than the Athenian snake-man Cecrops (whose name actually means 'face-tail') should have been remembered as serpentine remains obscure, but the Athenians were sure he was their founding ancestor whose only conveyance was a chariot. Erichthonius may have originally been a pre-Greek deity, given the tradition recorded by Herodotus that the Athenians were not of Greek stock. He writes that 'they were Pelasgians, who changed their language when absorbed into the Greek family of peoples'. Possibly in Erichthonius the Athenians recalled an indigenous earth god, not unlike Python, the earliest owner of Delphi and the victim of Apollo's deadly arrows. That they added a chariot to his myth only serves to underline the impact which a Mycenaean dynasty must have had on their early development. From the easily defended acropolis at Athens, such a royal house would have sent forth its chief members in chariots, on either tours of inspection or more robust activities such as war and the chase. So Erichthonius' chariot would have passed near its entrance a great tower from the top of which defending archers fired during an attack. Its foundations were traced in 1936 beneath the bastion now supporting the temple of Athene Nike, 'wingless victory'. The Athenian acropolis was indeed one of the few royal strongholds which never fell, a circumstance giving rise to the belief that its strong walls protected not only the people living in the surrounding countryside but also refugees from less lucky cities as far away as Pylos.

Archaeological evidence for the importance of the horse at this time comes from present-day Vrana, at the edge of the Marathon plain. There a tumulus, surrounded by a ring of stones like the grave circle at Mycenae, contained the skeleton of a horse. Its presence recalls the burial customs of southern Russia and the Caucasus, where sacrificed animals were placed on the roofs of kurgans, and especially those graves reserved for royalty. Since we know that the dispatch of a horse to accompany a warrior in the afterlife was an ancient Indo-European practice, the Vrana tumulus may well be the last resting place of a Greek-speaking dynast, or one of his chief followers. After the deceased human was interred, a horse was slaughtered over the stone slab of the grave, and then the earth forming the tumulus heaped over both the interment and the horse. Memories of these burial rites survive in Homer: his description of Patroclus' funeral pyre mentions the bones of slaughtered men and horses lying around its periphery. As Achilles says:

'Rejoice, Patroclus, even in Hades itself. I am keeping all the promises I made to you. I have dragged Hector's body here, for the dogs to devour, while at your pyre I shall cut the throats of a dozen Trojan youths of high standing, so as to avenge your death.'

Then an ox, a goat and a pig were sacrificed, and 'cupfuls of blood were poured all round the corpse'. The day after Patroclus was burned, there were funeral games: the first event was a chariot race, we are told, with splendid prizes for the winner. These were 'a woman skilled in fine crafts, plus a large tripod with ear-shaped handles'. They were promptly claimed by Sthenelus, Diomedes' squire, after Diomedes pulled up first in his gleaming chariot, 'with sweat pouring off the necks and chests of his horses'.

Both Achilles and Patroclus hailed from Thessaly, an exceptionally fertile part of Greece. To this great plain were attracted some of the earliest Greek settlers, who quickly learned how suited it was to the breeding of horses. Long after the chariot ceased to be an effective war machine, the Thessalian cavalry remained supreme. At Gaugamela, Alexander's final victory over the Persians owed a great deal to this elite force. The worst reverse it ever suffered occurred in an engagement with the Phocians some time prior to 480 BC. Then the Thessalians charged only to have their horses step into jars sunk in the ground, and break their legs. The surprise defeat had as much to do with poor observation as combat skills. The scarcity of archaeological remains in Thessaly is probably explained by the preference for building with mud brick. Stone is readily available near Thessaly's mountainous borders, but in short supply elsewhere. Only in the south at Volos, ancient Iolkos, and in the north at Yeoryikon, close to the Pindus range, were tholoi constructed. Yet the central role the Thessalians played in ancient Greek history does not depend on archaeological testimony alone. Much mythology originated in Thessaly, including stories about the mysterious Centaurs, a race of horse-men. One of them by the name of Chiron acted as Achilles' tutor. So revered was this wise horse-man for his knowledge of medicine that the Greeks associated him with the zodiacal constellation Sagittarius, which they borrowed from the Babylonians. The medical back-up which

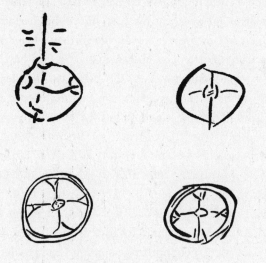

Linear B pictographs

Chiron's instruction of Achilles provided at Troy was noted in the *Iliad*, when the Greek champion cured Patroclus' wounds at the start of the siege. The father of Achilles was Peleus, king of Phthia in southern Thessaly, an Argonaut, one of the heroes who sailed from Iolkos with Jason in order to recover the Golden Fleece from the kingdom of Colchis, in the Caucasus. Jason, whose name means 'healer', led the Argonauts through numerous adventures, many of which descend from very remote times. The location of Colchis points to an old connection between Thessaly and the Caucasus that could well recall a migration westwards.

From the so-called Linear B tablets, which were baked during the burning of the palaces around 1200 BC, it is possible to gain an insight into the roles played by the horse as well as the chariot in ancient Greece.

In the 1950s a number of Greek words were identified on tablets recovered from both Crete and the Greek mainland. Named Linear B in order to distinguish it from Linear A used earlier by the Minoans, this script has been partially deciphered to reveal lists of stores and records of transactions conducted on behalf of the rulers of Knossos and Pylos. At the former, the seat of a Mycenaean king after 1400 BC, are listed bridles, harness, blinkers, chariot frames, wheels, armour, arrows, javelins and horses. It is calculated from the tablets so far understood that Knossos could put into the field some 200 chariots. But in addition to the tablets recording chariot equipment, others refer to fully assembled vehicles and their charioteers, suggesting that the final figure for chariotry there could be higher. Such a large force would hardly have been kept as a taxi service to the battlefield, nor would so many chariots have had a strictly ceremonial or religious purpose. As the high cost of their maintenance rules out both of these, they must have been employed for warfare, and for chariot battles like those fought in nearby West Asia and Egypt. The Knossian chariotry is thus documented as an up-to-date striking force similar to Ramesses II's Amun division. What the tablets most likely record, besides inventories of military stores, is the issue of extra equipment for seasonal manoeuvres. Whereas one charioteer received a corselet similar to the scale armour which saved Menelaus from a mortal arrow wound at Troy, a comrade-in-arms is mentioned as getting only horses with his chariot. Yet another was given two corselets, presumably for himself and the archer who rode alongside, and a pair of horses but no chariot. The view that these non-inventory tablets were scribal exercises rather than actual records of equipment issued to charioteers and chariot warriors cannot be proved or disproved, although the fact that the exercises took this form does suggest that they were based on actual methods of allocating military supplies.

At Pylos no tablets listing chariots have been unearthed. Wheels are often mentioned, along with comments on their effectiveness. Some are described as 'old' and 'thin', others as 'new' and 'serviceable'; there is even a tantalising reference to their strengthening with bronze. Obviously the king of Pylos possessed a chariotry, but until archaeologists find tablets carrying more detail we cannot judge its size. Possibly the smallness of the kingdom over which he ruled meant a smaller force was adequate, despite Nestor's rare grasp of how a chariot formation should actually fight together. As at Knossos, there was an armoury at Pylos complete with swords, spears and axes. It should be no surprise that unfortified Pylos still possessed enough weapons to equip an army. Bronze metallurgy tended to be a royal monopoly, except in Egypt where temple workshops were involved in the manufacture of military equipment. From the *Odyssey* we can deduce that royal palaces stored plenty of weapons, because one of the major problems confronting Odysseus in his assault on the suitors was how to get the arms out of the hall without being noticed. This was accomplished by Odysseus' son Telemachus: his father told him to 'stow the arms away, to the last weapon'. Should the suitors ask him about their removal Telemachus was to say that they had been tarnished by smoke. The Pylian armoury permitted Nestor to sail to the Trojan War with his 'first-rate foot soldiers', whom he stationed immediately behind his chariots. These were the kind of men who repulsed Hector's attack on the Greek camp. In what is almost a description of a phalanx, the standard infantry formation of later times, Homer relates how

> Hector ran into a solid block of men and stopped short; these Greeks lunged hard at him with swords and spears and thrust him back. Shaken though he was by this turn of events, Hector called out in a loud voice to his own men: 'Stand by me Trojans and Lycians, and you Dardanians who enjoy a fight hand to hand. The Greeks will not stop me for long, packed together as they are like stones in a wall. They will give way before my spear.'

The efficiency of the phalanx rested on standardised weapons and regular training. It would appear that its possibilities were first perceived by the half-legendary Pheidon of Argos in the eighth century BC. The patent superiority of the phalanx over the much looser formation favoured by aristocratic fighters was probably first demonstrated at Hysiae, where a Spartan expedition was overwhelmed by the Argives in 669 BC. Whether a Greek invention or an adaptation of West Asian tactics, the phalanx made the foot soldier the master of the battlefield, as Homer well knew. That is the reason for Hector becoming so exasperated by the refusal of the defenders of the Greek camp to fight as individuals. Once again we encounter in the *Iliad* a mixture of military periods: the older dismounted chariot warrior is thwarted here by a newer infantry unit. For the foot soldiers who drew their weapons from Nestor's armoury and sailed with him to fight at Troy would never have fought in a phalanx: their job was

to lend close support to the chariotry. They were the Greek equivalent of
the Egyptian 'runners', whose cut-and-thrust operations were directed at
enemy chariots and their Trojan counterparts. They only formed a solid
rearguard when Nestor's chariots stopped fighting and retreated.

The earliest Greek chariots, illustrated on shaft-grave markers at
Mycenae, date from the second half of the sixteenth century BC. The best
preserved of these stelae have charioteers armed with swords or daggers.
No archers are shown, but the military context is transparent from a dead
warrior with a large shield lying beneath a chariot. In a less well-
preserved carving a foot soldier appears to be thrusting a spear at a chariot
driven at speed. Within one of the shaft-graves, however, a gold signet
ring discloses the chief purpose of the ancient chariot as a fast-moving
platform for the archer. Though this particular representation of a
charioteer and a chariot warrior may well be that of a hunting scene, it
can leave us in no doubt over the familiarity of the Mycenaeans with the
composite bow as a chariot weapon. They would have employed its
power in the same manner as the Egyptians and the Hittites did on the
battlefield: arrows fired from chariots softened up enemy infantrymen
prior to an all-out engagement. As the Mycenaeans also sacrificed
protection for speed, concern for the safety of chariot crews and draught
teams meant that skirmishing chariots never charged an unbroken enemy

Mycenaean shaft-grave carving of a chariot

line. Except for scythed chariots, a late weapon developed with mixed success by the Persians and the Celts, charioteers were always careful to remain at a distance from ranks of foot soldiers. Quick turns at speed were the surest method of survival in chariot battle.

Objection to the gold signet ring as proof of Mycenaean use of mobile archers in warfare can be discounted. After all, there is no surviving illustration of the spear-thrusting tactics advocated by Nestor for his own chariotry. At first sight a stone seal recovered from the Vaphio tholos might suggest otherwise, but close examination does not support the notion of any superiority of the spear over the composite bow. This seal depicts a slow-moving chariot crewed by a charioteer and a spearman. The latter leans forward, holding a spear with both hands. But the weapon is tilted upwards as if about to be thrown like a javelin, which makes the scene reminiscent of Pandarus' abortive attempt to kill Diomedes while riding in the chariot belonging to Aeneas. In fact these tiny illustrations, one on the Mycenaean signet ring and the other on the Vaphio seal, are some of the few representations we have of weapons actually being used in ancient Greek chariots. Where such vehicles appear elsewhere, spearmen are not shown poised for action. Their weapons are carried. In other respects though, these chariots are almost identical with those found in Egyptian tombs. They comprised a solidly walled box with carved extensions or sides, the two-man crew apparently standing on a floor made from interwoven leather thongs or basketry. A carved stone ring from Avdou, to the east of Knossos, dating from the period of the Mycenaean takeover, gives a good impression as to the extent of a chariot's wings, in this case nothing more elaborate than a heat-bent wooden rail strengthened with a cross bar. Both the rectangular box at the front and the wings were usually covered with spotted oxhide, as dots reveal in surviving murals.

One purpose which Homer correctly assigned to the chariot was its central importance in games, and especially those connected with funerals or celebrations of the dead. Near the end of the *Iliad*, following the burning and burial of Patroclus, Achilles arranged for his deceased companion a splendid games, bringing from his ships prizes such as 'cauldrons and tripods; horses, mules, and sturdy cattle; grey iron and women in their belted gowns'. The first event was a chariot race; then came a boxing match, a wrestling match, a foot race, a spear fight, discus throwing, an archery contest, and finally spear throwing. Though the spear fight, the discus throwing and the archery contest may have been later additions to the epic, the other contests so readily entered by the leading Greek heroes descend from the very earliest times. Most of them are also found in Hittite texts, as is the consolation prize of a cup for the loser. At Troy Euryalus, son of King Mecisteus, was knocked out by the 'champion boxer' Epeius. While he lay senseless in his corner, Euryalus' friends had 'to go and fetch the two-handled mug for him'. Then Odysseus and the greater Ajax were stopped in their wrestling match by Achilles, because they were simply wearing each other out. Even more worrying was the spear fight, which the spectators halted before a serious injury

Chariot archer from the gold ring found in the shaft-grave at Mycenae

could be sustained by either Diomedes or his opponent, the lesser Ajax.

Armed duelling was obviously more dangerous and bloody than the rest of the contests, and its appearance later as an Italian custom seems to have had direct connections with funeral sacrifice. The Romans, who adopted gladiatorial combat from their Italic neighbours, recognised this from the start, when in 264 BC gladiators appeared at the funeral of Junius Brutus Pera. As a commentator noted, 'Women are accustomed in grief during funerals so to lacerate their faces that they satisfy the dead with their blood. Thus it became an established custom for victims also to be butchered at graves. Among the ancients men also used to be killed, but when Brutus died, and many nations sent captives to his funeral, his grandson paired them and they fought to the death.' Yet the other events held at Patroclus' funeral were not without the risk of dying: chariot racing, boxing and wrestling could lead to fatal accidents. And it has even been suggested how in Greek funeral games the pain and injury suffered by contestants were regarded as a service to the deceased. That contestants were once killed in ancient Greece is clear in the hesitation and embarrassment felt over the spear fight between Diomedes and the lesser Ajax. No fatality occurs during the games held in honour of Patroclus, despite the disruption caused by the gods to the chariot race. Off to the quickest start was the Thessalian Eumelus, whose horses had been bred by Apollo, the divine champion of charioteers in Asia Minor. When Diomedes made a move to overtake Eumelus, Apollo knocked the whip out of Diomedes' hands, but Athena gave it back to him. Worse still, the goddess pursued Eumelus

to break the yoke of his chariot, with the result that his mares ran off on their own. Then his draught pole struck the ground, breaking into pieces, while Eumelus himself was flung out of the chariot box and landed heavily near a wheel. The skin was torn off his elbows, mouth and nose; his eyes were filled with tears, and he was left speechless.

With the unfortunate Thessalian out of the race, Antilochus came in second behind Diomedes. Infuriated by Antilochus' reckless driving, Menelaus accused him of gaining the second prize by dishonest means. Their quarrel was settled only when Antilochus handed the prize to Menelaus who, mollified by this conciliatory gesture, gave it back to him. Homer makes no bones about Antilochus' determination to gain a prize, for we are told how

Menelaus kept possession of the track at its narrowest point, making it difficult for anyone to come abreast of him. But Antilochus did not keep to it. He drove a little to one side, and pressed Menelaus hard. When Menelaus protested about the danger, Antilochus, pretending not to have heard him, whipped his team and dashed recklessly ahead.

Antilochus, according to Menelaus 'the most appalling charioteer in the world', was none other than Nestor's son. Before the race took place his

old father had given him the benefit of his advice, expounding 'the whole
art of horsemanship'.

So under the spell of Homer was the Macedonian king Alexander in
334 BC that he associated the crossing of his army from Europe to Asia
with the Trojan War. On the European shore he sacrificed to Protesilaus
and prayed for a happier landing than this hero. 'He was the first of the
Achaeans to leap ashore, but fell victim to a Dardanian foe, leaving his
wife in Phylace with lacerated cheeks, and his house half-built.' The first
of his own expedition to reach the Asian shore, Alexander hurled his

The Vaphio javelin thrower

spear into the ground as a spear-won gift of the gods. Then passing Troy,
he sacrificed again and placed a wreath on Achilles' tomb, while his close
friend Hephaestion placed one on that of Patroclus. When Hephaestion
died in 324 BC after a brief illness, Alexander was as stricken by grief
as Achilles had been at Patroclus' death. A period of mourning was
proclaimed throughout Asia, a lavish funeral arranged with a festival of
arts and atheltic games to surpass all others, and during a whirlwind
campaign against the Cossaeans, fierce hillsmen living in modern Iran,
Alexander killed their young men as human sacrifices to the dead
Hephaestion. The exact details of Hephaestion's funeral games elude us,
but it is inconceivable that horse racing was not included. Alexander

could not have forgotten that the greatest event Achilles staged for Patroclus was the chariot race.

At Olympia, in the western Peloponnesian state of Elis, the Greek charioteer was to discover a perfect setting for his skills in the races staged there every four years, starting in 776 BC. A sacred truce between the normally warring Greek states covered these pan-hellenic games as well as a thirty-day training period, which may have been imposed on contestants in order to discourage the poor or less proficient. Though the emphasis of the Olympic Games was placed on athletics, the chariot race still held pride of place among the contests, perhaps because the event's foundation myth was the chariot race in which Pelops defeated King Oenomaus of Pisa and won the hand of his daughter Hippodamia, whose name means 'tamer of horses'. Said to hail from Asia Minor, Pelops gave his own name to the Peloponnese after beating Oenomaus, the ruler of the rich valley in which Olympia was to stand. It was this king's custom to make the suitors of his daughter attempt to carry her off in a chariot, while he pursued in another one and speared each of them in the back. Pelops won Hippodamia's hand only by bribing Oenomaus' charioteer Myrtilus to replace the linch pins of the king's chariot with new ones made of wax. As soon as Oenomaus set off in pursuit, the wheels came off and he was thrown to the ground. Then Pelops speared the king, just as later on he killed Myrtilus too. Possibly he felt remorse at Myrtilus' death because at Olympia, where games were inaugurated, Pelops erected a monument in his honour. An alternative version of the myth has Pelops borrow a chariot pulled by winged horses from the god of seas and waters, Poseidon. The curse pronounced by Myrtilus on his death fell heaviest on Atreus and Thyestes, two of Pelops' sons. It eventually cost Agamemnon his life on returning home from the Trojan War: his estranged wife Clytemnestra was assisted in this dark deed by Aegisthus, Thyestes' fourth son. His three brothers had been served to Thyestes in a stew prepared by Atreus, the father of Agamemnon and Menelaus, Helen's deserted husband. Putting aside the cannibalistic element in the Pelops story, we have here an account of a Mycenaean dynasty taking over large parts of the Peloponnese through the chariot skills of its founder. Besides Atreus and Thyestes, Pelops' other sons were Epidaurus, Sicyon and Troezen, from whom three states took their names.

Chariot races were also held at Delphi, whose Pythian Games celebrated the oracle there belonging to Apollo. The prize for the successful charioteer on the nearby Crisaean plain was a crown of bay-leaves cut in Tempe, a narrow valley in northern Thessaly. The source of the victor's crown reflected the prominence of the Thessalians and other northern Greeks among the chariot entries. Even Agamemnon's son, the matricide Orestes, drove Thessalian mares when he was supposed to have raced at Delphi. In Sophocles' play *Electra*, produced at Athens soon after 415 BC, Orestes persuaded an old man to tell those in his mother's palace that he had died in the chariot race. In the description of the crash we are told

> how Orestes, keeping his horses near the turning-post, each time grazed it, while trying to block off his pursuer . . . On the seventh round one driver crashed into another, and then the whole plain of Crisa was filled with the wreckage of chariots. Seeing this, a wily Athenian charioteer slowed his team and found a way through. Orestes, following behind him, was now confident of winning. Encouraging his horses to pick up speed, he drew level with the Athenian and the two charioteers remained close together through several turns . . . But Orestes relaxed his left-hand rein, and struck the turning-post, so that he broke the chariot box, fell over the rail, and was caught in the reins, before plunging to the ground.

This false report of Orestes' death, which Sophocles has the chorus in his play relate to the curse of Myrtilus, possesses more than an air of credibility. It is a reminder of the real dangers facing those in classical times who chose to imitate the ancient heroes. Though association with a heroic past ennobled and enhanced the prestige of races for both contestants and audience, charioteering was fraught with danger.

For there is no question that the chariot, long after Homer had pronounced it a conveyance fit for gods and heroes, retained a mystic status in Greece. The historian Herodotus cannot hide his amazement at the stupidity of the Athenians when Pisistratus claimed to be accompanied by the goddess Athena riding in a chariot. Having been expelled from Athens around 557 BC because of his tyrannical ways, Pisistratus devised a plan to seize the Athenian acropolis and become sole ruler of the city. Herodotus comments:

A Cretan chariot pulled by goats

The Greeks have never been fools. For centuries they were distinguished from other peoples by their intelligence, and of all the Greeks the Athenians are credited with the greatest sense. Yet it was at the Athenians' expense that Pisistratus' silly trick was played. In the village of Paeania there was a beautiful girl called Phye, nearly six feet tall, whom he fitted into a suit of armour and mounted on a chariot. Having got the girl to strike a pose, she was driven into Athens, where Pisistratus' agents had already told its citizens to welcome the would-be tyrant back, for the good reason the goddess Athena herself was bringing him to her temple on the acropolis. This nonsense was spread widely, and it was not long before villagers and townsfolk were convinced that Pisistratus was the object of divine favour. So they offered the goddess their prayers and received Pisistratus with open arms.

The theatrical coup did not secure for Pisistratus a permanent hold on Athens. When he returned a year later, his tyranny was backed by enough mercenaries and money to last until his death in 527 BC. Yet Pisistratus certainly touched a religious nerve among the Athenians with his imitation goddess. We know from other sources that warlike Athena, who relished manly deeds and joined warriors on the battlefield, was used to riding in a chariot. In winter a torch-lit procession conducted her cult statue down to the sea at Phaleron, and then back again, under the care of 'the charioteer of Pallas'.

For the Romans, who identified Athena with their own goddess Minerva, the chariot also maintained a critical role in their culture. The triumph, the ultimate accolade for a successful general, always involved the victor entering Rome in a chariot drawn by four horses. In AD 17 the future emperor Caligula, not yet five years old, rode in the triumphal chariot of his father Germanicus, whom the emperor Tiberius had recalled to Rome in the belief that his campaigns on the northern frontier, successful though they were, represented a drain on the empire's resources. Germanicus' death two years later in Syria left the young Caligula at Tiberius' mercy. Little is known about the years he spent on Capri with a Tiberius increasingly beset with the plots of his enemies, real or imagined. His survival gave rise to the famous epigram, 'Never was there a better slave or a worse master.' On his accession Caligula, the great-grandson of both Augustus and Mark Antony, was rapturously welcomed by the Roman people. And at once the young emperor's fascination with public display became evident, as Suetonius tells us in his *Twelve Caesars*, for Caligula was overjoyed with the stage-managed reception he received. 'A dense crowd greeted him with altars, sacrifices, torches, and expressions of affection like "star", "chicken", "baby" and "pet".' It did not take long, therefore, for Caligula to earn a dubious reputation of his own. A former consul, Lucius Arnuntius, had already committed suicide rather than become his subject. But Caligula's excesses never matched those of Nero, the last Julio-Claudian emperor, whom Suetonius said 'was above all crazed by a desire for popularity, and jealous of all who in any way excited the emotions of the mob'. It was this urge for fame which led him to race in person a chariot at the Olympic Games.

Once Roman aristocrats had followed the Greek practice of entering and sometimes driving their own chariots, but the custom had lapsed well before the republican period ended. There was no need of penalties for well-born Romans who tried to revive the practice, because charioteers had come to be seen as unworthy professionals. Most drivers in Rome were slaves. When a prominent Roman entered a chariot team, as both Germanicus and Tiberius did at Olympia, they were merely responsible for the finance. Rather like owners at present-day Ascot, they were acknowledged as the winners, but never confused with either charioteers or trainers: except for the emperor Nero, who had scandalised Rome by racing a chariot at Olympia during a tour of Greece. The Eleans hurriedly built a villa for him adjoining the stadium, along with a monumental gateway for the emperor to enter the sanctuary itself. So pleased was Nero to win all the contests he entered that he gave the judges such a huge tip that his successor, Galba, later ordered them to pay it back. Nero's only failure was with his ten-horse chariot. Driving this outsize team, 'he lost his balance and fell out and had to be helped in again; but, though he failed to stay the course and retired before the finish,' Suetonius tells us, 'the judges nevertheless awarded him the prize'.

On his way back to Rome, where he was obliged to commit suicide in the summer of AD 68, Nero would have recalled how his uncle Caligula had been assassinated when rumours were rife that he intended to appear on the stage. But his ambition to outshine everyone else caused him to become reckless, unbalanced his mind, and made him the victim of a military insurrection which swept away Rome's first imperial dynasty. Riding into the city in Augustus' own triumphal chariot was not enough to save Nero. That he chose this hallowed vehicle, the one belonging to the empire's founder, only serves to underline the potent symbolism the triumphal chariot retained in the popular imagination, even though the Roman army never had a chariotry of its own. Despite the silence of the historical record, the Romans probably first encountered the chariot as a war machine when they fought the Gauls. This Celtic people occupied what is today northern Italy in the fourth century BC, as the name Cisalpine Gaul acknowledged when finally the Romans succeeded in annexing it as a province. In 387 BC the Gauls sacked Rome and started a series of conflicts between the Romans and the Gauls which lasted until Hannibal's invasion of Italy during the Second Punic War (218–201 BC). Arguably it was the assistance the Gauls rendered to the Carthaginian invader that galvanised Rome into seeking firm control of the Po valley and the foothills of the Alps. It was quite possible to assert in the 50s BC, when Julius Caesar campaigned the length and breadth of Gaul, that the future dictator was dealing with an enemy who still threatened Rome. What he overcame one by one were Gallic tribes unable to unite against the Roman legions. Had they done so before Vercingetorix led a general rebellion in 52 BC, the outcome of the Gallic Wars might have been different. Using scorched-earth tactics and avoiding a pitched battle, the

Gauls outmanoeuvred the Roman army until at Alesia, near modern
Dijon, they were besieged in a strong defensive position. But the failure
of all attempts to relieve Alesia sealed the fate of the rebellion: the rebel
leader was executed in Rome after being paraded in a splendid triumph
in 46 BC.

Horses were always esteemed by Celtic peoples, whose recruitment as
cavalrymen was in imperial times one of the mainstays of the Roman
army. At barracks in Rome shrines dedicated to Epona, the Celtic horse
goddess, have been found. She is depicted as a horsewoman, with a cloak
billowing in the wind behind her head and shoulders. There she acted as
the protectress of horses, riders and grooms. Because of the refusal of the
Gauls to commit anything to writing, we remain ignorant of Epona's
religious significance, just as we depend on Roman and Greek accounts
of Celtic warfare. This one-sided picture hinders an appreciation of
Celtic chariotry, although there is in Caesar's *Gallic Wars* a description of
British chariots in action. During the first invasion of 55 BC, the Romans
encountered Britons riding in chariots on the Kent beach where they
landed, but the action Caesar describes in some detail took place after a
proper camp was built. Short of supplies, Caesar sent men from one of
the two legions with him to harvest grain. When guards at the camp
reported that they saw a large cloud of dust, reinforcements were quickly
dispatched in case these legionaires had been surprised by the Britons.

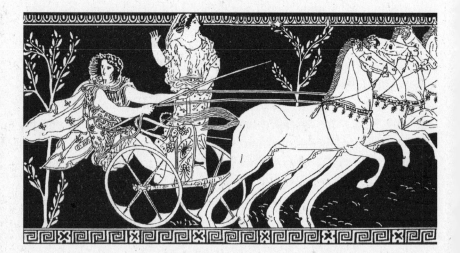

Pelops escaping with his bride-to-be

This was indeed what was happening when Caesar arrived on the scene: the scattered harvesters were having to fend off attacks by enemy chariots and cavalry. Although the Britons did not commit themselves to a major

The Celtic goddess Epona

engagement, and fell back with the arrival of the Roman reinforcements, their unusual chariot tactics impressed Caesar. He wrote

> how they drive their chariots in all directions, hurling javelins. Such is the terror caused by their galloping horses and the din of their wheels, they often succeed in making opponents panic before the action starts. They push their way through their own cavalry, then jump down from their chariots and fight on foot. Meanwhile the charioteers withdraw in such a way that if their masters are hard pressed by the enemy, they have an easy means of retreat to their own lines. Thus when they fight they have the mobility of horsemen and the staying power of foot soldiers; and with regular training and practice they have become so proficient than even on sloping ground they control their horses at full gallop, check and

turn them in a moment, run along the draught pole, stand on the yoke, and get back in the chariot in no time at all.

Earlier references to Celtic chariotry suggest a more traditional approach to warfare, with chariot pitted against chariot. Yet there is no mention of archers riding in chariots, even though Vercingetorix called up large numbers of them during his great rebellion. Caesar noted the way in which archers were dispersed among Gallic cavalry units, where they could check enemy attacks. In ancient China crossbowmen offered stationary cavalrymen similar protection from opposing foot soldiers.

The only battle in which we know large numbers of Celtic chariots were deployed took place in Asia Minor. In 278 BC, following a raid on Greece, Celtic tribesmen had migrated there and harassed the coastal areas prior to settling in what was later called Galatia. As the Seleucid rulers of the area could not ignore appeals for help, Antiochus I marched from Syria to confront the marauding Celts, who put 240 chariots into the field against him. How many chariots the Seleucid army included then is uncertain. Antiochus' father, Seleucus, had inherited a chariotry 120-strong when he founded his kingdom in 305 BC. Two years later he ceded northwestern India to Candragupta, the founder of the powerful Mauryan dynasty, in return for 500 war elephants. Ever since being in the thick of the fighting against those belonging to Porus, when he had commanded a wing of Alexander's infantry at the battle of Hydaspes river, Seleucus feared the military might of elephants. Possibly the Celts faced chariots as well as elephants in 275 BC, the year Antiochus drove them into the interior of Asia Minor. Carved reliefs commemorating the victory at Pergamum seem to indicate the use of scythed chariots on both sides. The Galatians, the name given to the surviving Celts, remained independent until their forcible inclusion in the Roman empire in 25 BC.

Whatever the shortcomings of the historical record, the association of the Celts with chariots is deeply ingrained in British folk-lore, as witnessed by Thornycroft's impressive statue of Boadicea riding in her scythed war machine, which stands today close to the Houses of Parliament. Queen Boudicca, as she is more properly called, may have attacked in such a chariot during the revolt she headed against Rome in AD 60. We cannot be sure, but archaeological finds have confirmed the prestige which the Celts accorded chariot warriors. There are enough burials with chariots, or parts of chariots, to show how important they were in this life and the next. Amid roadworks in 2003, a chariot with iron tyres was recovered from a limestone chamber at Ferrybridge in West Yorkshire. As the bones of over 200 cows were found there too, it is thought the find represents the grave of a tribal leader, whose followers celebrated his burial with a great feast. Another discovery earlier the same year, in the Evros region of Greece close to the Bulgarian border, is also a reminder of the incredible persistence of the chariot in ritual observance, and especially ceremonies connected with death. For archaeologists unearthed the remains of several richly decorated vehicles, along with those of two horses, concluding they once belonged to a Roman undertaker who used them for transporting the dead on their way to cremation. They date from the late first century AD.

5

India

The great warrior Kaunteya, riding a beautifully decorated chariot
with quivers and a battle-flag on top, with his sword in his belt, his
wrist guards put on, and his bow ready, set out in a northerly
direction. Relying on his strength alone, this enemy-slayer blew
mightily on his conch, so that the hair of his foes stood on end.

Mahabharata

When in early 326 BC Alexander descended on to the north Indian plain
from the mountains of Afghanistan, he thought he was entering the last
province of Asia. His tutor, the philosopher Aristotle, had told him that
the subcontinent projected eastwards into the great ocean which
surrounded the lands of the world, in the same manner that the
Cheronesus, the Gallipoli peninsula, jutted into the Aegean. One of the
surprises India had in store for Alexander and his men was its size, the
sheer scale of its kingdoms and their populations. For northern India was
a land of cities, with as many foundations as China then sustained. Two
centuries before Alexander's arrival, the Buddha had been very aware that
his mission was an urban one. His solution to the quest for enlightenment
was the abandonment of social entanglements prevalent in villages, towns
and cities: those who chose to follow his teachings were required to
accept monastic self-discipline. Though some members of Alexander's
train, like the sceptic philosopher Pyrrhon of Elis, took an interest in
religious ideas, the bulk of his followers were concerned with more
mundane matters, since the Indian climate was proving to be a real trial,
not just because of the intense heat but also the monsoon rain. Yet
Alexander's men did not lack enthusiasm for the conquest of India until
the enormity of the task they were undertaking dawned upon them. In
his history of the campaign, Plutarch recounts how

Alexander was worried about the amount of booty already collected. He saw that it slowed the progress of the army and so, on the day of the advance into India, after the baggage-wagons had been loaded, he first burned those belonging to himself and his companions, and then gave orders to set fire to those of the Macedonians. The business was not easily accomplished, for it angered some soldiers. But the majority greeted the decision with joyous shouts and war-cries, shared their goods with those in need, and what was superfluous they destroyed with their own hands, thus filling Alexander with joy and eagerness. Besides, he was greatly feared, and unyielding in the punishment of the disobedient.

By this time the men whom Alexander led were quite unlike the soldiers who in 334 BC crossed with him to Asia Minor. Then he commanded an army of 32,000 infantry and 5,100 cavalry raised from Greece and Macedon. Later at the decisive Gaugamela battle, when he broke the last vestiges of Persian power, his army numbered 47,000 men. Through subsequent recruitment of Asians its strength rose to 120,000, of whom the Macedonians were one-eighth and the Greeks one-third. This expansion was part of Alexander's policy to found a multiracial kingdom, albeit modelled on European lines. Practically all the peoples from the Adriatic to the River Indus were represented in his army.

Having sacrificed on both banks of the Indus, Alexander marched to Taxila, 'a realm as large as Egypt with good pasturage and orchards laden with choice fruit'. Its ruler, Taxiles, came to terms along with other kings, and after an exchange of gifts, Alexander pushed eastwards with an additional 5,000 Indian troops to engage Porus, a ruler who declined to send envoys. In the subsequent battle, which took place near the Hydaspes river, Alexander was challenged by an Indian army able to deploy elephants as well as chariots. The action was complicated because the river, a tributary of the Indus, had a turbulent and swift current swollen by melted Himalayan snow and heavy rain. Porus was surprised by a night crossing, which one of his sons tried in vain to thwart. According to Arrian, who also compiled a history of Alexander's conquests, in one of the conflicting accounts of this initial action,

Porus' son arrived on the scene with sixty chariots before Alexander

effected a crossing . . . In view of the fact that the crossing was no
easy matter even without opposition, he might have prevented it
altogether if his Indians had decided to leave their chariots and
assault on foot Alexander's leading troops as they scrambled up the
riverbank. But in point of fact he merely drove past, and let
Alexander cross without interference . . . Other writers state that
there was a fight at the landing place between Alexander's cavalry
and a force of Indians commanded by Porus' son, who was there
ready to oppose them with superior numbers, and that in the course
of the engagement he wounded Alexander with his own hand and
struck a blow which killed his beloved horse Bucephalus. Yet
another, more credible, account is provided by Ptolemy, who says
Porus sent his son . . . with 2,000 horsemen and 120 chariots to
oppose the crossing. Alexander was too quick for him . . . Against
this force he dispatched mounted archers, while he moved himself
with the cavalry, thinking that Porus himself was on his way to
attack him with the main strength of his army, and that he faced the
vanguard. But as soon as Alexander received an accurate report of
his enemy's numbers, he charged at once, and the Indians, seeing
Alexander there in person and his massed cavalry bearing down
upon them, broke and fled.

Among the 400 who fell on the Indian side, Arrian tells us, was Porus'
son. Chariots were also captured because 'speed was impossible, the
muddy ground rendering them useless'. Whatever the truth about this
skirmish, the loss of a son did nothing to weaken the resolve of Porus or
his seasoned troops, whom Alexander soon learned to respect for their
courage.

Porus drew his army up in the so-called garuda formation, one of the
standard ways in which Indian commanders arrayed their soldiers on the
battlefield. Its object in placing 200 elephants in front of his infantry was
to scare away Alexander's cavalry, which was standing in a compact body.
Both wings of Porus' army were protected by 150 chariots and 2,000
cavalry, while a screen of foot soldiers was thrown around the elephants
in order to deal with any skirmishers. But the unexpected mobility of
Alexander's troops decided the outcome, as they concentrated their
efforts on the left wing of the Indian army, making its superior numbers
irrelevant. The first troops to engage the Indians were 1,000 mounted

Prince Siddhartha, the future Buddha, riding in his chariot

archers, who routed the chariots and the cavalrymen. Into this confusion Alexander now sent the remainder of his cavalry, while his infantry closed with Porus' foot soldiers. This last move, however, was not easy to achieve because of the elephants. 'These monsters,' Arrian relates, 'plunged this way and that among the lines of infantry, dealing destruction in the solid mass of the Macedonian phalanx, while the Indian horsemen, seeing the infantry at one another's throats, turned to attack the Macedonian cavalry. Once again, the strength and experience of Alexander's men told, although for a while the battle hung in the balance. For the Indians nearly gained the upper hand through the havoc being wrought by the elephants. These fearful creatures trampled the Macedonian soldiers underfoot, lifting some in their trunks and bashing them against the ground, and impaling others on their tusks. But so tightly packed together with the Indian cavalry did the elephants become at this point that they ceased to fight with any cohesion. Many of their riders were dead, with the result that riderless, and often wounded, elephants set 'indiscriminately upon friend and foe alike'. The sign that Alexander had won came when these tired creatures 'began to back away, slowly, like ships going astern, with nothing worse than loud trumpetings'.

Nearly 20,000 Indian foot soldiers were killed, and about 3,000 cavalrymen and charioteers. The personal bravery of Porus drew Alexander's admiration because, Arrian tells us, 'unlike the Persian king Darius, he was not the first to flee, but so long as a single unit of his men held together, fought stubbornly on'. When Porus was finally persuaded to meet Alexander face to face, such was his noble bearing that he was restored to his throne by the Macedonian king. Thus Alexander gained his first victory on Indian soil, his army proving more than a match for its opponent in every branch of arms. Porus' chariotry had proved to be no more effective against him than the scythed chariots Darius deployed at Gaugamela, while Alexander's infantry had learned the hard way how to withstand war elephants. The Macedonians used their judgment, giving ground when charged and chasing after animals with javelins when they turned and lumbered away. Yet it was not long before the victory at Hydaspes was put into an Indian context. Within months the Macedonians refused to advance further eastwards, where the next enemy would be the Nanda, the rulers of Magadha, a state centred upon the populous Ganges valley. Disillusion gripped Alexander's most dependable soldiers, who were suffering from exhaustion and the effects of seventy days of continuous rain; for they felt that they had been misled and the promised end of Asia was nowhere in sight. It has to be said that Alexander himself was baffled by India's size and, even though he still wanted to advance into the Ganges valley, he recognised that this was now impossible and so he agreed to turn back.

One of the reasons for this enforced decision was the effectiveness of Indian military tactics. So incensed did Alexander become with the level of resistance he met that, on one occasion, he broke a truce in order to perpetrate a massacre, 'an act which adheres like a stain to his military career'. As Plutarch explains,

> the best fighters among the Indians were mercenaries, and they used to sell their services to different cities and defend them with determination, thereby causing much harm to Alexander's position. Having made a truce with them in a certain city and allowed them to depart, he fell upon them as they marched and slew them all . . . The philosophers, too, no less than the mercenaries gave him trouble, by abusing native princes who allied themselves to him, and by inciting their subjects to rebel. He therefore took many of these also and hanged them.

An even better reason to moderate Alexander's ambitions in the subcontinent was the realisation of how great were the military resources of the rulers who still chose to oppose him. Despite being overshadowed by the splendour of its successor, the Mauryan dynasty, the Nanda kings ruled over an extensive state. News had reached the Macedonians that the Nanda army comprised 200,000 infantry, 20,000 cavalry, 2,000 chariots and 4,000 elephants. Four years after Alexander headed west, the first Mauryan king, Candragupta, extinguished the Nanda dynasty and, Plutarch asserts, 'overran and subdued all India with an army of 600,000 men', of which 30,000 were cavalrymen. War was always a serious business in India. Alexander's brief intervention was not so much a military revelation to Indian rulers as a stimulus to someone like Candragupta to establish an empire of his own. Megasthenes, the Seleucid ambassador at his court, was amazed at the professionalism of the men who formed Candragupta's standing army. It was organised under a committee of thirty, divided in sub-committees which controlled the corps of infantry, chariots, elephants, navy and supply train.

The emergence of Magadha, modern Bihar, as a major Indian power had begun under the Nandas around the time Persia first subdued northwestern India and made it into the twentieth satrapy of Gandhara, which numbered among its famous cities Takshashila, or Taxila to the Greeks. The willingness of its ruler to accept Alexander's authority two centuries later indicates a tradition of foreign overlordship which started with the Persians in 530 BC. Counted among the most populous and wealthy parts of the Persian empire, northwestern India was a glittering prize for any ruler, but it remained under foreign influence – at first Persian, then afterwards Macedonian – until Candragupta took it from Seleucus I in 303 BC. The failure of Seleucus to hold on to the easternmost territories conquered by Alexander led to Megasthenes' embassy to Pataliputra, the Mauryan capital, and an agreement on borders. Pataliputra stood on a high bank of the Ganges and when the river was in flood during the monsoon the city looked like an island in the midst of flooded plains. From the outset it had the added advantage of proximity to Magadha's rich supply of metals, an essential resource for any state with serious military pretensions. Under the first Mauryan ruler, Candragupta (321–298 BC), the city of Pataliputra became the focus of an India empire, which stretched 'from the mountains to the sea'.

Ancient Indians regarded the subcontinent as a complete world and, although there were periods when foreign intruders briefly extended their horizons, Indian kings usually thought of foreign affairs in terms of handling their immediate rivals. This is true of the *Arthasastra*, the political handbook written by the brahmin Kautilya, Candragupta's first minister and adviser. The *Arthasastra* provides a detailed blueprint for the control of a state and the conduct of war. The civilian and military officials were to be well paid, necessitating a large state income derived from the land. The predictability of revenue from taxation on agriculture was regarded as the basis of fiscal security, as indeed it was in ancient China. Kautilya refers at length to the methods of tax collection and the need to keep an eye open for new sources of revenue. His linking of taxation, administration and military power was crucial to the establishment of a centralised empire, but it is doubtful whether the Mauryan state ever exercised the level of regulation proposed in the *Arthasastra*. If agriculture helped to build an empire, the latter in turn furthered another form of economic activity. The attempted political unification of the subcontinent, and the security provided by a stable government, encouraged a massive expansion of trade. The state itself employed large numbers of craftsmen, including armourers, chariot-makers and ship-builders, who enjoyed exemption from taxation. Others who worked in state workshops devoted to the manufacture of cloth, however, were liable to pay taxes. Excavations at Pataliputra have uncovered spacious brick-built houses and the stone foundations of the royal palace. They reveal the accuracy of Megasthenes' report of his stay in India, because also located by archaeologists are the massive timber defences he described. Prior to their discovery in the 1950s there was scepticism about this novel method of fortification, in spite of the advantage wood offered over brick and stone in the soft alluvial soil of the river bank.

War elephants and chariots

How Candragupta won his campaigns in north India remains a mystery. Apart from the narrative of Alexander's incursion, there are no surviving accounts of ancient Indian battles. Only with Candragupta's successors do we begin to have records of military engagements and by then chariotry had ceased to count on the battlefield. Even the battle at Hydaspes river showed the marginal role it came to perform in contemporary Indian armies. Chariots were essentially deployed there as scout cars or extra support for cavalry. That charioteers continued to fight on the battlefield at all may have had a connection with the prestige they were accorded in the Indian epics, the *Mahabharata* and the *Ramayana*, which had an equivalent status to Homer's compositions in the Greco-

Roman world. The first Mauryan ruler does not appear in any heroic poem. On the contrary he is remembered in religious tradition for his abdication in favour of his son Bindusara in 298 BC so as to become a Jain recluse at Sravana Belgola in the south of India. There today on a hillock, next to the main hill on which stands the giant statue of the Jain saviour Gommatesvara, is a record in bas-relief of Candragupta's life. It tells how the Mauryan king, like Gommatesvara, came to see the vanity of worldly triumph, and as a result sought release from the endless cycle of rebirth through meditation, prior to fasting unto death. Possibly because Candragupta was such a new phenomenon in Indian history – the usurper of power over an extensive area which had previously consisted of small kingdoms and republics – he could safely indulge his own preference for Jainism, a heterodox faith more austere than Buddhism in its rejection of Hinduism. Its tenets are located at the impersonal end of the spectrum of ancient belief, far removed from European notions concerning personality. Only through a sustained act of self-renunciation could a soul make its escape from the endless cycle of reincarnation. Quite opposite was the outlook of Bindusara, whom the Greeks knew as Amitrochates, 'the destroyer of foes', who accepted the determinist doctrines of the Ajivikas, which was another non-orthodox sect. As a dynasty the Mauryans were very eclectic in their religious beliefs: Candragupta favoured Jainism; in reaction Bindusara clung to the this-worldly approach of the Ajivikas; while Candragupta's grandson Ashoka became the world's first Buddhist ruler.

The reason for outlining the religious preoccupations of these Indian kings is to remind ourselves of a stronger sacred charge to be found in the Indian epics than in either the *Iliad* or the *Odyssey*. It is impossible to forget that the hero Rama is none other than an incarnation of the great god Vishnu. Such an event, in which part of Vishnu's divine essence became incarnate in a human or supernatural form, occurred whenever there was an urgent requirement to correct some great evil influence; in this case the threat to universal order came from Ravana, the demon king of Sri Lanka, who had gained extraordinary power through severe penances and austere devotion to Brahma, the creator god. In the *Ramayana*, and even more in the battle books of the *Mahabharata*, we encounter the combat typical of the early first millennium BC. Armies are composed of members of an aristocratic warrior class, who individually

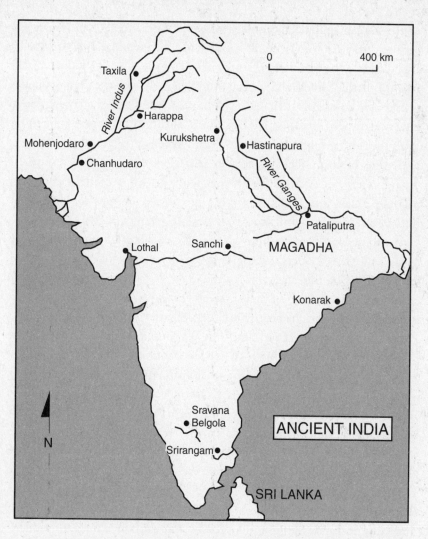

maintain horses, chariots and elephants, bringing them with them in the event of war. The epics contain statements that death at home, in bed with the illnesses of old age, is an utter shame for these warriors, even as it is to return from battle without wounds. Their duels usually comprise an exchange of arrows between warriors mounted in two-wheeled chariots, the favourite battle vehicles since the era of the *Rig Veda*.

The *Ramayana* is much shorter than the *Mahabharata* despite later additions. The original version is attributed to the sage Valmiki, who, like Homer, probably brought together bardic fragments and then reshaped them into poetry that set the standard for early Sanskrit literature. Study of the Indian epics demonstrates parallels with Homer, and especially between the *Iliad* and the *Ramayana*, which culminates with Rama's expedition to the island of Sri Lanka in order to recover his abducted wife Sita. Both the Greek and Indian storytellers must have drawn upon a shared mythological heritage, which was recast to suit the different historical experiences involved in the occupation of Greece and India. Well though he might have been a real Mycenaean king, Agamemnon's leadership of the Greek expedition has been absorbed into a story of divine rivalry, of gods and goddesses settling their personal disputes by backing either the Trojans or the Greeks. Yet even with Helen, the human cause of the conflict, we are dealing with a goddess rather than a wayward queen. Hatched from an egg, this daughter of mighty Zeus was an ancient tree goddess, whose cult encompassed abduction as well as rescue. One of the chief things the *Iliad* and the *Ramayana* have in common is the divinity of these abducted women, Helen and Sita. But it is among the lesser characters that the similarity is more striking. Just as Zeus is unable to save from death the Trojans' loyal hero Sarpedon, the Lycian commander and his own son, so Brahma has to tell the demon Indrajit that neither lengthy sacrifices nor supernatural weapons are proof against his dying on the battlefield. And only the monkey god Hanuman is able to revive Rama's charioteer Laksmana when a magic spear hurled by Ravana pierces his heart. In a parallel of the medical skills imparted to Achilles by the wise centaur Chiron, Hanuman fetches a special herb and Laksmana's life is saved. At the end of a long siege Ravana's Sri Lankan stronghold falls, like Troy, and Sita is reunited with Rama. Because he does not accept her back as readily as Menelaus, Helen's forgiving husband, Sita is swallowed by the earth as a testimony of her innocence and purity. Inconsolable, Rama follows her by disappearing into the Sarayu river, water being the element of Vishnu. Rama means 'that which on earth charms and shines', a reference to the ancient Indian notion of the first syllable of his name being the basic sound from which language issued.

Representations of Rama nearly always show him armed with a composite bow, not least because prowess as an archer is inseparable from the development of the *Ramayana* tale. Two trials with supernatural bows are imposed upon Rama at the beginning of the epic. In the first of these Rama, alone among princes and kings, was able to lift, wield and destroy the bow of Shiva which had been left in the possession of King Janaka of

Mithila, a kingdom situated in the middle Ganges plain. As a reward for this feat Janaka gave him in marriage his daughter Sita, meaning 'furrow'. Janaka says he found her as he was clearing a field; 'she sprang up from the earth during ploughing'. Because 'she was not born from the womb, Sita has been set apart as one for whom the only bride-price is great strength'. A fertility goddess like Helen, Sita does not appear to have been very important prior to the *Ramayana*, even though her marriage to Rama, the embodiment of righteousness, is in line with the agricultural responsibilities of ancient Indian kings. The interrelation between fertility, manly vigour and kingly power was first made clear in the *Rig Veda*, where the charioteers' champion Indra, the wielder of the thunderbolt, overcame the serpent of drought, Vritra, and released on to the earth life-giving waters. Rama's winning of Sita as a bride, losing her as a prisoner of the demons, regaining his wife on the fall of Ravana's stronghold, and then her final loss in the soil would tend to suggest that the epic embodies a fertility myth in its narrative of the heroic struggle between an incarnate deity and an immensely powerful demon. That she became the ideal of chastity – 'as pure as Sita' – fails to disguise her original connection with abundance. The royal ritual of ploughing the earth each year was likened to a symbolic coupling with the earth: Rama fertilising Sita. As we shall see in the ancient Indian institution of horse-sacrifice, everything revolved around the paramountcy of the king, the chief sacrificer.

Oppressed by the rulers who wished to marry Sita, a situation reminiscent of the pressures suffered by Penelope during Odysseus' long absence from home, hard-pressed Janaka was relieved at the willingness of Rama to try the bow. So the young king

affixed the bow string and fitting an arrow to it, drew it back. But, in doing so, the best of men broke the celestial weapon in the middle. There was a tremendous noise as loud as a thunderclap, and the earth trembled, as if a mountain had been split in half. Of all the spectators of this amazing deed, only the king and his closest advisers remained standing; the rest were thrown to the ground by the noise.

Wonder over the bow's destruction was of course soon balanced by amazement at this incredible revelation of strength; Janaka spoke for all

A royal procession emerging from a city gate

when he admitted his awe of such a 'marvellous and inconceivable'
might. Since no one there, not even Rama himself, was aware of the
incarnate power which had come into play, the divine significance of the
moment was missed. But Vishnu had disposed of one of his great rival's
weapons: indestructible Shiva, 'out of fear of whom the wind blows, the
sun shines, while the king of heaven, fire and death rush to their work',
had forfeited his great bow. The second trial was understood for what it
was, because the bow this time belonged to Vishnu, part of whose
essence resided in Rama. On his way back home to Ayodhya with his
new bride, Rama was challenged by his namesake, the terrible son of
Jamadagni, who also appears in the *Mahabharata*. Furious at the damage
done to Shiva's bow, he challenged Rama to try his strength against the
even mightier weapon of Vishnu, and then to a fight. 'Lotus-eyed'
Rama's anger so humbled the priestly Rama Jamadagni that he fled to his
mountainous retreat, in the knowledge of a lucky escape from the
incarnate deity.

Rama's skill as an archer, however, was severely challenged during the fourteen years he spent in the Vindhyan forests. Rama's stepmother wanted her son to succeed to the throne and successfully contrived to have Rama banished from Ayodhya. Accompanied by his wife and his younger brother Laksmana, the exile went into the vast forests then adjoining the cultivated lands of the Ganges valley. There the party was set upon by the man-eating demon Viradha, literally 'the insatiable one'. By means of severe penances he had obtained, like his greater counterpart Ravana, a boon of invulnerability from Brahma. Described as 'sunken-eyed, huge-mouthed, great-bellied, a massive, loathsome, deformed, gigantic, monstrous creature, terrible to behold', Viradha told Rama that he and his brother could go free on condition they handed Sita over to him. In response to this demand,

> Rama strung his bow, and quickly fired one well-honed arrow after another at the demon. From this taut-strung weapon seven arrows, gold-tipped with peacock feathers, flew swift as the wind and tore through Viradha, before falling to the ground dripping with blood. Seizing a spear like Indra's own weapon, the wounded demon let out a tremendous roar, looking for all the world like death itself with jaws agape. The spear resembled a thunderbolt or some blazing object in the sky, but two arrows from Rama, foremost of warriors, soon smashed it to pieces.

Disarmed and tottering, Viradha was seized by Laksmana and Rama, who broke both of his arms. In gratitude, the dying demon told his startled opponents that he was now free from a curse which had transformed him into a man-eater. Slaughter at the hands of Rama was his only hope of escape from his dreadful lot, as reincarnation would permit a different existence. So the brothers cast the demon into a pit and 'the pointed-eared Viradha let out a last monstrous roar, howling at the top of his voice'. Victorious though they were in this encounter, Laksmana was unnerved by 'the trackless forest' and persuaded Rama to visit the residence of the ascetic Sarabhanga, where Indra was conferring with the wise man. Seeing him approaching, the god informed Sarabhanga that Rama had 'a great deed to do, impossible for anyone else to accomplish'. Ignorant of the nature of Rama's task, the extinction of Ravana, the ascetic nonetheless recognised his divinity and contentedly expired on a pyre, from which 'he ascended to the world of Brahma'.

Although warned about the fighting abilities of Rama, who on foot could 'cut down an army with a shower of arrows', and Laksmana, 'the great chariot fighter, feared for his sharp arrows', the demon king Ravana went ahead with Sita's abduction. Rama organised an army for her rescue with the assistance of Hanuman, the leader of the monkeys, and a fierce battle was fought, in which Ravana and his forces were destroyed and his Sri Lankan stronghold was captured. Less extended than the battle scenes in the *Mahabharata*, the conflict in the *Ramayana* was conducted on traditional lines, as prominent warriors rode in chariots, dispatching arrows and javelins at opponents. The usual aim was the disabling of the horses or charioteer, so as to immobilise the chariot and make it easier to kill the warrior. The composite bow remained the chief offensive weapon, while hand-to-hand fighting was decided with axes, maces and swords. Despite the importance of his profession, the charioteer still occupied a position unmistakably lower than that of the chariot warrior. Yet the interdependence of a chariot crew was appreciated by those who had experienced the dangers of chariot battle. It was the charioteer's prime duty to protect the fighter in his chariot, just as the chariot warrior had to do all he could to guard the life of his driver. A chariot warrior, if wounded or exhausted, was hurried out of harm's way by his charioteer. Even proud Bhishma, whose name means 'terrible', had to admit his indebtedness to his charioteer. Near the middle of the *Mahabharata*, he relates how

Jamadagni loosed at me feathered shafts like fiery-mouthed snakes. Again and again I cut through them with honed arrows in the sky by the hundreds and thousands. Whereupon Jamadagni unleashed at me celestial weapons, but I warded them off trying to get the upper hand with my own, and all the while there was a mighty din . . . Then, moving his chariot to one side, the great brahmin, powerful Rama Jamadagni, struck me in the chest. I sank down in my fine chariot, and my charioteer, seeing my fallen countenance, quickly carried me off to the distance of a cow's bellow, smarting from Rama's arrow. When they saw me being taken away, wounded and losing consciousness, all the followers of Rama cheered . . . Recovering my senses, I ordered my charioteer to return to the duel . . . and angrily I covered my opponent with a mass of arrows in an effort to defeat him. But Rama . . . cut into two my straight-flying shafts by the hundreds on the battlefield. Then I shot one fiery, very shiny arrow, like time itself, to kill him, but it only tumbled him to the ground wounded.

On the following day, the battle renewed, it was Bhishma's charioteer who was killed by Rama Jamadagni. 'For a while,' conceded Bhishma, 'fear possessed me after my charioteer was slain. Then I fired my bow distractedly, but Rama pelted me with deadly arrows, one of which struck me, while I was still in shock at my charioteer's death. The blood-gorging bolt hit me through the collar bone.' Death would have resulted from another arrow had not Bhishma's mother, the river goddess Ganga, come to his aid. With an immobile chariot he was now entirely at his enemy's mercy.

Ganga had by the time the epics assumed their final form replaced Saraswati as the sacred river which demarcated the dwelling place of the gods and the first place of settlement for the invading Indo-Aryans in northwestern India. Later the Persians, their Iranian cousins, transferred the same river goddess westwards, where her name was eventually changed under Babylonian influence from Harahviti to Anahita. Both peoples reverenced running water, which is reflected in one translation of Saraswati's name as 'the flowing one'. Ganga's replacement of Saraswati was a reflection of ancient India's shift of political gravity to the Ganges valley, the setting of the *Ramayana* and the *Mahabharata*. But the river goddess could no more prevent the death of Bhishma in battle than the Greek gods at Troy were able to protect their favourites. He was eventually slain by the Pandu prince Arjuna, who riddled him with arrows. There was not a space of two fingers' breadth left unwounded on Bhishma's whole body, and when he fell from his chariot he was kept aloft from the ground by the arrows and lay as on a couch of darts. Even though mortally wounded, he had secured the right to fix the date of his own death, so he survived eighty-five days, and gave expression to his view of events. From the start of the *Mahabharata* Bhishma had sought to minimise conflict and, though he was drawn into the war between the Pandavas and the Kauravas on the latter's side, he still tried to introduce rules of combat which would lessen the horrors of fighting. His desire to avoid fighting Arjuna was not fulfilled, a circumstance Bhishma simply had to accept as his fate.

Two things stand out in Bhishma's military career: the effort he made to civilize warfare and the sheer brilliance of the chariot warriors' skills in archery he witnessed. The concern to limit unnecessary violence was a fundamental trait of his character. Notwithstanding his personal prowess as a chariot warrior, Bhishma tried to counsel moderation and peace between the Pandavas and the Kauravas, the two families whose bitter quarrel over the succession to Dhritarastra's throne propels the action of the *Mahabharata*. Because Dhritarastra was blind from birth, his brother Pandu ruled in his stead for some years, before retiring to a life of solitude in the Himalayas. Pandu, 'the pale one', had a skin ailment that could have been leprosy, so the entitlement of his five sons, the Pandavas, to the succession was as uncertain as that of the hundred sons Dhritarastra sired, when he came to the throne after Pandu's abdication.

As in ancient Greece, Indian kings were supposed to be without physical blemish. At Athens we know how magistrates, whose duties had previously been discharged by kings, in particular those who oversaw religious matters, were once examined to make sure of their physical perfection. Ideally Greek and Indian rulers had to be paragons of health. Aware of the seriousness of his condition, Pandu never consorted with his two wives, who presented the retired king with sons fathered by the gods. Arjuna, 'the bright or silvery one', the third son, had Indra for his father. On the death of Pandu, Dhritarastra welcomed the five Pandavas back to Hastinapura, his capital on the upper reaches of the Ganges, and nominated the eldest, Yudhisthira, as his heir. This was deeply resented by Dhritarastra's own eldest son Duryodhana, whose name means 'hard to conquer'. As a result of this conflict, the Pandavas went into exile. It was not to be their last, for they left Hastinapura a second time after Yudhisthira lost everything in a gambling match with Duryodhana: his possessions, the freedom of himself, his brothers and their joint wife Draupadi. In this tremendous win Duryodhana was abetted by his uncle Sakuni, an expert gambler and a cheat. He told Yudhisthira that the single throw of the dice would determine 'a stake of exile in the forest when you or we lose'. But the triumphant Duryodhana was persuaded with some difficulty to a compromise, whereby the Pandavas were permitted to retain half their possessions as well as Draupadi, provided they first went into exile for thirteen years. At the end of this period the

Kauravas were unwilling to let them rule, so the matter had to be settled through warfare. They battled for eighteen days, with breaks at night to refresh horses and men, on the plain at Kurukshetra, near modern Delhi. The battle consumed whole families as well as their followers.

Before this great clash of arms commenced, the leaders under Bhishma's guidance established the rules of warfare, prohibiting the killing of a warrior who surrendered, fell wounded to the ground, or fled. Mercy had to be shown, too, when an opponent lacked arms. It was agreed, in an interesting attempt to ensure fairness during a duel, that warriors should restrict combat to those who were similarly armed. And

King Ashoka visits a stupa

weapons were never to be aimed below an opponent's navel. It was also understood was that non-combatants were not to be attacked. However, the conduct of the battle was not entirely in accordance with these humane rules, for Bhishma himself was unfairly wounded. Not even Krishna was exempt from the mayhem of the battlefield; he would have abandoned his duties as a charioteer and made a dash for Bhishma had not Arjuna restrained him. An incarnation of Vishnu, Krishna was at first reluctant to join the Pandavas, being relatives of both them and the Kauravas. Krishna finally agreed to act as charioteer to his friend Arjuna, and it was to this prince he revealed his true identity just before the fighting began on the Kurukshetra plain. What prompted this revelation,

and Krishna's sermon known as the *Bhagavadgita*, the 'Song of the Lord',
was the faltering of Arjuna.

Seeing Arjuna overwhelmed with compassion and sadness, his eyes
flowing with tears, Krishna consoled him and encouraged his
manliness. 'How can I,' asked Arjuna, 'shoot Bhishma and Drona,
when the battle rages? Rather would I be satisfied with a beggar's
crust than kill these teachers of mine, these noble souls!' . . . In reply
Krishna told him not to be so concerned. 'The wise grieve neither
for the dead nor for the living,' said Krishna. 'There never was a
time I was not, nor you, nor these princes were not; there never
will be a time when we shall cease to be . . . Only the hero who is
unmoved by circumstance, accepting pleasure and pain with
equanimity, he alone achieves immortality.'

But Arjuna was still unconvinced by Krishna's words about the spirit
being 'indestructible, immortal, unchanging', and so the incarnate god
went on to explain the absolute necessity of the performance of duty. As
a warrior, Arjuna had no choice but to fight because his path to
enlightenment was through the way of action, not contemplation. 'It is
better,' Krishna assured him, 'to do your duty badly than to do that of
another well.' When questioned by Arjuna about Krishna's intimate
knowledge of such wisdom, which had been propounded by sages for the
earliest kings, he learned that his charioteer had lived then. 'My births are
known to me,' Krishna said, 'but you are unaware of yours.' No matter
the extent of the slaughter in the forthcoming battle, nor the grimness of
the hand-to-hand fighting, there was nothing any of the warriors could
do about the inevitable conflict other than take part, a fatalism which
recalls that expressed by King Priam of Troy when he and Helen
observed the Greek host drawn up outside his city. Underlying this
acceptance of war as endemic in ancient India were two beliefs:
reincarnation and immutable class divisions. In Indian society there was
no scope for individuals to change from the class into which they were
born. Except leaving civilization altogether and seeking self-knowledge
in the solitude of the forest, one's life was decreed at birth. So Arjuna,
'the great archer', rode on to the battlefield, finally sure that 'good
fortune, victory, happiness and righteousness will follow'.

The archery of Arjuna, and the other chariot warriors, is a notable feature of the fighting recounted in the *Mahabharata*. These chief men were bowmen par excellence. At the battle of Kurukshetra the quick thinking of Krishna alone saved the life of Arjuna from Karna's arrow by making the chariot team bend down on their knees, so sure was the aim. The duel between Arjuna and Karna is described as a terrific combat, in which the former nearly lost. A crescent-shaped arrow eventually felled Karna, who was later revealed to be a half-brother of the Pandavas. They showed their regret for his death by great kindness to his widows, children and dependants. It was insignificant that this son of Surya, the sun god, had sided with the Kauravas. For he had properly fulfilled his destiny in the performance of his duty as a warrior, something Arjuna now had the advantage of fully comprehending. Archery exchanges were not always as lethal, since opposing chariot warriors were skilled enough to hit their opponents' arrows in flight. Such impressive duels tended to become the focus of attention on the battlefield, so that there was often a lull in the chariot battle as others looked on. According to Bhishma, not all arrows reached their targets, through natural causes. 'By friction of the wind and the heat of the sun's rays,' he recalled, 'a fire sometimes broke out in the sky. Burning in the flames that sparked from themselves, arrows fell to the ground in ashes.'

The supreme weapon in the epics was of course the composite bow, which invariably decided the outcome of an armed encounter. Most effective were those made, as in West Asia and Egypt, from wood and horn, although smaller wooden bows also found a use. The latter were not quite self bows, because they contained several woods including bamboo. Bows belonging to heroes were frequently inlaid with figures of golden elephants, tigers and other animals. Arjuna's bow is described as backed with gold: it was a present from the Agni, the god of fire, who had received the weapon in turn from omniscient Varuna, the upholder of the moral order. Its original owner was Soma, a god who appears in the *Rig Veda*. Sometimes regarded as a deity, Soma usually refers to the ambrosial offering made to the gods, by which they sustained their immortality. This drink is the equivalent of haoma, the Iranian elixir of life, which was prepared from a fragrant and milky plant found growing wild on the sides of mountains. Indra's initial rise to prominence was facilitated by the soma he stole from a sacrifice performed by his father, Tvastr. After Indra had drunk the sacrificial Soma, Tvastr asked him, 'Is anything left over?' He was handed the remnant, which he threw on the fire, and Vritra was born. The victory Indra won over the drought-serpent Vritra was only achieved by 'a roaring thunderbolt which his father Tvastr had fashioned for him'. Some of the immense power that the gods derived from the drink soma may have infused Arjuna's bow, which was called Gandiva.

Bow strings were made from hemp or cowhide. Like composite bows elsewhere in the ancient world, they were usually left unstrung. In the *Mahabharata* there are cries of 'Oh' and 'Ah', when heroes are obliged to employ all their strength in order to bend and string their bows. So Karna let out a 'loud noise' as he drew out, prepared, and then fired his great bow. But it was the sound of Drona's bow which really frightened his enemies, for

> he drew his handsome weapon taut with the crackle of monsoon thunder. Stretching his terrifying bow till it looked like a circle of fire, Drona, the outstanding speaker in assemblies, shattered all the incoming arrows, and there was a smell like burning bamboo . . . So fast did Drona fire his bow that it appeared as if there was one single, continuous arrow flying through the air.

This renowned archer was the brother-in-law of Bhishma, after whose death he became the commander-in-chief of the forces belonging to the Kauravas. On the fourth day of the battle on the Kurukshetra plain he slew Draupada, the king of Pauchala. Long an enemy of Drona, the king had anticipated his end by siring a son who was courageous enough to avenge him. So Draupada's son on the fourteenth day slew and beheaded Drona, whose name means 'bucket'. Apparently Drona had been generated in a bucket, a start to life which does not seem to have adversely influenced him. For he became an expert in military matters and imparted his knowledge to the Pandavas as well as the Kauravas, who called him Dronacharya, 'Drona the teacher of war'. Acts of revenge like this apart, the fighting throughout the *Mahabharata* was not as savage as Bhishma feared it might become in the heat of battle. Opponents were invited to don their body-armour and mount their chariots before a fight started, and time was given for a hero surprised by a sudden setback. During a cattle raid Arjuna even gave a chariot warrior time to adjust, when he pierced his opponent's four horses rapidly with four, smooth, gold-feathered arrows shot from Gandiva. All the horses, hit with the sharp shafts like flaming serpents, reared violently, so that his adversary Kripa Saradvata lost his balance. When Arjuna saw how he had lost his footing, the slayer of enemy heroes refrained from striking him in order to preserve the other's dignity. When Kripa recovered his balance and fired ten heron-feathered arrows at Arjuna, the latter cut his bow in half with a single arrow and tore it from his hand. Next he blew off his opponent's corselet with sharp arrows that sought the weak spots in the armour, but he did not hurt his body. Without body protection, Kripa looked like a snake that had shed its skin . . . Second and third bows were likewise knocked by Arjuna's arrows from Kripa's hand . . . Then his determined opponent seized a javelin and hurled it like a blazing thunderbolt, but again Arjuna broke the missile into pieces with his arrows . . . Undaunted, Kripa stung Arjuna with ten sharp arrows from another of his bows, and in reply Arjuna loosed thirteen arrows with the splendour of fire; he smashed the yoke with one, finished off Kripa's horses with four, decapitated his charioteer with a sixth, struck the bamboo poles with three, the two axles of the chariot with two, and split a battle-pennant with a twelfth arrow. Then, laughingly, he hit Kripa full in the chest with a thirteenth arrow like a thunderbolt. His bows broken, his chariot wrecked, his horses lying dead next to his charioteer, Kripa jumped to the ground and threw a well-studded club at Arjuna, whose arrows stopped it in flight.

The contest might have gone on had not Kripa's followers intervened. They showered Arjuna with arrows and carried off the wounded, but unsubdued, chariot warrior. Of obscure identity, Kripa can stand as the heroic fighter of the Indian epics. The politeness displayed by Arjuna permitted him to live to fight on another day, but not for a moment could the obvious superiority of this Pandava prince dent Kripa's enthusiasm for chariot battle. For him this was the entire purpose of his existence, the duty he had to perform on earth.

Arjuna alone among the warriors in the *Mahabharata* was ambidextrous. Often called 'the left-handed archer', he could draw the bow string with either hand. Chariots were supplied with quivers full of arrows, while an archer always carried as a reserve on his back two quivers tied together. Arjuna's quivers were a gift from Varuna, but the source of his numerous arrows is not specified. These 'sharp and blood-thirsty shafts' were made from cane and tipped with metal or horn. Sometimes arrows were even poisoned. The occasional reference to an arrow being as long as a chariot axle suggests many were of great length, but shorter ones were also used in composite bows for close encounters with enemy chariots. The complexity of ancient Indian archery can be deduced from the variety of arrow-heads which are mentioned in the epics, such as 'boar-eared', 'crescent-shaped', 'calf-toothed' and 'frog-mouthed'. Crescent-shaped points seem to have been Arjuna's preference, as Karna learned to his cost at Kurukshetra. Razor-sharp iron arrows were fired by Arjuna when dealing with opponents mounted on elephants. In the same cattle raid which discomfited Kripa, he was charged by Duryodhana, the eldest Kaurava prince, mounted on a 'rutting elephant of enormous size'. From Gandiva, 'drawn wide to his ear full circle', Arjuna loosed 'a swift iron arrow which hit the beast on the front of its head'. The shaft having penetrated so deeply that only the feathers at the end were visible, the elephant staggered 'like a towering peak, cleft by one of Indra's thunderbolts, and collapsed on the ground'. Duryodhana took a shot in the chest with the same kind of arrow, but he was carried away to safety by his men. The body-armour this iron arrow pierced is not described, nor are there many references to defensive equipment in the *Mahabharata* or the *Ramayana*. Guards for the arms and the throat are mentioned, along with helmets and shields. Protection for the chest, like the corselet ripped from Kripa by Arjuna's arrows, receives hardly any notice in the battle narratives. In all probability Indian body-armour was similar to that worn by chariot warriors elsewhere: it comprised small metal plates, either bronze or iron, supported by a leather jerkin. In China corselets often incorporated sleeves for the charioteer, so that he could hold the reins without fear of any damage being inflicted on his outstretched arms.

As members of that privileged band of warriors, the chief men of the Indian epics, Kripa and Arjuna rode in two-wheeled chariots driven by a charioteer. Believing in the attainment of heavenly bliss through dying honourably on the battlefield, they were part of the incipient growth of a professional monopoly in fighting that led to the formation of the so-called martial classes of ancient Indian society. Born himself into a royal family dedicated to martial exploits, the Buddha was appalled by this outlook. His espousal of non-violence, non-killing, a doctrine he may have borrowed from the Jain faith, was a concerted effort at establishing the true path to enlightenment. The would-be sage had to learn spiritual self-mastery at a distance from human endeavour, not to say the turmoil of the battlefield. Once achieved, he could step again into the world of daily affairs as a superman, although never a warrior. As in West Asia and

Two Indian rulers, one sitting on an elephant, the other standing on a chariot

Egypt, the Indian chariot comprised a light wooden box with a leather or wickerwork floor, which rested on an axle projecting free of the vehicle on each side. The wheels were secured to the axle by linch pins on their outer faces. Some chariots are said to have wheels with four spokes, others eight. The number of spokes could have been increased over time here, as they were in Assyria, in order to strengthen chariots operating over rough ground or carrying heavier loads. The arrangement of the draught pole and yoke again followed West Asian practice, horses being fitted with neck-straps and not the better shoulder harness developed in China. In the *Rig Veda*, however, we learn that asses were used for pulling chariots as well, a reminder of early Sumerian representations of battle-cars. The animals hitched to the four-wheeled vehicles depicted on the Standard of Ur are more likely to have been asses than horses.

Whatever the draught teams initially employed by the Indo-Aryans, it was the dust and rumble of their chariots that announced their invasion of the subcontinent. This occurred hard on the heels of the extinction of the Indus civilization and obliterated city life for several centuries. Earlier raids may have already undermined the great cities of Mohenjodaro and Harappa, if the irrigation system was a casualty. Possibly dams were deliberately shattered. Warlike Indra, the chief deity of the Indo-Aryans during their occupation of northwestern India in the fifteenth century BC, was believed to have freed the waters by rolling away stones like wagon wheels. Although they eventually absorbed certain Indus valley preoccupations – personal cleanliness, yoga and the worship of the mother goddess, for example – the Indo-Aryans came as destroyers, and gained the upper hand over peoples living in walled towns and fortified cities through Indra's aid as 'the fort-destroyer'. The invaders apparently battled hard against the indigenous population, and at first they maintained a military supremacy based on the chariot. Yet the overwhelmed were not without a revenge, since their beliefs came to have a profound influence on the Indo-Aryans, for nowhere else in the ancient world do we find such an approval of asceticism. Quite unique were the Indian sages, divinely inspired seers who acquired their power from the practice of great austerities. Even a demon like Ravana, Rama's determined foe, could obtain supernatural strength by the same means.

The immediate home of the invading Indo-Aryans cannot be located with any certainty at the moment. The Asian steppes are one possibility. Another is eastern Iran where they may have lived as neighbours of their close cousins the Iranians, whom the Greeks knew as the Persians, the Romans as the Parthians and Sasanians. Despite the thorough recasting of Iranian religion by the prophet Zoroaster some time between 1200 and 1000 BC, the pantheons of the ancient Iranians and Indo-Aryans still had much in common. One of the three great deities of the Iranians was Mitra, who with Varuna was looked upon as a guardian of the moral order. In India the ethical side of Varuna's nature also came to receive emphasis, as the one whose rules of conduct had to be obeyed by other gods. For the Iranians though, Mitra was always more powerful than Varuna, in spite of Zoroaster's elevation of Ahura Mazda as the supreme deity, for Ahura Mazda and Mitra were regarded as the creator-preservers of the cosmos. Later on the cosmic role of Mitra was transformed in the mystery religion of his namesake Mithras into a cult which found favour among the Roman legionaries. Not only did his sacrifice of a bull keep evil at bay, but even more the bull's blood was believed to reanimate creation itself. An inscription discovered in a Mithraic shrine beneath the church of St Prisca in Rome reads: 'You have saved us by shedding eternal blood.' What is even more remarkable than this movement of Mitra's worship into the Mediterranean lands, and even remote Britain, where a temple devoted to this Iranian god was built next to Hadrian's Wall, is the fact that the earliest dated reference to Mitra comes not from India or Iran, but from nothern Syria. It occurs in the treaties agreed by Mitanni with other West Asian states. In the company of Indra, Varuna and the horse-headed Asvin twins, Mitra was invoked by a Mitannian king when making a hurried treaty with the Hittites, Mitanni's destroyers. Though not entirely identical to the Sanskrit of the *Rig Veda*, the words in Indo-Aryan form identified in Mitannian texts would seem to point to the presence of people living in ancient Syria whose tongue was Indo-Aryan.

How these horse-loving inhabitants of Mitanni got to settle there we cannot tell. But their obvious importance to the Mitannians, as witnessed in Kikkuli's training manual for chariot horses, has encouraged the idea that some of them may have been involved in the invasion of India. The *Rig Veda* provides no assistance in determining the route by which the Indo-Aryans arrived in the Indus valley, the area first occupied by the invaders. It is possible, therefore, that the Indo-Aryans came to India by way of Mesopotamia. Had they started on their journey from Mitanni, an easier way to reach the subcontinent than the overland route taken by Alexander would have been to go by sea. Merchants from the city of Ur traded with the Indus valley cities before their decline in the early eighteenth century BC. Thanks for a safe round trip are recorded in votive offerings to the goddess Ningal, whose temple at Ur seems to have been entitled to a share of the profits deriving from trade overseas. The enormous return made by seafaring merchants contrasts with the lesser one colleagues expected to obtain from caravan routes, which were more liable to disruption and robbery. Thus the riverine cities of southern Mesopotamia conducted an extensive trade with the Meluhhans, as the traders from India were called. An inscription from Lagash notes how 'the Meluhhans came up the river again from their country'.

Linguistic evidence is cited to support the proposition that the Indo-Aryans travelled to India by way of Mesopotamia. It is argued that, if the language of the Indo-Aryan speakers of Mitanni was ancestral to the language of the conquerors of northwestern India, then there is no reason to suppose they went east any other way. Yet it could as easily be suggested that these people in Mitanni were an offshoot of the Indo-Aryans, whose early speech happened not to be recorded anywhere else. No matter the eventual outcome of the debate, one thing is certain: the Indo-Aryans introduced the chariot to India. The civilisation of the Indus valley was familiar with wheeled transport, model carts having been excavated at Mohenjodaro, Harappa and Chanhudaro. A wagon from Chanhudaro with four solid wheels recalls the original construction method used in Sumer and Elam, an ancient state in present-day Iran known for its chariotry. The spoked wheels of later Elamite chariots had the luxury of bronze tyres. Except perhaps at Lothol, an ancient port in modern Gujarat, nothing suggests the use of a wheeled vehicle as an instrument of war before the arrival of the Indo-Aryans. For the model horses found at Lothol could have drawn a carriage instead of a chariot. This lack of evidence for the war chariot in the Indus civilisation is totally unlike the position of the Indo-Aryans, who were obsessed with charioteering. The chariot was just as central to the *Rig Veda*, the earliest statement of Indo-Aryan attitudes and beliefs, as it was to the *Ramayana* and the *Mahabharata*, the great epics.

Although the earliest realistic representations of chariots appear on the sculptured railings of the Buddhist monuments at Sanchi, in present-day Madhya Pradesh, and date from the early first century BC, there are references to the chariot in texts well before these were carved to illustrate scenes from the Buddha's mission on earth. As early as the *Rig Veda*, which assumed its current form at the beginning of the first millennium BC, it is transparent that this prestigious vehicle was reserved for gods, kings and heroes. Because the hymns in the *Rig Veda* were transmitted orally for centuries prior to the final formation of the collection, we encounter in them the first thoughts of the Indo-Aryans

A royal chariot

concerning the purpose of the chariot, which is described as an 'all-embracing' mode of transport for the gods. It could travel anywhere with incredible speed, like the three giant steps taken by Vishnu when he strode through the entire universe. As one commentator put it:

> But he who has knowledge, with thought, always pure, reaches the place where there is no rebirth. For the man who has knowledge as his charioteer and thought as the bridle, reaches the far end of the road, the ultimate step of Vishnu.

Here the goal of enlightenment, escape from the eternal round of reincarnation, is synonymous with handling a chariot. Such a gloss shows how the Indo-Aryans never forgot the critical role that chariotry played during their conquest of northwestern India. Even more explicit is the ancient idea of the mind as a wish-car, which if driven correctly took one to a spiritual destination as surely as a chariot accomplished its journey.

'The man who rides in a chariot drawn by his five senses and directed by his mind,' we are told, 'and who keeps the vehicle on the path of virtue, can never be diverted by his enemies – lust, wrath and greed.' That is to say, the person who rides in a car of good intentions is unstoppable like a chariot warrior. Always remembered was the 'Vritra-slaying chariot of Indra' for the invaluable service it rendered to the sky god when he battled against Vritra, a drought-serpent which had swallowed the cosmic waters and lay in coils on the mountains.

> Muddled by drunkenness like one who is no warrior, Vritra challenged the great god who had defeated the mighty and who drank soma to the dregs. Unable to withstand Indra's assault, Vritra was overcome, his nose crushed. Without feet or hands he fought against Indra, who from his chariot struck him on the nape of the neck with a thunderbolt . . . Then the serpent sank down . . . and, when Indra split open Vritra's stomach, the waters found an outlet to the earth.

Thus the chariot was literally all-conquering, the certain means of gaining control over 'the four quarters of the world'. Through this great act, one of two with which he was credited, Indra removed the obstruction standing in the way of fertility. Meaning 'resistance', Vritra was the chief obstacle to the development of creation. Indra's second task was propping up the sky with the tree of life, a separation of earth and sky achieved for the ancient Greeks by Kronos' emasculation of his sky father Ouranos, who held Gaia, mother earth, in too close an embrace. The two great deeds of chariot-riding Indra meant that charioteers invoked his assistance for their own vehicles: he was asked to protect the draught pole and axle from breakage, stop the harness and reins from coming loose, keep the linch pins in place, and prevent the wheels sticking in the mud.

One hymn in the *Rig Veda* recounts a strange chariot race. When thieves stole all of Mudgala's cattle but one old bull, he harnessed this animal to his chariot and set off in pursuit, brandishing a wooden club. Stranger still, Mudgala's wife acted as his charioteer. But 'Indra aided the husband of cows, and the humpbacked bull galloped' after the stolen herd, which Mudgala was able to recover. It was through 'the bull that he won as spoils of war one thousand one hundred cows'. Through his wife, too, the hymn says Mudgala succeeded in winning the race, while she, 'like a despised wife who wins back her husband', recovered his love apparently after a long period of neglect. The female charioteer had triumphed. She may have done so in fact, or possibly in fiction, if her wish was the chariot of Mudgala's success. Elsewhere in the *Rig Veda* there are references to 'chariots without wheels' in the minds of those who want or need something. Even sacrifice itself is termed 'a chariot of the gods'. In a different context, among the scrolls associated with the Qumran community, we find a similar association of the chariot with sacrifice. The fragment entitled *Chariots of Glory* mentions not only a divine chariot but also 'wheel-angels' responsible for the safe transport of 'the offerings of the land'. Dwelling on the shore of the Dead Sea, this first-century AD religious community destroyed by the Romans continued to use chariot imagery well after the vehicle had ceased to fulfil a military function in West Asia. As we noticed in the *Mahabharata*, the cattle raid suffered by Mudgala was a common occurrence in ancient India. Tending herds had never precluded agriculture, but it is interesting how the cow remained for the Indo-Aryans the measure of value after they settled down as farmers. 'Searching for cattle' was a euphemism for armed conflict, because the eating of beef remained an integral part of feasts, and especially when well-born guests were invited. A supply of meat had to be secured or safeguarded. Despite the Buddha's opposition to the killing of animals for sacrifice or food, the consumption of cattle continued without interruption.

Of even more significance to the Indo-Aryans than the cow was of course the horse. The *Rig Veda* is ecstatic over the horse-sacrifice. Identified with the sun and fire, the sacrificial horse was 'the swift runner of awesome birth'. It came to the slaughter, to 'the dwelling-place of its father and mother, where a welcome awaits among the gods'. Behind the animal 'walked the poets, the singers'. Along with a goat, the horse was killed and cooked, while those making the sacrifice were assured that it did not die, nor was it harmed. The horse went instead 'to the gods on pleasant paths, with two stallions and two mares as chariot companions'. The outcome of the sacrifice was expected to be 'good cattle, good horses, male children and wealth'. Apart from the hymns connected with the sacrifice of horses in the *Rig Veda*, there are details surviving about how the rite of horse-sacrifice was conducted later on. A Hindu ruler who had the circumstances of this rite cut in stone was Samudragupta, who died in AD 376. The second Gupta king, Samudragupta 'extended his dominions to the four oceans', although he seems to have struggled to impose his will on the Deccan, where rulers of smaller states combined against him. There he had to rely upon alliances rather than annexation. But wherever he triumphed in battle Samudragupta tended to reinstate defeated kings and accept gifts of treasure as a token of submission. Claims that the Sri Lankan king became his vassal are unfounded, since we know the purpose of the mission dispatched from the island to Pataliputra. The rich gifts sent to Samudragupta were intended to persuade him to look kindly upon a request to build a monastery and a resthouse for Sinhalese pilgrims at Bodh Gaya, the place where the Buddha attained enlightenment. Evidently the Gupta king chose to regard this as tribute. By the reign of Samudragupta the Buddhist faith was in decline, something the Chinese pilgrim Fa Xian was not slow to notice on his arrival in ancient India around AD 400. That this solitary foreign visitor could travel freely without fear of molestation by robbers, as he collected and copied Buddhist texts, shows how effective Gupta rule was then. To celebrate this auspicious state of affairs, Samudragupta asked his court-poet Harisena to compose verses for the occasion of the royal horse-sacrifice.

The rite was a perfect method for Samudragupta to demonstrate the extent of his authority, since it descended from a practice in remote times by which a chieftain asserted his ownership of herds and the grounds on which they grazed. When such an early ruler wished to announce himself as a paramount chief, he would do so by letting loose his best stallion. This splendid animal was allowed to wander where it liked, followed by a guard of young warriors, ready and able to defeat anyone who might attempt to drive the horse from his own grazing ground, or to make it captive. When the horse had wandered for a whole year, it was escorted home again to be slaughtered sacrificially. King Samudragupta's horse-sacrifice included this year-long roam as well as rituals designed to purify both the horse and the monarch. Before setting the horse free, the prospective victim was washed in a pool while a dog was killed and thrown into the water. Then the warriors accompanying the stallion made sure that there was no contact with mares, or further immersion in rivers or streams, during the year it wandered the world. Towards the end of the year a huge pyre was erected, and the king underwent a series of observances in readiness for the sacrifice. This lasted three days in all. On the second day, when the actual slaughter took place, the king drove in a war chariot drawn by the sacrificial stallion and three other horses. The victim was annointed by the king's three foremost wives, and its tail decorated with pearls. At the sacrifice of the horse, a sheep and a goat were also killed. Hundreds of other animals were often slain in supplementary ceremonies, but wild creatures among the intended victims were usually released unharmed. The stallion was smothered to death, presumably to avoid damaging its body, whereupon the king's first wife symbolically coupled with the sacrificed horse under covers, while the royal court gave her encouragement with obscene remarks. Afterwards the victim was dismembered and burned on the pyre.

Four-horse chariot

A not dissimilar rite, another horse-sacrifice, was practised in Rome every October. There the right-side horse of a chariot which had won a special race on the Campus Martius was killed with a spear. The inhabitants of two old parts of the city, Subura and Sacra Via, then fought over the head of the sacrificial horse; the winners were allowed to display the trophy on a prominent building in their quarter. By the time Hannibal threatened the city walls in 216 BC, Subura had become the centre of Rome. It was the place where Julius Caesar, as a young man, bought his first house. Notwithstanding the absence of an erotic element in this Roman horse ritual, there is a parallel between the sacrifice of horses among the ancient Indians and Romans, because in both cases the divine recipient was a war god, Mars and Indra. The Guptas seem to have favoured Prajapati, 'the lord of all creatures', over Indra in their horse-sacrifices, possibly because this creator deity rose in stature with the revival in India of what today we term Hinduism. Prajapati's new status may well have much to do with priestly dissatisfaction over existing creation stories. In Rome, however, it was always Mars who received the honour of the October horse. An implacable god with no proper temple in the city, perhaps because the dangers of the battlefield were his domain, Mars was the main beneficiary of spoils after a successful campaign.

Human sacrifice may once have been an appeasement for Mars, as an act of Julius Caesar suggests. In 46 BC, a mutiny of troops at Rome was ended by the dictator with the execution of one ringleader, and the killing of two others on the Campus Martius by religious officials, an event which could indicate that the Indo-European rite of horse-sacrifice was a late substitution for that of a warrior. Traces of human sacrifice lingered in ancient India, where a victim was said to be purchased from his family for 1,000 cows and 100 horses. After initial rites he was free for a year and humoured in everything except sexual pleasure. Like the sacrificial horse, the human victim was then slaughtered along with a sheep and a goat. Again the queen is supposed to have had intercourse with the dead or dying man and, rather than a menagerie of animals, people were killed as a supplement to the main sacrifice. These gruesome rituals are mentioned in the *Mahabharata*, but horse-sacrifices always remained the most popular celebration of the warrior ethic.

Even stranger than these sacrifices is the information Gerald of Cambrai provides about an Irish version of the horse-sacrifice. Outraged by what he learned about this pagan rite, he can barely control the language of the description, when he tells us of a remote Ulster tribe

which installed its ruler by means of a savage and abominable ceremony. In the presence of all the people, a white mare is brought into their midst. Thereupon he who is to be raised up, not to become a prince but a beast, not a king but an outlaw, steps forward in bestial fashion and couples with the mare. Afterwards the mare is killed and in the water used for boiling its flesh the king actually takes a bath. In the bath he even shares the cooked meat with his

The Buddhist wheel of enlightenment, which is based on a chariot wheel

people, who stand wide-eyed round him. Then, like a beast, he drinks the bathwater, not with a cup or his hands, but with his mouth. When this utterly disgusting ceremony is over, the king's reign begins.

The bafflement of the medieval chronicler at this ancient Indo-European rite, which somehow survived on the fringe of the Celtic world, is understandable. For what Gerald learned of was a ceremony tied into worship of the horse goddess, the same Epona to whom the Roman cavalry turned for support. Mating with a mare was in a sense mating with the goddess herself. Nothing quite like this is found in ancient India, although the wife of the Pandavas, Draupadi, remains an ambivalent figure in the *Mahabharata*. 'Her destiny is already declared,' says the sage

Vyasa, 'so let her satisfy all of Pandu's sons.' Possibly Draupadi could have once been a horse goddess whose sexual generosity was believed to sustain many chariot warriors. No more than hints are now available to elucidate the subject. In Greek mythology we have Centaurus, a son of Apollo, who mated with mares in order to produce the Centaurs, a race of horse-men. In Hittite law bestiality with horses was exempt from punishment, while stern penalties were prescribed for those who dared to couple with cattle, sheep and pigs. Among the Hittites though, there seems to have been no sacrifice of horses, with the exception of animals killed during warriors' burials. In Ireland the use of the chariot is uncertain. The Ulster hero Cuchulainn may be extolled in the Irish sagas as a fierce head-hunter, a daring cattle-rustler and a mighty eater, but there is no archaeological evidence for his chariot ever being 'graced with the bleeding heads of his enemies'. War chariots appear to have been absent from ancient Irish battlefields.

Where accounts of horse-sacrifice agree, other than the odd Ulster coronation ceremony, is in the importance of the right-hand stallion. The *Rig Veda* is the earliest document to explain the reason. According to one of its hymns, three horses originally formed the team for a chariot. The right-hand horse was yoked first on the instruction of the gods. A fourth horse ran alongside the team, unyoked but fully harnessed. After the first chariot race, this spare horse was added to the draught team. The change to a four-horse chariot is explained as threefold matters being properly the business of the gods, while fourfold belong to mankind.

6

China

When the Jin army returned home in triumph, the commander Shi Hsieh entered the capital after the others. His father said: 'Surely you knew how worried I was about you. Why did you delay your entry?' Shi Hsieh replied: 'The army won the victory and the people were greeting it with joy. If I had rode in my chariot ahead of the rest, I would have seemed to claim all the glory for myself.' Then said his father: 'Now I know you will come to no harm.'

Zuo zhuan

This conversation between father and son occurred shortly after the battle of An. One of the 'five great engagements' of the Spring and Autumn period (770–481 BC), An ended in a resounding defeat for the eastern state of Qi. The campaign had started with a Qi attack on Lu, a small state situated in the lower Yellow river valley. Neighbouring Wey was so concerned over the belligence of Qi that it mobilised and sent an official to the Jin capital to ask for additional troops. 'An official from Lu,' the *Zuo zhuan* relates, 'also went to beg troops from Jin.' China's oldest work of narrative history, the *Zuo zhuan* provides a year-by-year, often a month-by-month, account of happenings during the Spring and Autumn period. Like the *Iliad* and the *Mahabharata*, its narrative is focused on the exploits of aristocratic warriors who rode in chariots. The seventy-two foot soldiers who accompanied each chariot hardly receive a mention, even though some 56,000 of them ran alongside the 800 chariots which Jin dispatched against Qi. The combined forces of Lu, Wey and Jin confronted those of Qi just inside that state's territory in the summer of 589 BC. The Qi ruler

issued an invitation to the battle, saying, 'You have troubled yourself to enter my humble state with your ruler's troops. With the worthless forces at my command, I beg to meet with you tomorrow.' The Jin commander answered by saying that Lu and Wey were the brothers of Jin. He deplored, therefore, the violence Qi had displayed against their lands. 'Our ruler,' he said, 'moved by their plight, has sent his officers to request that you desist. We are instructed not to remain here long, so you need not trouble to incite us further!' After the ruler of Qi acknowledged the necessity

Terracotta horse's head

of battle, one of his warriors dashed into the Jin ranks and struck a man with a stone. After capturing him, he mounted his chariot, tied a mulberry tree to it and paraded his captive back and forth, as he shouted out: 'If any man wants valour, he may buy what I have to spare.'

Acts of provocation were normal on the ancient Chinese battlefield. They were intended to inflame, upset or intimidate one's opponents prior to the commencement of all-out action. It is not always obvious whether the bravado was planned or spontaneous. If judged on the outcome of the subsequent battle, this attack was ineffectual as Qi suffered a heavy defeat. More impressive was the display of the three Chu heroes, in 595 BC, at the battle of Bi. These daring warriors taunted the Jin lines and then escaped only through the politeness of their pursuers, to whom they presented a stag which had suddenly crossed their path as a token of respect. Implicit in the second challenge is an assumption of the moral superiority of the gift-givers, since their generosity revealed a truly amazing self-possession and confidence during the turmoil of fighting which elicited an equally civilised response from their opponents. That the Chu army went on and won a crushing victory only serves to underline the chivalry of the entire episode.

The battle of An seems to have been started with undue haste. Threatening to 'mow down' his enemies 'and wipe them out before breakfast', the Qi ruler 'drove into the field without waiting for his horses to be protected with armour'. In response to this early attack, the *Zuo zhuan* explains how the most experienced Jin commander, Hsi Ko, though severely wounded, raised the alarm by beating the war drum.

'I am hit!' he said. But his charioteer answered, 'When we first entered the fray, an arrow went right through my hand and reached my elbow! So I broke it off and continued driving. The chariot's left wheel is red with blood, but did I mention my wound? You must suffer the pain!' . . . Then he added: 'The eyes of the entire army are on our war-pennant and their ears listen to our drum. Advancing or retreating, the troops follow us. From this chariot one man can control everything. Just because you are wounded, would you bring ruin on our enterprise? When you put on armour and take up weapons, you should be ready to die. While your wound is not fatal, you must go on!'

With this stiffening of resolve and 'blood flowing down into his shoes', Hsi Ko let his chariot race forward 'so that no one could stop them, and the soldiers followed after. The Qi army was routed and its remnants chased away.' Afterwards a chastened Qi ruler offered terms for peace: an antique steamer used for ancestor worship and a set of jade chiming stones, plus the return of territory previously belonging to the

The cosmic archer Yi

state of Lu. These the representatives of Lu and Wey urged Hsi Ko to accept, since they considered it enough to have checked Qi's aggression. 'Remember that the fate of both Qi and Jin rests in the hands of Heaven,' they advised Hsi Ko. 'It is not Jin alone that enjoys favour from above!'

During the battle of An the Jin army had been led by three commanders, of whom Hsi Ko was the senior. Shi Hsieh commanded the left wing with distinction, but along with the two other commanders, Hsi Ko and Luan Shu, he disclaimed any responsibility for the defeat of Qi when back at home he was questioned by the Jin ruler. Such circumspection was a prudent policy, as Shi Hsieh's father quickly recognised, in the jealous atmosphere of a feudal court. How wise the three commanders were in their refusal to accept any personal credit for the victory became evident within two decades, for the next ruler of Jin was a wayward prince incapable of steady judgment. As Shi Hsieh later commented, after his return from the battle of Yenling, 'our ruler is arrogant and, now he has defeated his enemies, great problems will follow for our state. Those who love me would do well to pray for my speedy death, so I may not see the troubles ahead.' Fought in 575 BC between Jin and Chu, the battle of Yenling is the last of the *Zuo zhuan's* 'five great engagements'. It was precipitated by the switch of alliance of the tiny state of Chen from Jin to Chu, in return for a tract of land which the ruler of Chen had always coveted. Jin sent its army southwards under the command of Luan Shu and Shi Hsieh. When Chen heard of this advance, Chu was told the news so that it could send forces against Jin. Pleased though Chen was by Chu's rapid mobilisation, there was unease over the professionalism of the Chu commanders. 'They advance too fast,' noted one Chen official, 'and when they pass through a narrow place, they do not maintain proper order! Going at such a speed leaves no time to plan a campaign, and failing to keep the ranks in order leaves an army vulnerable. I am afraid Chu will be of no use to us!' All was not well, however, with the Jin army and Shi Hsieh advocated a withdrawal, but was overruled by Luan Shu, who told his subordinates:

'Chu is frivolous, its army is only halfhearted over this campaign. If we strengthen our position and wait three days, they are sure to withdraw. When they do, we can charge them in the certain knowledge of victory.' Agreeing with this analysis, another senior Jin officer said, 'We must not forget to exploit Chu's six weaknesses. Their commanders are at loggerheads. The ruler's personal guard has been long in the field. Chen's ranks are in disorder. Other allies are also not properly disposed. Every man looks behind him and none have a heart to fight. Above all, they have offended Heaven by drawing up for battle on the last day of the month.'

The reluctance of Luan Shu to begin the action certainly confused the Chu ruler, who tried to work out Jin intentions by a reconnaisance in

his own chariot. Yet this attempt to anticipate Luan Shu's plan of
attack lacked the precise details which the Jin commander-in-chief
had managed to glean about the disposition of the Chu army. He
had discovered how all the best enemy troops were concentrated
in the centre, leaving him free to overwhelm its wings before attacking them from the front and the sides. When divination confirmed the
advantage to Jin of such an attack, Luan Shu embraced the plan
enthusiastically.

On the day of the battle, the action at Yenling went according to Luan
Shu's plan, and the Chu army was forced to fall back through a narrow
valley. Unable to pursue it easily along this line of retreat, the Jin
chariotry halted. 'The battle began at dawn,' according to the *Zuo zhuan*,
'and was still in progress as the stars came out.' When both sides prepared
to continue the fight the next day, the ruler of Chu was the first to lose
his nerve, and he fled under cover of darkness with his personal guard.
Then 'the Jin troops occupied the Chu encampment and for three days
ate the stores of grain there'. Grateful to have won at Yenling, the new
Jin ruler was for a year more appreciative of his ministers and
commanders but he soon threw off all restraint and began executing those
who offered him uncongenial advice. In desperation Luan Shu staged a
coup, and executed the ruler. There is no doubt that incessant warfare
between ancient Chinese states did much to undermine feudal obligations
and weaken the position of rulers, even in successful states like Jin. The
nominal ruler of all China, the Zhou king, could do no more than watch
as the struggle for supremacy pulled down one feudal house after another.
At the start of the seventh century BC there were 200 feudal territories; by
500 BC that number had dropped to fewer than twenty. During the
Warring States period (481–221 BC) the internecine strife became so bitter
and so intense that only seven feudal states were able to concentrate
enough resources for war. After the break-up of Jin in 403 BC, when
continued internal problems split it into the three separate states of
Han, Wei and Zhao, the northwestern state of Qin was best placed to
dominate China. By 221 BC the strength of Qin was sufficient to destroy
all its rivals and unify the whole country in one empire. The last Zhou
king was pushed from his throne by Qin troops in 256 BC.

Prior to the domination of Qin an alternative method of government
was tried, the hegemon system which coincided with the chariot's
greatest era on the Chinese battlefield. The first hegemon fully

ANCIENT CHINA
during the Spring and Autumn period

recognised by the Zhou king was Huan, the ruler of Qi (685–643 BC).
Though its economic power was securely based in what is today
Shandong province on salt, iron and irrigation, the elevation to leadership
of China resulted from the energetic measures Huan took in dealing with
barbarian incursions and inter-state rivalry. On the advice of his chief
minister Guan Zhong, Huan called conferences to discuss matters of
mutual interest, such as sharing rivers, and alliances were formed against
truculent states such as semi-barbarian Chu in the south. Signatories of
the agreements were charged with punishing the unfilial, defending the
principle of inheritance, honouring the worthy, respecting the aged,
protecting children and strangers, choosing talented officials instead of
relying on hereditary offices, abstaining from putting officials to death,
and avoiding acts of provocation, such as the construction of barriers, the
unannounced placing of boundary markers, and the restriction of the sale

of grain. But these good intentions had to be backed by force: in the forty-two years Huan was hegemon he went to war no fewer than twenty-eight times.

Huan always claimed to act on behalf of the Son of Heaven, the Zhou king, but his protestations were really a cloak for his own policies. While he preferred to settle problems through diplomacy rather than on the battlefield, the events of his life reflect the uncertainties of the times. Violence surrounded his accession to power and followed his own death in 643 BC: he had to kill his brother at the outset of his reign and the struggle between his sons delayed his funeral until the condition of the corpse became scandalous. Worms were seen crawling out of the room in which Huan's body lay, and so putrid was its flesh that preparations for burial could not be undertaken in daylight. Yet as the first hegemon, Huan endeavoured to make sense of what was a great turning point in the ancient history of China, and he was ably assisted in this task by Guan Zhong, whom he spared as a supporter of his brother – an arrow fired by the distinguished minister had struck the clasp of Huan's belt during the fighting over the succession. Even though the observations associated with his name were not written down until long after his ministry, Guan Zhong's ideas appear to have been seminal for Chinese political thought, because his elevation of the ruler anticipates legalist notions, in particular those of the Qin chief minister Shang Yang (who died in 338 BC); they indeed look forward to the centralised order of the empire, which Qin inaugurated in 221 BC.

Starting in 375 BC the Qin government attempted to control and exploit the population by forcing them to register their names. This seems to have been the first time ordinary people were given names. Control was extended in 359 BC when a system of collective responsibility was enforced. For Shang Yang

ordered the people to be organised into groups of five and ten households, mutually to control one another's behaviour. Those who did not denounce the guilty would be cut in half; those who denounced the guilty would receive the same reward as if they had beheaded an enemy; those who concealed the guilty would receive the same punishment as if they had surrendered to an enemy. Families with two or more grown sons not living in separate households had to pay a double tax. Those who distinguished themselves in battle were given titles by the ruler, in strict order of merit. Everyone had to assist in the fundamental occupations of tilling and weaving, and only those who produced a large quantity of grain or silk were exempted from labour on public works. Those who occupied themselves with trade were enslaved, along with the destitute and lazy. Those of noble lineage who had no military value lost their noble status. The social hierarchy was clearly defined and each rank allotted its appropriate fields, houses, servants, concubines, and clothes. Those who had value were distinguished with honours, while those without any value, even if they were rich, could have no renown whatever.

The implementation of these regulations was by no means easy, but dissension did not outlast the shaming of the heir to the throne. When the crown prince transgressed one of the new laws, Shang Yang demanded at least he should be given a token punishment. The Qin ruler therefore agreed that the prince's guardian be downgraded and the face of the prince's tutor tattooed, presumably on the grounds that these nobles shared responsibility for the prince's misbehaviour.

Such fanaticism cost Shang Yang dear. Unloved, and feared by the nobles and the common people alike, he was safe as long as his patron remained on the throne, but after the death of the king in 338 BC, Shang Yang's enemies swiftly accused him of sedition and officers were sent to arrest him. There is marvellous irony in the story of his attempted flight. When the ex-chief minister at first tried to hide in an obscure inn, the innkeeper, in ignorance of his identity, told him that under the new laws he dared not admit a man without a permit for fear of punishment. So it was that Shang Yang learned of the thoroughness of his own law code. Realising that escape was impossible, he returned to his own estate where, as an example to the rebellious, Shang Yang was torn limb from limb by chariots, and all the members of his family were slain. After his death, however, the new laws were not abolished, for Qin rulers were aware of the political and military advantages of centralised power, a disciplined bureaucracy and a strong army. Shang Yang's belief, that it had to be made worse for someone to fall into the hands of the police than go to war, was to serve the expansionist ambitions of Qin well. By hastening the tendency of the age towards authoritarian government and despotism, he turned comparatively backward Qin into the strongest feudal state.

During Huan's lifetime this tendency was not so marked, despite the reforming zeal of Guan Zhong. After his death, the family feud over the succession in 642 BC ruined Qi and allowed the hegemony to pass first to neighbouring Song, and then in 636 BC to Jin, the biggest state of all until its disintegration. Jin included large parts of present-day Shaanxi, Hebei and Henan provinces, and some of its rulers felt independent enough to summon and dismiss the Zhou king without ceremony. A similar disregard for rank is transparent in the intrigue and violence prevalent within competing states themselves, an incipient disorder which became even more pronounced during the subsequent Warring States period.

An early chariot battle was the Qin defeat of Jin at Han in 645 BC. What interests the *Zuo zhuan* most is the aftermath of the engagement, for the situation was complicated by the fact that the wife of the victor, the Qin ruler Hui, was the eldest sister of the captured ruler of Jin. Hui's wife indicated that she would kill herself and her children if any harm came to her brother. While the feudal states fought each other, generation after generation, trying to extend their authority over their neighbours, and absorbing larger and larger tracts of land, their ruling houses were closely related through marriage alliances. In theory, they were all subordinate to the Zhou king, whose sacrifices to the heavenly powers were supposed to guarantee the safety of ancient China, then known as the Middle Kingdom, but in practice the vying feudal lords kept an eye on the activities of rivals so that they did not lose out in the shifting balance of power. After considerable debate over the wisdom of releasing the ruler of Jin, Hui took the line of least resistance and sent his difficult brother-in-law home. For us the battle of Han is more interesting because of the mishap that befell some of the Qin chariotry. War between the states of Qin and Jin had come about during a famine: whereas the former sent grain when the latter was suffering from a serious shortage, Jin hoarded its own stocks when Qin in turn ran into difficulties. The refusal of aid was enough for Hui to attack Jin after divination signalled eventual success on the battlefield. But Hui chose to ignore the oracle's warning about the danger likely to threaten his own chariot. The diviner explained the apparent contradiction thus:

Chariot and horse burial

This means good luck. Following three defeats, you are bound to capture the ruler of Jin, for it is predicted that after a thousand chariots have set out three times, they will take the fox prisoner. And being a pest, the fox is none other than the ruler of Jin.

So it happened that the Qin army suffered three defeats and retreated as far as Han. When Hui divined to see who should drive his chariot in the fourth engagement there, he refused to accept the advice that his usual charioteer would be 'lucky', because this man had dared to criticise his previous tactics. Instead, another charioteer took over the reins of a team of horses presented to Hui by an ally, the state of Chen. Prophetically the deposed royal charioteer commented how

> 'in the past chariots have been drawn by horses native to Qin. Born and trained locally, these animals always knew the desires of their drivers, were at home with their commands, and were fully accustomed to the terrain. Therefore they only needed guidance in order to accomplish what was required. But if foreign-bred horses are used in military operations, as now our ruler intends for his own chariot, they are likely to go against the command of the driver. In their confusion they will grow unruly, their blood will rise, and their veins will swell and stand out. Then their strength is bound to fail, so that the chariot can no longer be driven properly.'

Refusing to heed this comment, Hui mounted his chariot and the forces of Qin and Jin fought on the plain of Han, where his chariot team 'swerved in the mud and floundered to a stop'. A squadron of chariots guarding the ruler of Qin seems to have got into trouble as well. Luckily for Hui, however, other Qin chariots led by the rejected charioteer arrived in the nick of time and he escaped capture. Not so the ruler of Jin, who was taken prisoner as the diviner predicted.

The incident could have led to Hui losing the battle of Han, since he arrogantly brushed aside the advice of his greatest charioteer. This man was obviously the ancient Chinese equivalent of Kikkuli, the renowned trainer of Mitanni's chariotry. What he was trying to get Hui to appreciate was the critical importance of a close and trusting relationship between a charioteer and his chariot team, something which could only be fostered by a long period of training. They quite simply had to live together. A regime of training could never safely be delegated to anyone else: the charioteer had to be involved during every stage of a horse's commitment to a draught team. He was the putative mother and father of every animal specially 'bred and raised in the midst of the state's lands and waters'. Only then would it be possible for him to bring to perfection a team of horses capable of anticipating the swift commands so essential to success in a fast-moving chariot engagement. Just as the chariot changed the face of warfare elsewhere, in the late second and early first millenniums BC it transformed the Chinese battlefield into a series of rapid manoeuvres that largely decided the infantry contests which followed. The 70,000 or 80,000 foot soldiers who accompanied the Qin chariotry would have been dismayed at Hui's capture in a stranded chariot. They would have not gone on to disperse the Jin army, after suffering three successive defeats. Nor would they have won for Qin lands belonging to Jin. 'For the first time,' the *Zuo zhuan* reports, 'the state of Qin began collecting taxes from an area of Jin east of the Yellow river, and also established officials there to oversee the operation'. Valuable though this acquisition was to Qin, its major period of expansion occurred after the ministry of Shang Yang. In 330 BC Qin forces expanded its holdings east of the Yellow river at the expense of Wei, one of the states which emerged from Jin's collapse, and in 316 BC they thrust southwest to annex Shu, a large portion of modern Sichuan province. Besides outflanking Chu, the great southern state based on the Yangzi valley, the Shu conquest added valuable agricultural resources to Qin once irrigation schemes were introduced on the Chengdu plain, thereafter called 'sea-on-land' in recognition of the vast extent of the water-conservancy projects undertaken.

Less inclined to such large-scale schemes, Chu was still well endowed with natural resources. With a mild southern climate suited to intensive farming, there was no real need for Chu rulers to exploit agriculture in the determined way Qin did in the harsher northwest. It is not impossible that the loess soil of the north China plain, with the consequent reliance on irrigation, constituted the lever by which the Qin ruler could move his people as a united body, whereas the ruler of Chu required less social cohesion in order to produce a reliable agricultural suplus. Another factor working against centralisation may have been an apparent scarcity of cities. While town and city sites in Chu compare favourably with those excavated in northern states, only a few have been located so far. From tomb finds, however, it is clear that the state of Chu possessed an advanced economy, which included bronze and iron manufacturing; the discovery of weapons amongst these funerary goods confirms the fear expressed by chroniclers about the iron-tipped arrows of Chu, 'sharp as a bee's sting'. A feudal order shallowly founded as in Qin naturally inclined Chu towards the authoritarian doctrines of the so-called School of Law, but no Shang Yang appeared to give the sprawling state an organisation robust enough to withstand the political storms raging at the time.

Though it was not until after the conquest of Chu in 223 BC that Qin could be certain of final victory over all the feudal states, the growing strength of its army was signalled in a series of defeats inflicted on Chu during the earlier campaigns of 280 and 278 BC, which resulted in the annexation of large tracts of the Yangzi valley. These defeats were a humiliation for Chu, whose ruler had been the last hegemon between 613 and 591 BC. Only the struggle against Wu, a state near the estuary of the Yangzi, had given Chu as much grief. Matters were made worse by the defection of Wu Chen in 584 BC to Wu. This renegade commander taught the soldiers of Wu to use up-to-date weapons and fight in formation. An equally distinguished citizen was obliged to seek refuge in Wu over half a century later. An unscrupulous minister persuaded Bing, the ruler of Chu, that Wu She was contemplating a usurpation along with a prince. In 522 BC, Bing summoned Wu She to court and subjected him to examination. Wu She had two sons, Wu Shang and Wu Yun, and the ruler was advised to summon the sons to court as well so that they could not plot against him. Bing ordered them to appear on pain of death of their father. Out of filial piety the eldest son, Wu Shang, answered the summons in the knowledge that both he and his father would be killed. But he urged his younger brother Wu Yun to flee to Wu. 'I will do the dying,' Wu Shang said, 'you can do the avenging.' Vengeance indeed became Wu Yun's sole aim, for it really shaped the refugee's life as well as the lives of the people caught up in the terrible war he engineered between the states of Wu and Chu.

As the ruler's military adviser, Wu Yun helped to put Wu on a permanent war-footing. In 506 BC the fall of Ying, the Chu capital, shocked China. Five times the Wu army routed the superior forces of Chu, who were unable to drive back downstream the water-borne invaders. The arrival of reinforcements alone, from an incredulous Qin, halted the advance and after seven engagements forced a Wu evacuation. 'At this moment,' a chronicler relates, 'employing strategies Wu Yun suggested, Wu crushed the powerful state of Chu in the south, filling Qin and Jin in the north with awe.' The *Zuo zhuan* offers a description of one of the battles between Chu and Wu, which took place at Pochu. Rather than allow an encirclement of the Wu army to take place, through a cleverly devised sweep by a Chu commander close to the Yangzi river, Nang Wu, the general in charge of the force blocking the enemy advance on the city of Ying, was persuaded by his officers to launch an immediate attack. One said: 'The war chariots of Wu are made entirely of wood, while ours use plenty of leather and, in these rainy conditions, they will not last for long. You had better attack at once!' Another officer added: 'The people of Chu already admire the general who is outflanking the Wu army. If he succeeds in destroying its boats, before falling on it from the rear, then he alone will get the credit for the victory. You had better

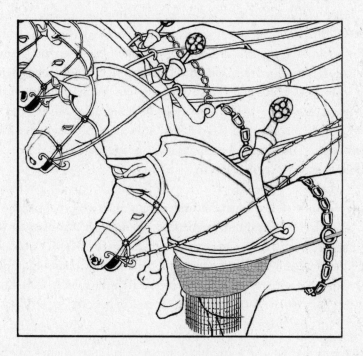

The efficient breast-strap harness

attack now, or afterwards you may be censured for your inaction.' Worried by what these officers had said, Nang Wu ordered his army forward and met the Wu invaders at Pochu. But Nang Wu's reputation was as poor in Wu as it was in Chu, for it was the view of the Wu high command that he was 'a heartless man and none of his officers have any intention of dying for his sake'. As the ruler of Wu was still uncertain whether an attack on Nang Wu's forces would disperse them as easily as his commanders believed, one of them acted on his own and 'led the five thousand men under his command and initiated hostilities by charging the Chu lines'. This unauthorised action threw Nang Wu's troops in confusion and they fled. Wu won a great victory. Nang Wu fled the battlefield, and his home state of Chu, but one of his officers mounted Nang Wu's chariot, pretending to be the runaway general, and died trying in vain to rally the troops. The Wu army pursued the broken Chu forces to a tributary of the Yangzi. This time none of the Wu commanders rushed into an attack, because they all recognised the best moment to strike was when the Chu army was crossing the river. They adopted this plan and once more inflicted a heavy defeat. Then the Chu soldiers who had already crossed the river and had begun preparing a meal were surprised when the men of Wu arrived on the scene. They also fled. The Wu troops ate the meal and then set off in pursuit once more, defeating the Chu army several times before they reached the Chu capital at Ying . . . When the Wu army entered the city, the commanders occupied the Chu palaces in accordance with their respective ranks.

In the meantime the commander undertaking the sweep behind the Wu army, Shenyin Hsu, had some success. He routed the Wu rearguard, but was himself wounded in the action. Although in two subsequent engagements he still got the better of the Wu soldiers opposing him, the severe wounds were having an effect on Shenyin Hsu, who feared being taken prisoner by the Wu forces. So he asked his officers,

'Who will see to it that my head does not fall into enemy hands!' One replied, 'I am a man of no rank, but will I do?' Shenyin Hsu said, 'In the past I've misjudged your worth. You will do fine.' So the general fought on and collected even more wounds, until he said, 'I am no more use now.' And the loyal officer cut off Shenyin Hsu's head and, having wrapped it carefully in a cloth, stole away.

With the loss of Shenyin Hsu, his men drifted back to their families. The Chu ruler had already abandoned his state to the Wu invaders so there was little they could accomplish on the battlefield. The ruler's final order, before he took flight, was to have 'elephants with lighted torches tied to their tails stampeded in the direction of the Wu army'.

Fleeing from one place to another, the Chu ruler was at last obliged to seek assistance from Qin. 'The state of Wu,' he told his host, 'is a long snake little by little eating away at the states of China proper . . . If it should become your neighbour, your border lands will surely be

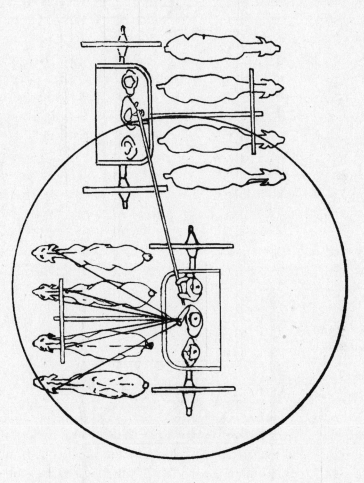

A halberd being used to disable a passing chariot

troubled. Before Wu has time to digest its conquest, you should come and take your share of territory, for if Chu is to be destroyed, its lands had best become yours.' Responding to this intriguing mixture of threat and enticement, the Qin court agreed to dispatch 500 war chariots to restore the Chu ruler to his throne. In a hard-fought campaign the Qin expeditionary force pushed Wu out of Chu. The restored Chu ruler put on a brave face, but there was no way of disguising his dependence on

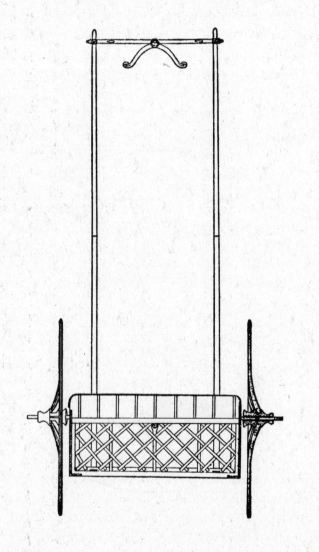

Dished wheels, a Chinese advance in chariot design

Qin military support. It took the southern state generations to regain the strength and wealth it had enjoyed before Wu Yun started his war of personal revenge. No matter how 'barbarian' Wu might seem to Chu or Qin, in some respects semi-sinicised states themselves, the fact remains that through Chu refugees this power had mastered the ancient Chinese art of war. Tactics during the Spring and Autumn period, as we have seen in the *Zuo zhuan*, revolved around chariotry. Armies combined chariots with infantry, the former being the preferred fighting vehicles of a warrior aristocracy in pitched battles located on plains. Infantry, composed of the lower orders living in cities and peasants who accompanied their noble masters to war, served for skirmishes, protection of chariots and their crews, storming fortifications, fighting in rough terrain, and guard duties. The most important weapons were the composite bow for chariot warriors and the halberd for infantrymen. The latter was a lethal combination of spear and battle-axe. Tied to the end of a shaft, often a length of bamboo, its sharp point extended to one side by as much as 40 centimetres. Judging from extant remains, the metal used for weaponry right down to the Qin unification of China in 221 BC was bronze, and not iron as was once thought. Further excavation may justify the view that the shattering victories of Qin over the other feudal states were achieved by means of low-grade steel weapons, but for now there is no archaeological proof.

It appears that the halberd, or a special adaptation of it, was also part of a chariot's standard weaponry. This halberd usually measured well over 3 metres in length, which meant that a chariot warrior wielding it sideways could strike down the charioteer in a passing chariot. Such an event could happen only when opposing chariots passed close to each other. At speed these passes were very dangerous for the crews of both chariots, not least because there was a real chance of protruding axle hubs hitting each other. The three-man crew of a Chinese chariot comprised the charioteer who stood in the middle of the chariot box, directly behind the draught pole; to his right was stationed the halberdier, to his left the chief chariot warrior who was armed with a composite bow. Body-armour was at first made out of treated sharkskin and animal hide, metal mail-coats appearing only in the sixth century BC. For reasons of safety there were occasions when the bowman and the halberdier swapped sides. The *Zuo zhuan* records this happening once as the result of a warning given in a dream. A bowman was warned of his approaching death, if he remained in his accustomed position in the chariot.

Besides the long halberd, there was a shorter spear for repelling infantry attacks on the chariot crew or the team of horses. For hand-to-hand combat all members of a chariot crew carried 'horse-head knives', daggers for stabbing anyone rash enough to mount the chariot. As in Indian and West Asian chariot battles, the prime weapon of attack and defence was the arrow fired from a composite bow. Its power, we are told, was enough 'to pierce seven layers of armour'. Everything possible was done by the arrowsmith to ensure ease of firing and trueness of flight. The best arrow shaft was said to come from a cane exposed to the sun on one side only. This gave the sunward-side a greater density, which combined with balanced fletching allowed a near perfect trajectory. All arrows were covered in a layer of lacquer, as indeed were composite bows. In ancient China the archer acquired an almost cosmic significance. So impressive was the strength and accuracy of the composite bow, prior to the invention of the even more effective crossbow, that it was believed the legendary Yi once used this weapon to save the world from destruction. This sage-king had to deal with nine extra suns, scorching the earth almost to a cinder. They were the wayward children of the sun god Di Jun, who until then had been able to ensure that they only crossed the sky one at a time. When Di Jun realised the catastrophe his children were about to cause, he reluctantly handed over a vermilion bow capable of shooting them down, which Yi did 'to the relief of the myriad people, who were grateful enough to recognise him as the first ruler of China'. In early illustrations Yi is usually shown aiming a composite bow, while the suns he has already shot down perch in the tree of life as crows. In a later version of the myth the fallen suns are said to have formed in the eastern seas a fiery rock, which continually belched out smoke and flames.

But whatever the value of the halberd or the arrow in disabling an opponent's chariot, the splendour and the exhilaration of chariot warfare never ceased to fascinate the ancient Chinese. The chariot itself was the subject of innumerable eulogies; the following poem dates from the early eighth century BC.

> On my chariot, small but swift,
> And safe with decorated straps
> Whose five bright silver rings harness
> The handsome horses to the yoke,
> I stand, tiger skin at my feet,
> Relaxed and ready for the fray.

The assurance of the poet, chariot warrior or charioteer, in the performance of his vehicle is not unlike that of the fighter pilot during the Second World War. Confidence in the Spitfire, in its easy handling and top speed, gave the Royal Air Force the edge in combat over southern England throughout the summer of 1940. Like chariot battle, aerial combat relied on teamwork and quick reactions. There was no room for hesitation and uncertainty. Once battle was joined the fighter pilot and the charioteer had to know exactly what their war machines could, and could not, accomplish. Failure to do so meant disaster, even death.

Excavation of ancient Chinese chariots has confirmed the descriptions of them in the earliest texts. Wheels were constructed from a variety of woods: elm provided the hub, rose-wood the spokes and oak the felloes.

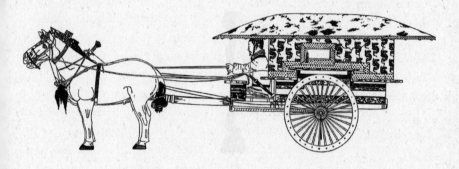

Bronze chariot from the tomb of the first emperor at Mount Li

The hub was drilled through to form an empty space into which the tampering axle was fitted, and between the two a tampering bronze bearing was inserted, the whole being covered with leather to retain lubricating oil. Though the number of spokes varied, a wheel by the fourth century BC usually had thirty-two of them. Records show how elaborate was the testing of each completed wheel: flotation and weighing were regarded as the best measures of balance, but even the empty spaces in the assembly were checked with millet grains. One outstanding constructional asset of the ancient Chinese wheel was dishing. This final development of the wheelwright's art did not appear in the West until the Middle Ages, at about the time the collar harness also came into use. Dishing refers to the dishlike shape of an advanced wooden wheel, which looks rather like a flat cone. Such wheels give extra strength against sideways thrusts occasioned by uneven or rutted surfaces. Referred to as 'cake wheels', the advantage they provided was fully understood and utilised by Chinese chariot-makers. On occasion they chose to strengthen a dished wheel with a pair of struts running from rim to rim on each side of the hub. As these extra supports were inserted separately into the felloes, they would have added even greater strength to the wheel. The first horse-drawn chariots appeared at Anyang, one of the capitals of the Shang kings who ruled ancient China between 1650 and 1027 BC. These vehicles were of the pole-and-yoke type, the standard chariot model of India, West Asia and Egypt. Within a millennium, however, Chinese chariot-makers had developed a vehicle with shafts, the precursor of the true carriage or cart. This design did not make its appearance in Europe until the end of the Roman empire. Because the shafts curved upwards, and the harness pressed against a horse's shoulders, not his neck, the shaft chariot was incredibly efficient. An example, unearthed at Changsha in Hunan province, could be pulled by a single animal. It dates from the first century BC.

Better harnessing seems always to have been typical of the Chinese chariot. The breast-strap harness had almost certainly been invented by the Spring and Autumn period, the era of the *Zuo zhuan* chariot battles. Its perfection during the later Warring States period (481–221 BC) in all probability explains the survival of chariotry, alongside cavalry, on the battlefield. So efficient did the war chariot remain that, in 221 BC when the ruler of Qin became the first emperor of China, he expanded the plans for his tomb to include an army of life-size terracotta warriors, including charioteers, as a protection in the afterlife. More than 700,000 workers were drafted to build China's first imperial palace and its first imperial tomb complex. In one of the underground chambers at Mount Li, the burial site, there is a unit of war chariots and cavalry, with some unmounted support. The remarkable speeds attributed to Chinese chariots must have resulted from a more effective harness. One charioteer is praised for the ability of his team of horses to maintain a gallop on sand, a surface likely to slow down or even stop a chariot. Though not directly connected with the improvement of the harness, a story about the philosopher Mo Zi's attitude to invention is revealing. He lived some time after the death of Confucius in 479 BC, and held high office in Song, where his expertise in defensive strategy would have been an asset to this minor state. According to the story, a gentleman in Song constructed a bird from wood, and when completed, it flew. For three days it stayed in the air, and the inventor was proud of his skill. But Mo Zi said to him, 'Your achievement in constructing this bird is not comparable with that of a carpenter making a linch pin for a chariot. In a few minutes

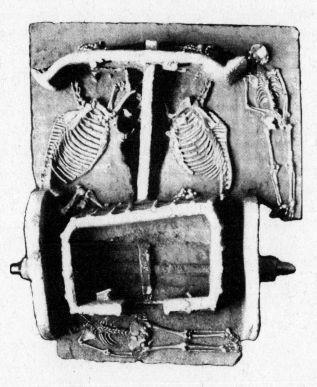

The Anyang burial with two men

he cuts out a tiny piece of wood which can carry a great load. Indeed, any achievement which is beneficial to man may be said to be skilful, while anything not beneficial may be said to be clumsy.'

For the philosopher the chariot was the supreme example of success; its lightness and speed remained the wonder of ancient China. The display of aeronautics he discounted because of its unreality, its lack of practical application to a contemporary situation. In Lu, his native state, Mo Zi ran a school, and from there his followers intervened in political squabbles, offering both ethical exhortation and practical aid. The power of his appeal was indeed his interest in the technical rather than the moral side of statecraft. Almost as if government was a machine, he sought methods of improving its working and warned rulers of the dangerous strains introduced by wars; he said that states should seek ways of self-defence and self-preservation only as long as aggression troubled China. That humble craftsmen later on transformed the breast-strap harness into the modern standard, the collar harness, would not have surprised Mo Zi.

The remains of pole-and-yoke chariots at Anyang, the site of the last capital of the Shang dynasty, come from burial pits associated with major tombs. The number of chariot burials excavated so far is twenty. Most were found to contain one or more chariots, usually with horses, but sometimes also with charioteers. Chariot burial was a sure method of asserting social superiority, a privilege restricted to the upper reaches of Shang society. The earliest chariots buried at Anyang are not well preserved, little besides their bronze fittings having survived. But in later burials it is possible to discern the outline of chariot construction – the box, the draught pole, the axle and the wheels. In one pit archaeologists uncovered a chariot, the skeletons of two men, and the skeletons of two horses. It is evident that the men had been killed and laid in the pit before the chariot was lowered into place. The wheels, axle and the draught pole fitted into trenches that allowed the chariot box to rest on the bottom of the pit, taking the weight of the wheels and protecting them from damage. No weapons were placed in this pit, or in half of those so far excavated. What is perhaps most significant about this find concerns the draught pole, which has the upward curve common in the Chinese chariot. The wheels possessed eighteen spokes, and were secured to an axle capped in bronze with wooden linch pins. At this stage of chariot construction though, the wheels were still not reinforced with metal fittings. Chariots belonging to the Zhou kings, who ended Shang rule in 1027 BC, had bronze on their felloes and hubs. No bits or cheekpieces were found in the pit, but both are known from other Anyang chariot burials. By both West Asian and Egyptian standards, Anyang chariots are large. The six chariots preserved in Tutankhamun's tomb were intended to carry two passengers at the most. Their floor dimensions are 100 cm wide and 50 cm front to back, while their wheels measure 95 cm in diameter. For Anyang chariots, the floor measurements are 135 by 85 cm, while the wheels exceed 135 cm. And their floors were usually made of wood, like the chariots of Wu described in the *Zuo zhuan*.

The first Chinese dynasty for which there is a conclusive archaeological trace, the Shang was reputedly established by the semi-legendary Tang around 1650 BC. A royal genealogy preserves the names of seventeen monarchs who together reigned for half a millennium, until they lost the heavenly mandate to rule. 'Because of his arrogance,' one of Tang's ministers said of cruel Jie, the last king of the legendary Xia dynasty, 'Heaven viewed him with disapproval, caused our Shang to receive the mandate, and employed Your Majesty to stir up the people.' It has to be noted that the cruelty of Jie is minor in comparison with that practised by Di Xin, the last Shang king. But as both rulers are described as being almost the same, we should guard against a tendency among Chinese chroniclers to explain a change of dynasty in terms of virtue sweeping aside corruption. Ancient historians perceived events as moving in cycles, whereby a new cycle began when a new hero-sage toppled the worthless tyrant of the old house and set up a new rule. Whatever the truth behind the savage deeds of Jie, tradition is unanimous in its praise for the just overthrow of an unworthy ruler by Tang, who was admired for both his military exploits and the attention he paid to domestic affairs. Efficient government coupled with the promotion of increased agricultural output upon which, during campaigns, he could support his army, now equipped with the chariot, gave supremacy to the new Shang house. The period which Tang inaugurated marks the emergence of civilization in China, as the Shang people distinguished themselves in handicrafts and technology; they introduced stone carving, bronze-casting, chariot warfare, systematised oracle-taking, urban palaces, kingship, nobility, massive public works, an accurate calendar, a pantheon of deities, and great tombs replete with treasure and sacrificial victims. Yet above all else, the Shang gave ancient China a centralised realm that was capable of embracing all the tribal groups living north of the Yangzi river.

It was during the first season of excavations at Anyang, from 1929 to 1937, that archaeologists started to wonder about the possibility of an importation of the chariot. Its abrupt appearance there and the striking similarity Chinese models, though larger, bear to West Asian and Egyptian types led to speculation about the transfer of this war machine across the Old World. But for many years it proved impossible to find archaeological sites in Central Asia which pointed to such a decisive transfer of ancient technology eastwards. The great steppe of Central Asia, running from the western reaches of the Yellow river all the way to the Caspian Sea, has long been the home of peoples famed for their horsemanship. Domestication of the horse, as we have already suggested, took place on the steppe, if not here, then further west in southern Russia. And so it would not be unreasonable to expect the steppe peoples to have experimented with all kinds of horse-drawn transport, including the chariot. While horses remained small in size, a chariot team offered the swiftest means of travel. Only when they grew larger under domestic care and selective breeding was there scope for cavalry. This was the military situation of the Assyrian kings, who in the eighth century BC deployed cavalry in addition to chariotry. Prior to this development, chariots remained the chief means of mobile warfare. Speaking of the Sigynnae, who dwelt beyond the Danube, Herodotus claimed their 'horses were snub-nosed with shaggy coats. They could not carry a man, but are very fast in harness, with the result that chariots are the rule.'

It is highly probable that the shift from driving a chariot to riding a horse repeated itself many times as different peoples bred their native stock to riding size or imported larger animals from peoples who had begun the process earlier. By the end of the western Roman empire, in the fifth century AD, it appears that the chariot was nowhere used on the battlefield. At the time of the chariot's arrival in ancient China, however, there were no cavalrymen to challenge its supremacy. The ruler of Anyang then, King Wu Ding (died 1189 BC), was delighted with his new acquisition, and for its manufacture and maintenance he set aside workshops manned by privileged craftsmen. Craft production in ancient China was always the preserve of rulers and their trusted supporters, who supplied specialists with the materials they required in order to make a complex item like a chariot, provided them with food and shelter, and perhaps even freed them from all other duties.

Archaeological testimony for the progress of the chariot eastwards to China is twofold. First, there are the chariots unearthed from burial mounds in the western part of Central Asia, and especially the Caucasus region. The second piece of evidence we now possess is more or less realistic rock paintings of chariots from the eastern part of Central Asia. The very oldest Central Asian chariots were discovered in 1972 near

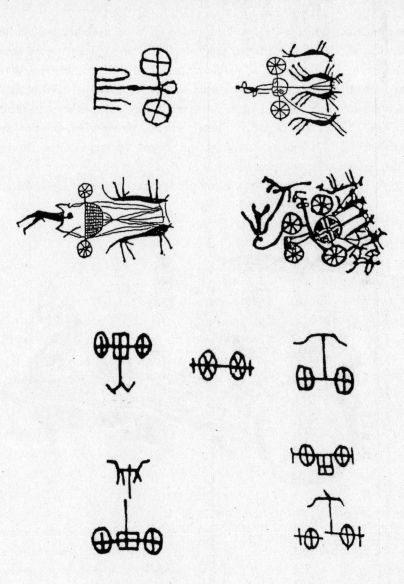

Rock drawings and Chinese pictographs of chariots

Rimnikski, a Russian city to the east of the Ural mountains. There among the graves were the remains of five chariots, plus the skeletons of horses. Despite the poor state of their preservation, the vehicles indicate that before 1500 BC chariotry was in operation among Central Asian peoples. These finds relate to the Lchashen discoveries, the wagons, carts and chariots which so excited historians in the 1950s because of the obvious parallels between these ancient Armenian vehicles and Chinese ones. Wheel construction in particular seems much alike. Whereas West Asian and Egyptian chariots at first had wheels with four spokes, later moving to six or eight, Lchashen wheels were made with up to thirty spokes, a number favoured in China. An even closer technique used by Armenian and Chinese chariot-makers could be seen in the bronze clamps used to strengthen felloes.

No chariot burial has come to light in the eastern part of Central Asia,

Chinese carriage showing the breast-strap harness and the upward carving shaft

but what have been found in great quantities, and across a wide expanse stretching through the Pamirs into Mongolia, are stylised rock drawings of horse-drawn chariots. The drawings do not attempt to show wheels with a large number of spokes, but nor does the Shang ideogram for a chariot. The latter was drawn in very simple fashion – two wheels and a draught pole. Horses were never shown, unlike in the Central Asian rock drawings. Some of these ancient drawings even indicate that the horses yoked to chariots were stallions, while others depict charioteers struggling to hold the reins. Draught teams vary between two and four horses, the former being the most common, presumably for the good reason that they were easier to draw. Difficult though rock art is to date, the general view is that the numerous chariot paintings range from the late second to the early first millennium BC. Confirmation for this dating is believed to have been found at Arzhan, where Russian archaeologists excavated in 1971 a royal tomb containing horses with riding saddles. This eighth century BC burial is taken as proof of the existence of a mature horse-riding culture in far eastern Central Asia, a stage of equine evolution that must have come after the driving of chariots. Horseback riding always followed on from the employment of horses as pullers of vehicles, whether they were carts or chariots.

From the Central Asian chariot burials and rock drawings it is possible to conclude that no feature of the first Chinese chariots was unique to China. Oracular inscriptions from the reign of Wu Ding indeed reveal the alacrity with which this foreign import was adopted for the purposes of warfare and hunting. One inscription tells of the king pursuing 'a rhinoceros' when his chariot collided with another and 'the king's chariot overturned'. Again we are told how the king was 'driven by his charioteer' on a hunting expedition with greater success this time. 'The chariot' suffered 'no harm'. On the battlefield oracular inscriptions show an interest in military formations, as we learn of chariots being accompanied by hundreds of foot soldiers. They also note the booty collected after a victory. 'Captured from Wey twenty-four men, from Erh 1,570 men, from Fan . . . horses, two chariots, 183 shields, fifty quivers, and . . . arrows'. This inscription then goes on to mention the sacrifice of captured noble opponents to various deities. Victims were not restricted to those of high rank, however, as beneath the foundations of ceremonial buildings at Anyang were placed the bodies of ordinary prisoners-of-war. Human sacrifice lingered on after the fall of Anyang, gradually declining before the humanist teaching of Confucius and his followers. In the first century BC a prince was severely punished for forcing slave musicians to follow him into death: his lands were confiscated and his son disinherited by the emperor. Despite the insight Shang oracles provide for the earliest use of the chariot, they throw no light on how it actually came to be imported. From whom the ancient Chinese learned of this revolutionary war machine there is no mention. But today a people canvassed for the introduction of the chariot from the Causasus into north China are the Tocharians.

The realisation that a hitherto unknown Indo-European language, Tocharian, was once spoken in the present-day Chinese province of Xinjiang amazed linguists and historians alike when it was deduced from documents recovered from ruins near the cities of Kucha and Turfan in the Tarim basin. The texts, in various states of preservation, are largely concerned with the Buddhist faith, although a few commercial documents also survive. The Indo-European language in which they are written has a closer affinity with the ancient languages of Europe, Celtic, Italic and Greek, than the speech of the Iranians and the Indo-Aryans. Yet it was the discovery of the Sanskrit word tokharika, meaning 'a woman from Kucha', in a bilingual text, which confirmed the name of the Tocharian people. The most startling evidence for an Indo-European people living in the Tarim basin as early as the second millennium BC, however, is the mummified bodies housed in the Urumchi museum. They came to the world's notice in the 1990s through the curiosity of American scholars visiting archaeological sites in Xinjiang. To their surprise the Caucasoid-looking mummies were not wizened and eviscerated like the swathed occupants of Egyptian tombs; instead, they were people dressed in their everyday clothes. So well preserved were the bodies, and others subsequently removed from graveyards around Urumchi, it was indisputable that they represent ancient Indo-European settlement of the Tarim basin. A wealth of artefacts was recovered from the graves, not luxury goods but simple items of daily use such as combs, needles, hooks, bowls and bridles. Disc wheels were unearthed too. No spoked chariot wheels have turned up yet in a Xinjiang excavation, which is odd considering that at Nonhong, to the south east in Qinghai province, one has been found and dated to 1200 BC. The survival skills of the Tocharians – some of whose mummified remains we now know are on exhibit at Urumchi – would have been honed in chariot battle, as they were elsewhere by Indo-Europeans seeking to secure the lands they had settled.

Like the Indo-Aryans in northwestern India, the Tocharians needed to be expert in horse-breeding as well as chariot manufacture in order to hold their own against rivals on the steppe. Hence the good fortune of the Shang kings in learning from them, or from others who copied their war technology, how to exploit the potential of the chariot. For the vehicle made its appearance in China already fully formed, unpreceded by any stages of development. There appear to have been no wheeled vehicles there at all prior to the chariot's arrival. Thus the ancient Chinese were able to jump a whole series of technical innovations without effort. What Chinese craftsmen quickly demonstrated though, was an ability to improve on the chariot's design: by the time of the engagements recounted in the *Zuo zhuan*, chariots were both larger and more robust in construction thanks to their solution of the harnessing problem that thwarted chariot-makers elsewhere.

The western origin of the chariot may not have been entirely forgotten by the ancient rulers of China. Looking westwards to Central Asia for answers to military shortcomings continued to be a policy as late as the reign of the Han emperor Wu Di. Its fine horses attracted this ruler's attention during his prolonged struggle with the nomadic Xiongnu, whose raids south of the Great Wall were a perpetual danger to the Chinese empire. An expedition was dispatched there in 104 BC, and after a three-year campaign, a Chinese general advanced beyond the Pamirs and obtained enough horses for stud purposes. The whole area, the so-called 'new territories' or Xinjiang, was declared a Chinese protectorate, though the city states based on its oases vacillated between the Xiongnu and China according to which side pressed them hardest. Nonetheless, the advent of Chinese arms in Central Asia disturbed the old balance of nomad power and this in itself weakened the Xiongnu, cousins of the Huns who later harassed Rome. Wu Di's imported horses additionally permitted the deployment of heavy cavalry against them, just as imported chariots had earlier assisted the Shang king Wu Ding in dealing with the Qiang, a northern people perpetually at war against him. Before the Great Wall was built the northern frontier was anything but static, which obliged the Shang dynasty to watch its various peoples with extra care. As the horse-breeding Qiang also had access to chariot technology, there was an arms race underlying their belligerence that only ended in a Shang victory through its greater concentration of resources. Surrounded by hostile peoples, Shang kings increasingly mounted campaigns to the north and the west, by means of which they established links with Central Asia.

Whether or not Shang kings had direct contact with Tocharian rulers we have no means of knowing. But a recently made suggestion that Indo-Europeans penetrated the Shang court as magicians and fortune-tellers, though still unproven, points to a way by which chariot expertise may have arrived in China. Chariot-makers could have been enticed to take up residence in Anyang, or they may have been brought there as

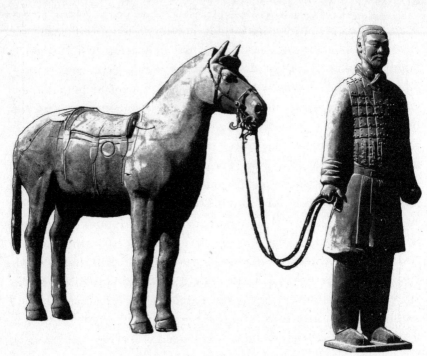

Cavalryman holding a horse

captured slaves. Qiang prisoners, for instance, were respected for their skill in the preparation of oracle bones. The cult of ancestor worship was intimately connected with divination from the cracks that developed in scorched animal bones, usually the shoulder blades of sheep, cattle and pigs, but sometimes deer. Questions put touched upon the business of state as well as family matters. Even though Qiang skill was not used in the actual rite of oracle-taking itself, this privilege being restricted to members of a lineage, there was no ritual reason for stopping a foreigner building a chariot for a Shang king or nobleman, not least because the ancient Chinese did not adopt the Indo-European practice of funeral games. Building, or maintaining, a chariot could therefore have been a task undertaken by a Tocharian, or another inhabitant of the Central Asian steppe familiar with Tocharian craftsmanship.

King Wu Ding deployed his newly acquired chariots in widespread campaigns. Their necessity signalled all was not well with Shang rule, which suffered under his successors a steady decline in authority until the last ruler, Di Xin, controlled little more than the environs of the capital.

According to the *Book of History*, an ancient collection of documents edited in the fourth century BC, Di Xin and his queen Dan Ji delighted in hurting others to such an extent that at last they alienated the Shang nobility. Dan Ji devised two new instruments with which to punish those who had accorded the throne inadequate respect. One was called 'the heater' and consisted of a piece of metal, made red hot in a fire, which accused persons were obliged to grasp with their hands. The other was a metal pole, greased all over, and placed above a pit of burning charcoal. The victim had to walk across the pole and when his feet slipped and he fell into the flames, Di Xin would burst out laughing. This was called 'roasting'. As intolerant of opposition was Di Xin when he gave vent to an uncontrollable rage against his uncle Pi Kan. Prince Pi Kan had decided that the situation was grave enough to risk death by reproving the Shang king. Consumed by anger, Di Xin exclaimed, 'I hear the heart of a sage has seven holes' and had Pi Kan cut open in order to see if he were one.

Such actions pleased few. 'The commoners complained and some of the nobles broke away.' Significantly, we are told how the 'senior and junior ritualists of Shang went to Zhou, carrying ritual and musical paraphernalia. Thereupon Wu, lord of Zhou, led his followers in a war these against Di Xin!' The defection of these experts in ritual would have been regarded as tantamount to a public declaration that the heavenly mandate to rule no longer resided with the Shang kings. The invading host of Zhou, which numbered 45,000 troops and 300 chariots, was confronted by the royal army in the wilds of Mu, west of Anyang. 'On a bright and clear morning, Zhou rose like an eagle', a poem tells us, 'and attacked the great Shang, its chariots pounding across the battlefield.' The chariot charge routed Di Xin's forces, but there seems to have been a certain amount of assistance from dissident Shang officers too. For 'those in the Shang front rank turned their spears and attacked those behind until they fled'. The stratagem would have been the work of nobles secretly in contact with Wu. As his enemies approached the capital, Di Xin 'climbed the Deer Platform, put on his precious jade robes, and went into a fire to his death'. The charred corpse was duly pierced with three arrows and the severed head hung on the top of a flagpole. In spite of the general hatred felt towards Di Xin, it was not until after Wu's death that the new Zhou house was effectively founded. The person responsible for this event was his younger brother Tan, who acted as regent during the minority of Wu's son. Well acquainted with the Shang nobility from his many years as a young man at the Shang court, this elder statesman has received great praise for the wisdom of his government. Looking back on these early years from the growing confusion of his own lifetime, Confucius (551–479 BC) regarded this age as a lost ideal. Tan suppressed a rebellion, drew up laws, established a central bureaucracy, organised schools throughout the realm, and showed proper respect for the fallen royal house by arranging for the continuation of ancestral sacrifices. His most conciliatory gesture was finding employment for Shang officials, a precedent that during subsequent changes of dynasty freed scholars from any slavish devotion to a royal lineage.

Even with the excellent start Tan gave the Zhou kings, they soon found themselves facing military difficulties similar to those that had dogged their predecessors. Fighting on too many fronts simply weakened Zhou arms. In 957 BC six armies were lost against Chu through an unnecessary drive southwards. Internal problems also arose under King Li (853–828 BC), whose suspicions of senior members of the nobility persuaded him to put his trust in a magician, 'who claimed to be able by his sorcery to point out anyone, no matter how remote from the palace, who had spoken ill of the throne'. After three years of this terror the people rose in rebellion, drove the king into permanent exile, and almost extinguished the dynasty. Only the steadiness and the self-sacrifice of a leading noble, the duke of Zhao, saved the heir apparent: to placate the rebels and preserve the royal house the nobleman magnanimously handed over – to their fury – his own son, who was about the same age as the prince. Although the dynasty recovered and in 788 BC was strong enough to withstand a severe defeat by barbarian tribesmen living in present-day Gansu province, the reign of the fifteenth Zhou king led to such a disaster that feudalism was put into irreversible decline and scope provided for the rise of autonomous states during the Spring and Autumn period. This king named You was, according to chroniclers, 'a thoroughly bad and unprincipled man'. In 771 BC the capital of Hao, just west of modern Xi'an in Shaanxi province, was sacked through an alliance of barbarian tribesmen and relations of the queen, who had been set aside because of You's preference for a concubine. The king was slain but, once again with the aid of great vassals, the dynasty survived the catastrophe, though a new capital had to be built in a safer position at Luoyang, some distance down the Yellow river. Royal power was shattered, and real power, real energy shifted to the nobles who held the largest fiefs. 'Another unwise act,' which tradition asserts helped to diminish the authority of the crown, 'was the ennoblement of the chief of the Qin people. Out of gratitude for sending soldiers to guard him on his way to Luoyang, the new king, the rejected queen's son, not only raised him to noble rank but also gave him sufficient land to sustain his position, the chief city of which was the old capital which he had just abandoned.' From this first warden of the western march would eventually descend Zheng, the first emperor of a united China.

With hindsight it was easy for ancient Chinese historians to conclude that this decision brought inevitable danger, for the reason that 'the very duties ennobled Qin would be called upon to perform could only develop his ambition, since the military capacity of his people was improved by their constant struggles with raiding tribesmen along the western frontier'. But the inevitability of the decision was caused by the extreme weakness of the throne. In 707 BC the alteration of political reality became transparent to all in the humiliating defeat inflicted upon the royal army by a tiny territory previously under direct Zhou control. Yet from the late tenth century BC onwards it seems hardly likely that a Zhou ruler exercised much influence at all over his chief vassals. Bows and arrows, along with war chariots, were regularly presented to one or other of these great lords on their appointment as commanders of expeditions against peoples, Chinese or foreign, who were deemed to be a danger to Zhou rule. One splendid chariot is described as having

> bronze fittings, with a decorated cover on the handrail, scarlet breast-trapping of soft leather for the horses, a tiger-skin canopy with a brown lining, painted leather axle coverings with gilded brake fittings, a fish-skin quiver, bright harnessing, and a scarlet pennant with two bronze bells.

The vehicle, the Zhou monarch said, was 'for service on the battlefield'. Chariot engagements prior to the better documented Spring and Autumn period seem to have been quite small, with numbers of chariots on each side rarely reaching 300. After 770 BC there was a great increase in the size of chariotry, the combined strength of all Chinese states approaching 10,000 vehicles. Before the Spring and Autumn period ended in 481 BC though, cavalry had already made its first appearance along China's northern border, introducing a radically new style of warfare, which in association with the crossbow, was to eclipse the chariot as a war machine. Several states with northern frontiers adjacent to the steppelands constructed walls as a method of dealing with nomad raiders. So serious did the threat become to Zhao, one of the three states formerly part of Jin, that its ruler disregarded the derision of his Chinese neighbours and bade his people adopt barbarian dress, for he took over not only nomad cavalry tactics but even the trousers worn by these fast-moving horsemen.

The Warring States period (481–221 BC) witnessed, as its name implies, an unprecedented level of warfare as well as a fundamental change in its nature. The mannered skirmishes of chariot-riding aristocrats were soon a thing of the past. For the decline of the chariot, in the face of the deadly crossbow, destroyed the link between aristocracy and war. Battles turned into large-scale infantry actions, with massed armoured columns of foot soldiers supported by crossbowmen, cavalry and chariotry. The new riveted iron mail-coats were far removed from the padded jackets or treated sharkskin and animal hide used in the lifetime of Huan, the first hegemon. With the demise of the hegemon system war became not just more professional and serious, but also very expensive as larger states absorbed their smaller neighbours and diverted more resources to military purposes. The powerful states of Qin and Chu could each put into the field over a million soldiers. Because the core of the contending armies consisted of highly trained and well-equipped regulars, rulers were anxious not to waste in unprofitable engagements what was a considerable investment. Sun Zi's *Art of War* cautions the eager commander against taking unnecessary risks. The realism of this fifth-century BC strategist stemmed from his appreciation of logistics, and their heavy cost. As he pointed out,

operations inevitably require 1,000 chariots, 100 supply wagons, and 100,000 mail-clad foot soldiers. When provisions are transported for 1,000 kilometres the expenditure at home and at the front, including entertainment of allies, the cost of materials such as glue and lacquer, and sums spent on chariots and armour, will amount to 1,000 pieces of silver a day. Such is the outlay required to put into the field an army of 100,000 men. When the actual fighting commences, and a victory is slow in coming, the weapons of troops grow dull and their morale weakens. Again, if a campaign is protracted, the resources of the state will prove unequal to the strain. When your weapons are dulled and morale is weakened, your strength exhausted and your treasure spent, others will take advantage of your distress. Then no adviser, however clever, will be able to save your state.

Yet the furious determination of Sun Zi himself in military affairs is not to be underestimated. When hostilities broke out between the states of Lu and Qi, he offered his services to the duke of Lu, who hesitated to accept Sun Zi's expert advice because of his marriage to a native of Qi. The issue of loyalty was settled by killing her. Sun Zi said he could find another wife more readily than an opportunity to direct a campaign.

This cold-blooded murder can stand as a symbol of the Warring States period. The ruthlessness of the battlefield could be disguised no longer: 'blood for the drums' ceased to be the occasional execution of a handful of prisoners after the fight when, in 260 BC at Chang Ping, the Qin commanders ordered the wholesale slaughter of Zhao prisoners. Allowing for anti-Qin exaggeration on the part of chroniclers, it is still apparent that the Qin army inflicted staggering casualties on opposing forces. From the records of battles we possess the combined total of enemy soldiers it killed in action amounts to nearly two million. Even this casualty list is incomplete, because the wounded are excluded, as well as enemy losses sustained in the campaigns for which no figures are given. The policies ultimately responsible for the new aggression were those of Shang Yang who, as we have noted, saw war as the sole purpose of a state. But this determination was merely the extreme expression of a general trend in political and military affairs, which was destined under the early Chinese empire to cause a reaction against glory on the battlefield that permanently subordinated the army to civilian control. Sun Zi's *Art of War* reflects earlier realities and relates how severe the code of discipline had become. When a Chu officer succeeded in taking a pair of Qin heads prior to an attack, he was himself beheaded for acting without orders. As the Chu commander-in-chief remarked, 'I am confident he is an officer of ability, but he is disobedient.' No room was left on the battlefield for the acts of valour so beloved by noble chariot warriors. All combatants were now expected to follow orders, presumably because the changing

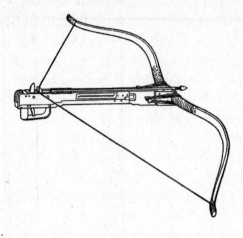

Crossbow

composition of armies had replaced the dominance of a warrior nobility
with a professional officer corps, which received without demur strict
obedience from the conscripted peasants who formed the infantry, the
bulk of the soldiers.

Crossbowman

Such a hierarchy based on military service grew out of the increased specialism evident towards the close of the Spring and Autumn period. Crack companies of soldiers were raised then as the personal retinues of rulers, and trained to move at speed to points of danger. By the period of the Warring States we know that these elite units were expanded as shock-troops capable of surprise thrusts. Wearing heavy armour, they could carry crossbows, swords and halberds, plus rations, over 100 kilometres in a day. Soldiers like these comprise the terracotta army buried alongside the tomb of the first emperor at Mount Li. Number one pit, which contains an infantry formation of 3,000 men commanded by chariot-borne officers, is known to be modelled on an actual elite unit, as excavators have found no two faces are alike. A degree of standardisation is apparent in each life-size statue's modelling, but the treatment of the heads by the potter-sculptor is unique. The formation stands ready for action in three armoured columns, to the front of which are deployed 200 sharpshooters drawn up in three ranks. Their clothing is light cotton because these bowmen and crossbowmen were long-range fighters, who discharged their arrows and bolts well before hand-to-hand engagements began. The three ranks would have taken turns at firing, so as to keep up a continuous stream of missiles. The majority were armed with crossbows, whose range exceeded 200 metres. These underworld guardians of Zheng, the Qin ruler who overcame all opposition and united ancient China, wore 'no helmets and attacked the enemy with untold ferocity', a chronicler records with amazement. 'Whereas the soldiers of the other feudal states when they entered the fray wore heavy armour which was clumsy and impeded their movements, the Qin soldiers threw away their coats of mail and charged headlong.' Armour was considered useful by them as long as it gave protection from arrows; once they clashed with opposing infantrymen it was better to freely swing the halberd. Into this mayhem chariots ventured at their peril, as indeed did any mounted soldiers.

The single most important technological development of the Warring States period was of course the crossbow, a weapon which greatly exercised Christendom on its arrival in the West. Prejudice against the crossbow, in 1139, led the Second Lateran Council to condemn it under anathema, except for use against non-Christians. In China the weapon was widely deployed by the end of the fourth century BC. Already Sun Zi was aware of its potential when he chose the crossbow as a metaphor for correct timing in battle. Speaking of an effective commander, Sun Zi argued

> that the momentum of one really skilled in war is irresistible, because his overwhelming attack is precisely determined. His ability to strike exactly when required resembles a drawn crossbow, for he is as quick as the release of the trigger.

So powerful and accurate were even the earliest crossbows that it was possible for a single crossbowman to match dozens of opponents armed

Terracotta depiction of a Chinese carriage

with other weapons. The overriding advantage of the crossbow lay in the chance of firing a bow far beyond the strength of the archer by reason of the mechanical release and holding of the bow string. Once bronze trigger mechanisms reached perfection, and sights were added, the crossbow ruled supreme. Fixed crossbows were tried on chariots with mixed success, but by the third century BC chariotry had been replaced by cavalry as the mobile arm of ancient Chinese armies anyway. Effective offensive weapons, whether composite bows or crossbows, had an inevitable impact on attitudes to warfare, especially in the absence of good body protection. In the *Zho zhuan* there are countless stories of feudal lords being killed by arrow-shots. Because the peasantry later came into possession of such a potent weapon as the crossbow, and their superiors lacked a foolproof means of defence against it, the balance of military power was never as one-sided in China as it always was in Rome. There disciplined legions equipped with excellent bronze and iron armour were able to hold at bay Rome's enemies and keep down a very large slave population, which had access to neither legionary equipment nor strong bows. The principal Roman weapons were the javelin and the short sword. When the enslaved managed to obtain substantial stores of weapons, as in the revolt led by Spartacus between 73 and 71 BC, the legions struggled to regain control. In ancient China it was quite different, with no clear superiority belonging to any section of society. Well before the chariot ceased to count on the battlefield, political wisdom accepted that the people of China had to be persuaded, rather than cowed by force of arms. Military might remained the ultimate argument but, as the Qin emperors were to discover, what was gained by force could not be kept by force alone. Mencius (372–288 BC), Confucius' greatest follower, could reasonably argue that the will of the Chinese people was a decisive factor which might express itself in justified rebellion against tyrannical government. This democratic theory, a kind of safety-valve in the Chinese constitution, meant that approval did not apply solely at times of dynastic changeover when the people could indicate the choice of a successor by resisting or accepting him, but also in ordinary times the major policies of government had to reflect popular opinion. Continuity could thus be guaranteed only through the ruler's adherence to traditional values, once the first imperial house of the Qin was pulled down by a nationwide rebellion of the enraged peasantry.

Despite the crossbow, nomad pressure on the northern frontier was a perennial problem for ancient China, as the Han emperor Wu Di's war against the Xiongnu between 134 and 91 BC proved to be beyond the empire's strength. Losses were high and the Xiongnu seemed forever capable of reviving as a potent enemy. A part of the problem was the terrain on which campaigns were fought. Supplies of food, weapons and fuel to deal with winter cold had to be transported long distances, and often commanders were left with inadequate supplies. These difficulties were graphically illustrated in the surrender of one of the best Chinese generals in 99 BC. Bereft of cavalry support, Li Ling managed with only 5,000 infantrymen to hold out against a vastly superior force of mounted nomad-archers. He positioned his crossbowmen behind a wall of shields and spears so that their bolts could outrange arrows shot from Xiongnu bows. The effect was devastating, and Li Ling showed that properly armed foot soldiers could defeat mobile archers. But without adequate food provisions and with crossbow bolts running low, he ordered his men to find their way back to the Great Wall as best they could. Only 400 soldiers reached the safety of its gateways, Li Ling himself being taken prisoner. This encounter is worth recalling because it is one of the few documented cases of direct competition between the crossbow and the composite bow. At Carrhae, fifty years later, a much larger force of Roman legionaries under the command of Marcus Licinius Crassus was unable to offer any resistance to mounted archers. They had nothing with which to return the fire from composite Parthian bows. Not only would Chinese crossbows have kept the Parthians at a safe distance, but even more their bolts would have ripped through armour and shields belonging to Rome's less mobile enemies. As ancient Chinese charioteers had long known, speed was no longer enough to keep a chariot safe from the attentions of the crossbowmen.

To deal with the Xiongnu, and other nomad peoples, defensive walls were extended and friendly relations established with some tribal groups, while in the north east a number of commanderies were formed on the Korean peninsula, the largest of which, Lolang, was administered from the site of modern Pyongyang. It is in Korea that we find the most easterly evidence for the chariot, although its use on the battlefield there remains undocumented. In tombs constructed during the era of the first purely Korean state, Koguryo, which asserted its independence from China in AD 12, there are numerous remains of harnesses and chariot fittings.

7

The End of the War Chariot

He advanced against me intent on combat. I defeated him, I
shattered his warriors, 3,000 of whom I slew. With their blood I filled
the wide plain. His arms, his royal treasure, his cavalry, I took away
from him. To save his life he climbed a steep mountain . . . Over the
plain I thundered like Adad, the storm god. Now my harsh rule is
established over Urartu.

Assyrian inscription

The first blow to the chariot's supremacy as a war machine fell in the
eastern Mediterranean during the twelfth century BC. This setback was
inextricably bound up with the widespread destruction then visited upon
cities throughout the region, a catastrophe usually blamed on the so-
called Sea Peoples. The name was coined in the late nineteenth century
to refer to the invaders from across the sea described by Ramesses III
(1198–1166 BC) in his account of their repulse from Egypt. Yet it is a
misleading name, for not all the perpetrators of violence came from
islands or even coastlines. One of these peoples, for instance, the Teresh,
whom the ancient Greeks called the Tyrsenoi, were inhabitants of Lydia,
a land-locked state in the western part of Asia Minor. The Teresh have
been linked to the Etruscans, Rome's northern neighbours. In 1200 BC,
according to Herodotus, there

was a great famine in Lydia. King Atys tried to distract the minds of
the Lydians from the famine but after eighteen years divided the
population in two. One half, under his son, Tyrsenos, emigrated.
They went first to the sea where they built ships which they filled
with provisions. They then sailed in search of new lands and
eventually settled in Italy, founding cities they still live in. They
called themselves Tyrsenoi after their leader.

Unreliable though Herodotus' date is, the tradition of migration he records is worth attention. Scarcity at home sent the Tyrsenoi abroad, so that by the eighth century BC their Italian settlements had coalesced into a league of city states capable of dominating early Rome. Another migration could have seen the Teresh seeking land in Egypt, just as it propelled the Peleset in the same direction from southwestern Asia Minor. But famine was not the only cause of instability and population movement. The Hittite practice of resettling large groups of rebellious vassals in new locations had an adverse influence on border areas, since they offered sanctuary to disaffected subjects. It was a problem that would later confront Assyria in its own heartland: there the policy of enforced resettlement came close to threatening the Assyrian way of life. In the Hittite empire, however, it always seems to have been the outlying territories that were the source of danger. This was particularly true in the western part of Asia Minor, where rivalry between Hatti and Ahhiyawa, the Hittite name for ancient Greece, had long been a feature of local politics. Hittite records note how, in the fifteenth century BC, a 'man of Ahhiya' campaigned alongside rebellious vassals with a force of infantry and 100 chariots. At this stage there was as yet still little Ahhiyawan settlement on the Aegean shore of Asia Minor – Greek colonisation really got started in the eighth century BC – but the city of Miletos certainly had Greek inhabitants. Cretan legend claims that Miletos was a colony of present-day Mallia, whose ancient name may have been Milatos. King Sarpedon of Mallia quarrelled with King Minos of Knossos and had to flee the island of Crete in order to escape his brother's wrath. Either Sarpedon or one of his followers took over an existing settlement on the site of Miletos and turned it into a major trading port.

Documents from the the reign of Mursili II (1321–1295 BC) mention the defection of Millawanda, a Hittite subject state, and its alliance with Ahhiyawa. If Miletos and Millawanda are the same, then we possess a rare insight into ancient Greek–Hittite relations as well as the increasingly unstable condition of Hatti's western frontier. Trouble started when a local ruler named Uhhaziti endeavoured to persuade other Hittite vassals to join him in a revolt which had the support of Ahhiyawa. Against the rebels Mursili sent 'troops and chariots' with some success, but his commanders proved unable to stop Uhhaziti interfering with Hatti's affairs as the rebel king continued to provide asylum for refugees from Mursili's authority. So at the head of a large army, supplemented with

An Egyptian ship battles against the Sea Peoples

levies from Syrian allies, Mursili marched against Uhhaziti confident in the outcome of battle, for the reason that his troops saw a thunderbolt, a sign that 'the mighty storm god . . . and all other gods were well disposed' towards the campaign. Illness prevented Uhhaziti taking the field himself, leaving Mursili to defeat his son instead. Afterwards Uhhaziti sought refuge on 'the islands', the Hittite records state, 'and there he remained'. What this actually means is shelter being provided for the deposed king on an Aegean island belonging to an Ahhiyawan ruler. About the fate of Millawanda we are uncertain and it is quite possible that Mursili ceded the city as a diplomatic move intended to satisfy Ahhiyawa and insure against future aggression in western Asia Minor. When Mursili's successor, Muwatalli II, drew up a list of potential troublemakers as he prepared for his confrontation with the Egyptians in 1274 BC at Kadesh, neither Millawanda nor Ahhiyawa were on that list. If this interpretation is correct, the diplomatic strategy failed, as Ahhiyawa did nothing to deter raids on Hittite territory. But Hattusili III (1267–1237 BC), the Hittite king who concluded peace with Ramesses II, sent a letter to a king of Ahhiyawa, whose sovereignty over Millawanda he recognised, to ask for the surrender of Piyamaradu, a Hittite renegade who was launching raids from the city. This approach worked: Piyamaradu left Millawanda, although he avoided Hittite custody through an escape by sea.

The disaster which struck Hatti around 1200 BC gave no advantage to Ahhiyawa, because the ancient Greeks were faced with calamity as well. Palaces and cities on mainland Greece were destroyed and abandoned. At first Miletos and the Aegean islands escaped the spreading destruction and remained prosperous. Then in the 1050s BC Miletos suffered assault, its eventual revival occurring when the Ionian Greeks migrated across the Aegean after the collapse of Mycenaean civilisation. The Athenians never doubted that their kinsmen were responsible for this second settlement of Miletos. Revolt in Ionia, between 499 and 493 BC, put this belief to the test, because Persia, then the dominant Asian power, crushed the rebel Greek cities with extreme force and installed compliant governments against the wishes of their inhabitants. Athens' Ionian policy vacillated dramatically. An Athenian squadron was withdrawn from the rebel fleet at the end of the first campaigning season. And in 494 BC a playwright was fined for writing about the Persian sack of Miletos. Although the fine was supposed to have been imposed because the Athenians were deeply distressed at the reminder of Ionia's misfortune, the actual reason was most likely a wish to avoid annoying the Persians any further. What this conflict represents is a repeat of the frontier difficulties faced by Hatti, which struggled less and less effectively at controlling the Aegean seaboard as well as the hill peoples who lived immediately behind it. Added to all this was the long-standing threat from the Kashka in the north, not far distant from Hattusha, the Hittite capital. These troublesome peoples were not in themselves the cause of Hatti's overthrow, any more than others like them were solely responsible for the end of city states such as Ugarit in Syria, but rather they brought pressure to bear on an empire already in the process of disintegration and accelerated its downfall. The strength of Hatti was a great source of stability in the eastern Mediterranean: its sudden fall reduced many places to a pre-civilized level of existence.

The idea of some kind of coalition bringing about the general destruction derives from Ramesses III's depiction of his defence of Egypt against peoples moving south from Syria by sea and by land. On the walls of his memorial temple at Medinet Habu, the pharaoh records how in 1182 BC foreigners

> made a conspiracy in their islands. All at once the lands were on the move, scattered in war. No country could stand before their arms, from Hatti . . . to Alashiya . . . They were advancing on Egypt . . . the Peleset, Tjeker, Shekelesh, Denyen and Weshesh, united lands . . . Against them I readied my troops and made the mouth of the Nile into a strong wall of ships . . . manned with picked man. The chariotry comprised the best runners and every accomplished chariot warrior.

Most of these attackers were new enemies. When in 1218 BC the Libyans had raided the Nile delta, their northern allies were the Shardana, some of whom had served as a bodyguard for Ramesses II, but whose homeland is unknown. The Teresh came from Lydia while the Shekelesh were most probably the Sicels who gave their name to Sicily. The Tjeker in Ramesses III's inscription seem to have hailed from the Troad and worn their hair in the distinctive upright fashion favoured by the Peleset. The Denyen were no strangers to the Egyptians, since letters in the Amarna archive refer to the 'land of Danuna'. It was situated to the north of Ugarit. Like the Shardana who also wore pointed helmets, the homeland of the Weshesh remains a mystery. Even though we can dismiss any notion of co-ordination amongst these peoples, the evidence suggests that Asia Minor was the epicentre of a storm of destruction which then swept across Syria and Palestine, before coming to a halt on the Egyptian frontier. A variety of peoples were attracted by the opportunities for plunder and land this great disturbance offered, once Hatti had collapsed.

The Hittites were in difficulties before the onslaught of the Sea Peoples. Their last ruler, Suppiluliuma II, had to deal with serious unrest in Hatti itself, as a result of intrigue over the succession. Suppiluliuma was the brother of Arnuwanda III, who in 1207 BC died after a very brief reign without descendants. Disunity at home did not assist the new king who found himself opposed by rebellious vassals as well. A letter addressed by him to the ruler of Ugarit complains about his lukewarm attitude to Suppiluliuma's succession. So weak had the Hittite crown become in Syria that it appears the viceroy in Carchemish was now virtually autonomous. But it was not the eastern vassals who worried Suppiluliuma most; his campaigns were directed against rebels and raiders in the western and southern parts of Asia Minor. The southern province of Tarhuntassa, opposite Alashiya or Cyprus, was vital, because its port of Ura handled imported grain from Egypt and Ugarit. Tarhuntassa may have ceased to acknowledge royal authority, because not only did Suppiluliuma restore control over the strategically important territory but he also conducted sea operations from Ura against Alashiya, previously a vassal of Hatti. It is possible in the three sea battles, and the one land battle, fought during this campaign that the defeated enemy was not Cypriot. Raiders could have been using harbours on the island as temporary bases in an early phase of the movement of the Sea Peoples.

Whoever the enemy, the Hittites prevailed with the assistance of the Urgaritian fleet. Correspondence between Ugarit and Cyprus at this time reflects a growing concern over a threat from the sea. The king of Ugarit is advised to 'fortify your towns, bring troops and chariots into them, and wait for the enemy with firm feet'. In reply the king had to admit the weakness of his military position, with both his army and navy on active service with the Hittites in southwestern Asia Minor. Neither Hatti nor Ugarit managed to weather the storm of the Sea Peoples. The sacking of Hattusha destroyed Hittite power, leaving only vestiges of its influence in Syria, where a number of small states continued to use the hieroglyphic script developed by the Hittites. One by one they succumbed to the powerful Assyrian army and by 700 BC they had all been incorporated into the Assyrian empire. Ugarit was abandoned like Hattusha, a joy for modern archaeologists but a nightmare for its inhabitants caught in the devastating sudden attack.

On Cyprus there were also sacking and burning at Kition and Enkomi, but on this densely settled island the lesser scale of destruction made it a refuge for those who fled from Ugarit. In Palestine the Sea Peoples' progress south along the route from Syria to Egypt took a heavy toll. The coastal city of Ashdod was destroyed along with a host of towns. For the Israelites Ashdod was one of the five great cities of the Philistines. The others were Ashkalon, Ekron, Gath and Gaza, the pillars of whose chief temple a sightless Samson pulled down and crushed his Philistine captors. After failing in their assault on Egypt, the retreating Sea Peoples split up, some entering the Jordan valley where the Denyen could well have become the biblical tribe of Dan, others like the Peleset settling on the coast. So close are the words Peleset and Philistine linguistically that there can be little doubt that the descendants of the Peleset were the Philistines,

The Shardana bodyguard of Ramesses II

the formidable enemies of the Israelites. At first the Philistines probably formed no more than a ruling warrior-class, but by the time of King David (1000–960 BC) they had become indistinguishable from the rest of the population. Prior to David's success against the Philistines, they had almost destroyed Israel. At this moment of crisis the prophet Samuel had chosen Saul as the liberator from the Philistine yoke. Saul's election as king, 'as all other peoples have', steadied the Israelites, although it was his successor David who founded a strong kingdom. Relations between the two war leaders were bad enough for David to hire out his personal following to the Philistines. They excused him from taking part in the battle of Aphek, which was fought beneath Mount Gilboa, a dozen kilometres south east of Megiddo. Taking advantage of the broad valley at the foot of the mountain, the Philistine chariotry tore through the Israelites,

> who fled before the Philistines, and many fell on Mount Gilboa. The Philistines overtook Saul and his sons; and the Philistines killed Jonathan and Abinabab and Malchishua, the sons of Saul. The battle pressed hard upon Saul; the archers found him, and he was badly wounded by them . . . So Saul and his three sons and his armour-bearer and all his men died together on the same day. When the men of Israel who were on the other side of the valley and those beyond the Jordan saw that the men of Israel had fled and that Saul and his sons were dead, they forsook their towns and fled; and the Philistines came and occupied them.

After this devastating victory, the Philistines captured the symbol of Israel's faith, the Ark of the Covenant, and razed to the ground the sanctuary at Shiloh. Hearing of Saul's death, David seized control of the southern part of Israel, and following the assassination of Ishbaal, the surviving son of Saul, he united all the Israelites in a single kingdom. Under David, and his son Solomon, Israel became, for nearly a century, a militarily powerful state. As the young David had told Goliath before their famous duel, he had killed lions and bears and the Philistine champion would die like them for having dared to taunt the ranks of an army under divine protection. Along with the Philistine dead Goliath's giant corpse would be devoured by birds and beasts.

When in 1182 BC the Peleset advanced on Egypt in the company of other Sea Peoples their identity was less clear. To the Egyptians they were nothing more than barbarous invaders. The first encounter between the Sea Peoples and the Egyptians was a land battle on the borders of Egypt and Palestine. Ramesses III's depiction of the action shows a confused mass of infantrymen and chariot warriors: the Egyptian troops and chariots and their Shardana auxiliaries struggle with an enemy also equipped with chariots. Yet it is not the fact that some of the Sea Peoples rode in chariots which is surprising, rather it is the presence of ox-carts loaded with women and children which seems so out of place on the

Peleset prisoners-of-war

battlefield. Either the Egyptian attack fell suddenly on a camp of the Sea Peoples, or caught the invaders on the march, thereby preventing them from deploying separately from their families. In the inevitable mêlée the Egyptians were at a considerable advantage. That there were two-wheeled carts drawn by oxen present reveals that this southerly movement of people comprised uprooted farmers seeking new land. They were not raiders, nor were they rootless nomads passing through areas of settled agriculture on the lookout for loot. The design of ox-cart and the humped oxen point to Asia Minor as these displaced farmers' homeland. After turning them back into Palestine, the Egyptians had to deal with another group of Sea Peoples moving south on water. In the sea battle, which took place in the Nile delta, the invaders were routed again. At Medinet Habu this victory is vividly depicted with Egyptian boats sinking enemy craft or driving them ashore where bowmen wait to finish off any survivors. These Sea Peoples are depicted sporting upright hairstyles as well as horned helmets, and carrying swords, javelins and large round shields.

So complete was the Egyptian repulse of the Sea Peoples that Ramesses III could boast how he 'overthrew those who invaded' Egypt's boundaries, and 'slew the Denyen, while making ashes of the Tjeker and the Peleset'. As Mesopotamia was spared an all-out assault, probably because the strength of Assyrian arms acted as a deterrent, there has been a tendency to give ancient Egypt undue credit for its defeat of the Sea Peoples. For in some ways the two victories marked the final glory of its power. The successors of Ramesses III were hard-pressed in maintaining Egyptian influence outside the country, and inside its borders there was a sharp reduction in the number of monuments erected by pharaohs. One reason for Egyptian weakness was dependence on foreign mercenaries, which was quite as damaging as the Hittite reliance on the forces belonging to powerful vassals and allies. At Kadesh in 1274 BC King Muwattali II of Hatti had needed to hire many mercenaries too. Ugarit seems to have heavily supplemented its forces with mercenaries, a practice fraught with danger.

Some of the best foot soldiers in the Egyptian army were the Shardana, who participated in 1218 BC in the Libyan attack on the Nile delta. Described in an Egyptian inscription as 'rebellious at heart', Shardana warriors were enlisted by Ramesses II, who even let some of them serve as his personal bodyguard. He had problems with certain mercenaries, but the Shardana are not mentioned as being among them. There is no reason to suppose, however, that Shardana warriors-turned-Egyptian-auxiliaries could not tire of their role in a regular army and turn into raiders again. A group of them migrated to Sardinia to which island they gave the name. Bronzes unearthed there reveal people with an appearance similar to Ramesses II's mercenary recruits. It does seem likely that integration of mercenaries like the Shardana into the armies of the great powers of the eastern Mediterranean, and especially as fast-moving foot soldiers who fought alongside chariotry, opened up new and terrifying possibilities for various semi-civilised peoples who previously had no connection at all with cities. Chariotry was discovered to be vulnerable to assault by the so-called 'runners' armed with javelins and swords. For at Kadesh Ramesses II had sent his Shardana 'runners' with success against Hittite chariots which came close to his besieged camp. These hillsmen fought with cunning and dash, as they avoided arrows fired from the composite bows of chariot warriors and disabled chariots through the injuries they inflicted on charioteers or chariot teams. Apart from this infantry intervention at a moment of crisis for the Egyptians, the battle of Kadesh was decided by chariotry alone. As in the battles recorded by the *Mahabharata* and the *Zuo zhuan*, the outcome was determined by two chariot forces charging against and past each other and then circling back to charge each other again. In ancient India the accuracy of the archers was decisive, whereas in China passing chariots could deploy the halberd as well as the composite bow. No infantry engagement occurred at Kadesh, once the Hittite king realised the extent of his chariot losses. Neither is there any mention of infantry action at the battle of Megiddo until Thutmose III was obliged to besiege the city itself. The implication is obvious: chariotry always started a battle, and then the advancing infantry behind exploited whatever tactical advantage had been gained. Otherwise the infantry halted and endeavoured to hold back an enemy advance, if its own chariotry had been worsted in the initial action.

Assyria was unusual in placing its trust in infantrymen. Mountainous terrain along its northern and eastern frontiers encouraged the development of a sizeable Assyrian infantry unmixed with mercenary levies. When enemies descended from these mountains and hills on to the plain though, the Assyrian king would use chariotry to defeat them. Thus Shalmaneser I (1273–1244 BC) dealt with the Gutians, a people inhabiting

A mercenary cutting off the hand of a slain Hittite charioteer

the Zagros range. The Gutians were frequent raiders. In the late third
millennium BC they briefly overran southern Mesopotamia, but their
stronghold was in the north opposite Assyria. Shalmaneser's chariot
victory over the Gutians is a reminder of the continued deployment of
chariotry in the Assyrian army wherever the terrain was suitable. From
records discovered at present-day Nimrud in Iraq, it is evident that
chariotry remained in the seventh century BC an important element in
Assyria's armed forces, notwithstanding the development of a corps of
mounted archers. Innovation in the breeding of horses had produced
larger mounts in Urartu, whose core was the Lake Van area to the north
of Assyria, and in Nubia, Egypt's southern neighbour. Horses were first
imported from the latter by Tiglath-pileser III (744–727 BC).

Egyptian weakness ensured by this Assyrian king's reign that Nubia
had been an independent kingdom for several centuries with its capital at
Napata, well to the south of Kerma. There the Egyptian god Amun was
still worshipped on the lines established by Thutmose III, the recon-
queror of Nubia. It was fortuitous for the Nubians, as their king Pianky
dominated Thebes, the site of Amun's great temple. In fact Pianky
tolerated a number of petty Egyptian kings as his subordinates, terming
them 'governors'. He had come to the Nubian throne in 747 BC, and his
sway in southern Egypt led him to revive the pyramid as a tomb for the
Nubian royal family on his return to Napata. Although he boldly stated in
his inscriptions that Amun had appointed him as ruler of Egypt, Pianky
preferred to spend most of the time at Napata, from which he played one
petty Egyptian king off against another. Not that this worried the
Assyrians, whose chief concern was the regular supply of Nubian horses.
Their trade enriched the Nubians and allowed the Assyrian army to
develop its cavalry. The successor of Tiglath-pileser III, Sargon II was
guarded on the battlefield by 1,000 cavalrymen.

Another factor in the rise of mounted soldiers was the bronze bit,
which gave early riders a certain degree of control. Once the more
sophisticated snaffle-bit came into general use, there existed an effective
means of communicating a rider's intentions to his mount, although the
absence of stirrups left the mounted archer or javelin thrower vulnerable
in the event of a collision. This shift from chariotry to cavalry began
shortly after the catastrophe brought about by the Sea Peoples. Then the
vulnerability of the chariot to infantry assault seems to have become
transparent. Fast-moving infantry, whom the Egyptians called 'runners',

Assyrian foot soldiers

had always accompanied chariotry for a number of purposes. They gave
chariots moving in column a degree of protection from enemy
skirmishers, stood guard over an encampment in which chariot horses
were unyoked and fed, and on the battlefield their presence ensured that
support was available for disabled chariots and wounded crews. The *Zuo
zhuan* does not dwell on the lesser duties of the 'runners' in comparison
with the heroic actions of charioteers and chariot warriors, but there is no
suggestion in its narrative of ancient Chinese battles that they could have
been fought without the services of these infantrymen. Each Chinese
chariot relied on the back-up provided by seventy-two foot soldiers,
whose speed of movement ensured timely assistance to a stranded vehicle.
The politeness displayed by chariot warriors to their opponents may have

The Nubian king Senkamanisken

had something to do with the presence of such infantry support. They could afford to be magnanimous in situations where an adequate degree of protection was available, for themselves as well as their opponents. But this early Chinese approach to chariot battle did not preclude hand-to-hand combat between foot soldiers from each side, nor did it stop them attacking enemy chariots in a mêlée. As warfare intensified towards the end of the Spring and Autumn period (770–481 BC), the old courtesies were replaced with a code of discipline which underlined a growing professionalism on the battlefield. In the eastern Mediterranean there never appears to have been an equivalent of the mannered chariot encounters so beloved by Chinese chroniclers. Chariot battle there was always more intense, with 'runners' expected to be in the thick of the fighting. Possibly the foreign recruitment of the 'runners', either as mercenaries or prisoners-of-war, led to this more pugnacious role, since they were used to irregular tactics. Ramesses II's Shardana recruits had a fearful reputation for hand-to-hand combat.

In reliefs cut at Abydos we can see how closely the 'runners' co-operated with chariots at the battle of Kadesh. Besides countering the activities of Hittite 'runners' during the assault on the Egyptian camp, the Shardana skirmished amongst the Hittite chariotry, finishing off immobilised enemy charioteers and chariot warriors. Their dispatch was clearly the job of the 'runners', who also severed enemy hands in order to number the dead. The presentation of hands to an Egyptian scribe after the battle was over may have been rewarded by a better share of the booty. From the account of Kadesh which Ramesses II had carved on various temple walls it can be deduced that Egyptian soldiers rarely acted as 'runners'. The same conclusion may be drawn from Ramesses III's record of the repulse of the Sea Peoples, not least because he deliberately chose to hire mercenaries rather than recruit men attached to Egyptian temples. Traditionally the pharaoh called up one in ten of the entire male population in time of war. The Egyptian infantry consisted of three main groups: conscripts, regulars and shock-troops. These were divided into formations of 200 men, and commanded by officers who bore a standard. Four junior officers, each responsible for fifty men, helped the commander of a formation in handling his troops. Many of Ramesses III's shock-troops would have been mercenaries like the 'runners' who served with the chariotry.

The Hittite kings maintained a regular army larger than that of the

Egyptian pharaohs, but they often had recourse to allies in order to supplement their forces. These were recruited from Ugarit and other Syrian states as well as from border areas settled with pacified rebels or tribesmen. The northern Kashka tribes were famous for their ferocity, a circumstance which caused the Hittites to employ the more amenable of them with care. Only in emergencies were the troops belonging to the great vassals inside Hatti required to join the royal army. Ugarit's military capacity was slight, although the Hittites were grateful for its navy. It would appear the Ugaritian army numbered less than 4,000 men, which indicates that its strength lay in chariotry, not infantry. According to Egyptian records, Muwatalli II stripped his treasury bare in order to hire mercenaries for the showdown at Kadesh. That the battle ended in a draw, or a partial Egyptian victory, must have been a disappointment for him and his troops, as there was no booty to help to defray the heavy cost of the campaign.

The involvement of foreign mercenaries in regular campaigning was of course dangerous for Hatti, Ugarit and Egypt, not least when they were used almost exclusively to support chariotry. For these hired troops could be as threatening to their own side's chariots as those of the enemy. But such an occurrence was unlikely as long as their numbers remained small, which seems to have been the situation down to the arrival of the Sea Peoples. Wandering bands of warriors were not a new phenomenon in the eastern Mediterranean, for these men were one of the sources of mercenary recruitment. They turned into a serious threat only when their numbers were great, or when they made common cause with mercenaries already in the pay of the countries they entered. 'Swarms' and 'hordes' were how the Sea Peoples appeared to those they attacked, probably because the defence of cities had previously relied on a small body of professionals. Swarming over chariotry, however, was the method by which these invaders revealed its battlefield limitations. They literally overwhelmed chariot warriors through sheer numbers. Where they failed to make headway was on the border of Egypt and Palestine. In the battle there the Shardana 'runners' of Ramesses III did not waver in their loyalty to the pharaoh, whose commanders seem to have surprised the Peleset, Denyen and even Shardana warriors in this column of Sea Peoples. Egypt escaped invasion, as did Assyria: both countries had good traditions of infantry warfare, despite the growing dependence of the pharaohs on foreign recruitment, and this may have been enough to see them through the crisis.

Afterwards chariotry continued to play a key role in conventional warfare, but its days of glory were numbered in West Asia and Egypt. No more could an army afford to rely on its performance to open the way to victory, when infantrymen were becoming the arbiters of battle, albeit supported by chariots and horsemen. Indicative of the changing face of combat was the engagement at Qarqar, in 853 BC, between the Assyrians and a confederation of Syrian and Palestinian states. The Assyrian king Shalmaneser III had commenced a campaign to subdue the lands west of the Euphrates, after those to the east had been subjugated. From military records the size of the Assyrian army at this period was still under 60,000 strong. A century later Tiglath-pileser III had at his disposal over 75,000 men, while under Sennacherib (704–681 BC) the number jumped to more than 200,000. But Shalmaneser III's army already had a large contingent of cavalry to fight alongside its chariotry. Horsemen were often deployed in mixed units with foot soldiers, which skirmished prior to the action and pursued fugitives after a victory. Exact figures are unavailable for the composition of the Assyrian army at Qarqar, which makes the detailed breakdown of its opponents' forces so interesting. Shalmaneser's scribes enumerated the Syro-Palestinian army as follows:

An Assyrian campaign against Arab raiders

Hadadezer: 1,200 chariots, 1,200 horsemen, 10,000 foot soldiers; Irhuleni of Hamath: 700 chariots, 700 horsemen, 10,000 foot soldiers; Ahab the Israelite: 2,000 chariots, 10,000 foot soldiers; Que: 500 foot soldiers; Musri: 1,000 foot soldiers; Arqad: 10 chariots, 10,000 foot soldiers; Arvad: 200 foot soldiers; Usanata: 200 foot soldiers; Shian: 30 chariots, 10,000 foot soldiers; Ammon: 1,000 foot soldiers; Gindibu the Arab: 1,000 camels.

In total, Shalmaneser faced 3,940 chariots, 1,900 horsemen, 1,000 camel troops and 52,900 infantrymen.

The prime movers of the coalition were Ben-hadad II, whom the Assyrians called Hadadezer, and Ahab, who was an uneasy ally of this Syrian king. Ben-hadad made demands on King Ahab of Israel that exceeded those considered acceptable in a relationship between dominant and subordinate powers. War ensued and the Israelites won, after which Ben-hadad promised to restore territory taken from Israel. Though he subsequently chose to hold on to a strategic strip of land along his southern border, the seriousness of the Assyrian threat obliged the two rulers to put their differences aside. The encounter with the Assyrians at Qarqar, on the Orontes river, was indecisive, but it was only a prelude to a series of attacks from Assyria, until in about 732 BC Tiglath-pileser III conquered Syria and installed pro-Assyrian rulers. The temporary withdrawal of the Assyrian army left Ben-hadad and Ahab free to pursue their feud. It ended in 841 BC at the battle of Ramoth-gilead, on the eastern side of the Jordan. Fearful of Ahab's skill as a tactician, Ben-hadad ordered his best squadron of chariots to seek out the Israelite king and 'fight him only'. The wily Ahab avoided its attention, fighting throughout the day in spite of an arrow wound. He feared that his men might mistake his absence from the battlefield in order to receive treatment, no matter how quickly he returned, as a sign of impending defeat and break ranks. 'So the king of Israel,' the Old Testament reports, 'stayed himself up in his chariot until the evening: and about the time of the sun going down he died.'

Qarqar shows how chariotry still retained a major role on the battlefield. The 1,900 cavalrymen on the Syro-Palestinian side, however, were heavily outnumbered by the Assyrian host, perhaps by as much as three to one. Cavalry was already well developed by the Assyrians and, by the middle of the seventh century BC, it would take over completely the mobile role performed by chariotry in their army. Before the battle of Qarqar it was not unusual for the Assyrians to campaign without chariotry. King Ashurnasirpal II (883–859 BC) had 'set off with cavalry and light troops' when he conducted a series of raids in a region of the Zagros mountains called Zamua, because its rugged landscape was 'unsuitable for chariots'.

The inscriptions of Ashurnasirpal are some of the most important in Mesopotamian history for their length and detail. They are indeed the first to describe individual campaigns. At Kalhu, the biblical Calah, which was some distance from the major Assyrian cities of Ashur and Nineveh, Ashurnasirpal built a new administrative centre for the growing empire and in the temple dedicated to the war god Ninurta there he placed huge stone reliefs inscribed with his victories. Their justification of violence as an expression of the divine will remains chilling. After heaping praises on Ninurta, 'the strong, the almighty, the foremost of the gods, the perfect warrior whose attack in battle is unequalled', the royal texts tell of the treatment Ashurnasirpal meted out to his enemies. Not only did he 'stand on the necks of his foes' and 'with their blood dye the mountains red like wool', but more precisely he 'cut off noses, ears and extremities' of captives, 'gouged out eyes', 'burnt prisoners', 'slashed the flesh of rebels' or 'flayed' them alive. One disloyal ruler had his skin 'draped over the wall of Nineveh'. Massacre, pillage, wholesale resettlement – these were the instruments of Assyrian domination, whose sovereignty was 'made supreme by Ashur and Adad, the great gods'. Harshness was taken for granted by Ashurnasirpal: his campaign accounts readily report flaying 'as many as rebelled' and placing 'their skins on stone monuments' or 'on stakes'.

What allowed this ruler to behave without apparent restraint was the power of the Assyrian army. Although he chose to describe himself as an 'attentive prince, worshipper of the great gods' and the 'designate of the warrior god Ninurta, destructive weapon of the great gods', Ashurnasirpal knew that his own position as a 'strong king' relied on the annual campaigns his soldiers waged against external and internal opponents. It was their efforts which provided the deportees to fill the city of Kalhu, modern Nimrud. Having rebuilt this dilapidated settlement, the king relates how he 'took people . . . from conquered lands', from cities over which he had dominion, and 'settled them there'. During his reign the Assyrian army was more homogeneous than in later years, but it

Tiglath-pileser III watching prisoners from Astartu

already contained allied troops as well as forcibly incorporated prisoners-of-war. Light is thrown on this practice of foreign recruitment by the 'horse lists' unearthed at a military building in Nimrud known as Fort Shalmaneser. Most of them date from the time of Sargon II (721–705 BC) and comprise among other things muster rolls, inventories of weapons and dockets for fodder. On one tablet there is information about a unit consisting of deported foreigners noted for their horsemanship. Some of its members were Israelites captured on the fall of Samaria in 721 BC.

Sargon II, who had just usurped the Assyrian throne, was keen to establish himself as an aggressive king, and so the reluctance of Hoshea to pay tribute provided a welcome opportunity for war. The Assyrian army captured the Israelite king and then laid siege to his capital Samaria. Once it was taken by storm, Israel ceased to exist and the country was annexed by Assyria. Where the old allied relationship was still feasible, Assyrian rulers seem to have stuck to this method of control but, wherever vassal kings proved consistently unreliable, they abolished local dynasties and, like the Romans, progressively annexed conquered territories, ruling them with an administration supported by strategically located garrisons. Opposition to Sargon's usurpation in Assyria itself had encouraged King Hoshea to defy the new Assyrian ruler. He may have received support from Egypt, for the Old Testament says that Hoshea 'had sent messengers to So, king of Egypt, and offered no tribute to the king of Assyria'. The prophet Isaiah took notice of Hoshea's lack of faith in divine assistance, and denounced him for putting his trust in Egyptian arms. The identity of So is problematic, and different interpretations have been put forward. All that can be concluded is the possibility of an alliance between Israel and a petty Egyptian kingdom in the Nile delta. Perhaps troops were sent from Egypt because in 720 BC Sargon enjoyed a victory over an Egyptian general named Raia. But this success was not sufficient to place the Egyptian ruler under any tribute obligation to Assyria, which became a direct threat to Egypt during the reign of Esarhaddon (680–669 BC). In 671 BC this Assyrian king overran the Nile delta and advanced upriver to seize Memphis. A rebellion incited by the Nubians brought Esarhaddon back to Egypt in 669 BC. As the Assyrians were unable to administer the northern part of Egypt themselves, they left this task to local collaborators who soon asserted their independence. Esarhaddon's son, Ashurbanipal, replaced these rulers with one pharaoh, Necho I, whose son Psamtik was to found the last Egyptian dynasty prior to the coming of the Persians in 525 BC. They were the inheritors of Assyrian dominion in Egypt and West Asia.

The inhabitants of Samaria who survived the siege were resettled in Assyria, where Sargon compelled enough of them to form a unit of 200 chariots which was added to the Assyrian army. There is disagreement over the composition of this unit: was it solely chariotry or did it include cavalry as well as chariots? The nub of the problem is the Assyrian use of the term 'commander of teams' for both chariot and cavalry officers. Its mention in connection with a unit largely, if not totally, recruited from Samarian deportees does nothing to clarify the situation. This means that Sargon could have created a mixed force of chariotry and cavalry. From records of his campaigns against the Medes, originally overlords of the Persians, it can be seen that he was pleased to capture horsemen as well as horses. On the eastern frontier of Assyria groups of Indo-European

people including the Medes and the Persians had begun to occupy the
mountainous terrain and impede Assyrian control of the region. Towards
the end of the seventh century BC, increased pressure from these people
helped to bring about the fall of the Assyrian empire. Its vulnerability was
augmented by a weakening of royal authority over powerful nobles who
seem to have been more concerned with their own estates than about
national defence. Another factor was the restlessness of a forcibly resettled
population, which dreamed of an escape from oppression. How foreign
units in the Assyrian army responded to the general uncertainty can only
be guessed. Assyrian cities fell one by one until Nineveh was taken and
destroyed in 612 BC. As one Israelite commentator said, the jubilation at
this event was inevitable because all had known Assyria's 'endless
plunderings' and 'unrelenting cruelty'.

That a 'commander of teams' could be either a chariot or a cavalry
officer is an indication of the profound change taking place in the
Assyrian army. While larger horses from Urartu and Nubia permitted the
Assyrian chariot to carry a four-man crew – a driver, two archers and a
shield bearer – they facilitated too the expansion of cavalry. First evident
in the mid-ninth century BC, horsemen had improved their battle skills
sufficiently within 150 years to exploit their advantage over chariotry in
all types of terrain. While cavalry replaced chariotry as a mobile striking
force, for skirmishing, flank attacks or hot pursuit, the new heavy
Assyrian chariot acted primarily as a firing-platform for archers, although
it was less mobile than before. The bigger wheels gave its crew one
notable advantage in compensation for the loss of speed: by raising the
chariot's floor they gave the archers a much better view. Assyrian kings
were quick to see how this higher firing-platform could be used for
hunting purposes. Huge stone reliefs from Nineveh record the pleasure
Ashurbanipal (668–627 BC) discovered in the chase. He can be seen firing
his bow from a heavy chariot during a lion hunt. One sculpture shows
the king shooting ahead, while two guards ward off with spears a
wounded lion attacking the chariot from the rear. This heroic encounter
is somewhat undercut by another relief, which reveals a gamekeeper
about to release from a cage a captured lion. As the monarch reserved to
himself the right to kill lions, they were collected in the wild and taken to
the palace for royal sport. Over the millennia kings have often chosen to
restrict the hunting rights of their subjects, for prestige as much as the
table. Yet there was at least an element of danger to Ashurbanipal's

Assyrian punishment of rebels

hunting. Not so for Napoleon, who suffered the indignity of a rabbit shoot which went hilariously wrong. One thousand tame rather than wild rabbits were supplied and, when the emperor arrived, they mistook him for the man who fed them their daily lettuce. Instead of fleeing to be shot they mobbed him and he was forced to dash to the safety of the imperial carriage. Where Ashurbanipal really surpassed Napoleon was in hunting on horseback, since one stone relief has him shooting wild asses pursued by hounds.

Doubtless these hunts were as carefully prepared as the ones with lions. Herds would have to be found for him without wasting too much time. More fascinating for us is his use of a bow on horseback. Even though a squire rides next to the king with a supply of arrows, the confident archery of Ashurbanipal marks the arrival of the mounted archer as the supreme wielder of missiles. The presence of the squire could well illustrate how Assyrian cavalry developed. A squire may have held the reins of a mounted archer, like a charioteer, when he first galloped into battle. Better reining would explain Ashurbanipal's ability to free both hands and fire a bow. With greater control over a horse, perhaps through a new type of bit, a mounted archer was thus able to spend more time in action and less worrying about falling off. To the Assyrians credit must be given for realising the potential of cavalry, and of the impact mobile archers could have on the outcome of infantry battle. They owed much to foreign horse breeders, but their readiness to concentrate on the development of cavalry altered methods of warfare and enabled Assyrian kings to remain masters of the battlefield until the close of the seventh century BC. In doing so they ended the career of the chariot as a war machine in West Asia and Egypt. Where it lingered on, its auxiliary function was no more decisive than the command vehicles employed for the direction of infantry formations during the Warring States period (481–221 BC) in China.

The Spring and Autumn period (770–481 BC) there differed in many ways from that of the Warring States, but they shared one thing in common: the frequency of fighting. Whilst the former witnessed the heyday of chariot battle, with engagements sometimes settled within the course of a single day, during the latter they were more prolonged as armies grew in size through the addition of massed infantry and cavalry. Manoeuvring and the ability to call upon reinforcements caused a number of Warring States' battles to exceed a week. Conflicts themselves tended to stretch over several years. In 314 BC Qi took advantage of internal problems in Yan to attack that northeastern state, and overran it in a swift campaign. According to the *Zhanguo ce*, a collection of historical anecdotes concerning the Warring States period, this military opportunity arose because of the weakness of the Yan ruler, who preferred to leave everything to one ambitious minister named Tzu Chih. We are told that

the ruler of Yan called in all the senior officials' seals of office and gave them to Tzu Chi. Then Tzu Chi faced south and was acknowledged as ruler. The former ruler pleaded old age, abdicated, and became a subject, while Tzu Chih conducted all affairs of state. In the third year of Tzu Chih there was a great rebellion in Yan, for its people had suffered, and they resented him . . . General Shi Bei and the heir apparent, Bing, attacked the palace with their supporters, but they failed to defeat Tzu Chih. In all this turmoil the common people even turned against Bing. General Shi Bei was

The impressive wheel on Ashurbanipal's chariot

King Ashurbanipal huntig wild asses on horseback

killed and tens of thousands followed him to the grave. At last Yan became afraid and its people rallied to the heir apparent . . . By then troops from Qi had made an attack on Yan. Not a soldier nor an officer opposed them, nor were gates closed against them. So Qi gained a great victory, and Tzu Chih fled. Two years later the people of Yan raised the heir apparent to the throne, and Bing saved the state from extinction.

Although Yan put up no resistance, the ruler of Qi boasted that a miracle must have enabled him to conquer a state in 'only fifty days'. Wars were obviously expected to last a long time. Thirty years after the Qi invasion a more conventional conflict occurred, when Yan revenged itself by attacking Qi, capturing the Qi ruler, and occupying half his territory. But Qi continued to resist and after five years of struggle the Yan army was finally expelled.

The bitterness between Yan and Qi, though more pronounced than the rivalry between the other feudal states, goes far in explaining why the northwestern state of Qin was allowed to expand its borders until they encompassed the whole of ancient China. Mutual antagonism made forming an alliance against Qin impossible until it was too late. The *Zhanguo ce* records the fear of Qin, which

shares customs with the barbarians. It has the outlook of a tiger or a wolf; it delights in cruelty, is keen to make gains and knows nothing of good faith, ritual, or virtuous behaviour. If an advantage appears, Qin will seize upon it with no regard to what happens to her kin, just like a wild animal. All China is aware of this . . . and the fact that Qin is a state which dislikes inactivity.

As this advice to a feudal ruler intent on attacking a small neighbour concluded, such a border war could only serve to weaken opposition to Qin, so that 'the day when all face west as its vassals will not be far off'. In the event the logic of the argument prevailed and no war was started, but steps were not taken to strengthen resistance against Qin ambitions. Another northern state accused of barbarian tendencies was Zhao, one of the three states into which Jin had split. So difficult did the Zhao army find repelling nomad raiders that in 307 BC its ruler, Wuling, decided to introduce a thorough military reform. Not only was a large corps of cavalry formed but even more trousers were borrowed from the nomads in order to make it easier for horsemen to ride and shoot their composite bows. Wuling's momentous decision is fully related in the *Zhanguo ce*.

One day Wuling said: 'The way of rulers is to be mindful of the virtue of their ancestors while they are on the throne; the rule for ministers is to devise ways to enhance their rulers' powers. Thus it is that a virtuous king, even when totally inactive, can guide his people and conduct his affairs with success; when active he can achieve such fame that it may exceed the past, to say nothing of the present . . . Now I intend to extend the inheritance I have from my forebears and make provinces out of barbarian lands; but though I shall spend my life in this enterprise, my eyes will never see its completion. I propose to adopt the horseman's clothing of the Hu nomads and will teach my people their mounted archery. Just think how the world will talk! But though all China laughs, I shall acquire the lands of the Hu and the Chungshan nomads.'

When a distinguished and loyal minister expressed reservations about this policy, Wuling frankly told him of the vulnerability of Zhao along its northern border. 'We share in the west river borders with the state of Qin and the Chungshan,' the ruler said, 'but command not a single boat upon them. From Chungshan to the state of Yan in the east, our border with

the Hu has not a single mounted archer. Therefore I have collected boats
and boatmen to guard the first, and deployed mounted archers in suitable
clothes to guard the second.' Abashed, the minister apologised for not
appreciating the ruler's reasons and instead having 'the temerity to mouth
platitudes'. A delighted Wuling immediately presented him with Hu
garments.

Afterwards the balance of forces in the Zhao army tilted towards
cavalry. Chariots are not mentioned again and the size of its infantry was
actually reduced in number. Even though there were continued protests
about these changes, Wuling stood firm in the knowledge that the terrain
over which his forces had to operate was best suited to mobile archers. As
he pointed out,

> 'My ancestor built a wall where our lands touch on those of the
> nomads and named it the Gate of No Horizon. Today heavy
> armour and halberds cannot go beyond this wall. Since benevo-
> lence, righteousness and ritual will not subdue the barbarous Hu, we
> must go and defeat them.'

So it was that Wuling, 'dressed in barbarian garments, led his horsemen
against the Hu leaving the Gate of No Horizon'. The stunning success of
this campaign opened up to Zhao the possibility of acquiring vast new
territories, 'even a thousand kilometres across'. Derision greeted Wuling's
innovation throughout China, but in the two other northern states facing
regular nomad incursion, Qin and Yan, the advantages offered by the
new cavalry were not entirely missed. They could see how greater
mobility was the means to dominate the steppe and the marginal tracts of
land adjoining it. Mounted archers remained, therefore, the specialised
troops of the northern frontier, and especially for forays beyond the
defences which eventually became incorporated in the Great Wall. One
of their greatest triumphs happened in 121 BC when Huo Quling, a
favourite general of the Han emperor Wu Di, led a six-day advance
across the steppe with a cavalry force and captured the Xiongnu leader
and 40,000 of his followers. But such victories were gained at enormous
cost in terms of human and animal losses, which meant the line of the
Great Wall was China's effective northern defence.

Cavalry was used by all the feudal states during the Warring States

ANCIENT CHINA
during the Warring States period

period, although not as mounted archers as in Zhao. The standard cavalry weapon became the halberd, perhaps as a result of the arrival of the toe-stirrup from India. Yet cavalry was not the cause of the chariot's decline, for purely Chinese battlefields were never dominated by horsemen: quite the reverse, the new power lay with armoured infantrymen, some of whom had in the crossbow a weapon capable of outranging the composite bow. Possibly because ancient China had such a variety of landscape, from the steppe in the north, through the great plain of the Yellow river valley, to the wet rice-growing areas of the south, its armies were bound to have developed in several distinct ways. Infantry rose to dominance first in the lower Yangzi valley, where lakes and swamps limited the use of chariots. The defection of Wu Chen in 584 BC to Wu, the feudal state straddling the estuary of the Yangzi, is usually cited as the reason for its early military success. This Chu turncoat in all probability brought the forces of Wu up to a high level of efficiency by introducing new tactics and ensuring a standardisation of weaponry, but he seems to have built on an existing infantry tradition. The Wu army under Wu Chen's direction also improved its chariot skills, as the state of Chu was to discover to its cost by the close of the sixth century BC, but the tremendous punch it delivered in battle came from infantrymen. They were as famous as their equivalents in the northwestern state of Qin for a ferocity and determination that left opponents aghast. As one chronicler noted: 'At this time Wu, following the advice of outsiders, crushed the powerful state of Chu in the west, filled Qi and Qin to the north with awe, and in the south forced the people of Yue to submit.' The struggle with Yue, a state situated to the south of Wu, had long been a thorn in its side, not least because Yue's strength resided in foot soldiers too. In 494 BC Yue was reduced to a dependency of Wu. The Yue people were not so easily subdued, however, and a sustained rebellion ended in the destruction of Wu. After 473 BC it was the Yue infantry which dominated the lower Yangzi and Huai river valleys, until in 333 BC a recovered Chu conquered the whole area. By then there were only seven

King Ashurbanipal leading two horses

major powers left: Han, Zhao, Wei, Qi, Chu, Yan and Qin; their loyalty to the Zhou king, the ruler of no more than a large estate at Luoyang, in the middle Yellow river valley, had entirely evaporated.

These were literally the warring states, whose conflicts lasted down to the Qin unification of China in 221 BC. Rising military expenditure was thus a factor in the replacement of chariots by infantry. Chariots were expensive to maintain, so that an army consisting mostly of them could be an impossible financial burden for a feudal state. An answer to the cost problem was an expansion of the infantry, which in turn lessened the importance of the war chariot. As a consequence of this change, a typical army comprised 'one thousand chariots, ten thousands of cavalry and hundred thousands of foot soldiers', according to the *Zhanguo ce*. Another reason for the replacement of chariotry by infantry concerned its vulnerability when assaulted by fast-moving infantrymen. In a parallel to the catastrophe experienced by West Asian and Egyptian chariotry, albeit on a smaller scale, a Chinese general suffered a serious reverse in 714 BC at the hands of northern barbarians fighting on foot. His chariots were almost overwhelmed by these lightly armed infantrymen. Well before Zhao abandoned chariotry for cavalry, Jin, the state from which it sprang, had realised the uselessness of chariots along the same northern border. Its earlier military solution was to form flying columns of infantry capable of intercepting the hit-and-run attacks of barbarian hillsmen. Their gradual reduction in previously unpenetrated mountainous terrain had the effect of removing a buffer zone which stood between the original core of China, the Yellow river plain, and the nomads who roamed the northern steppelands. The resulting increase in nomad raids explains the pressure on Zhao, which led its ruler Wuling to adopt mounted archery as a new means of defence, and also conquest.

So it was in the far north of China that cavalry came to enjoy a supremacy matched by infantry in the south. Over the Warring States period these new military formations steadily squeezed out chariotry. The aristocratic warfare of chariot-borne archers finally gave way to infantry tactics using armoured foot soldiers advancing with swords, halberds and crossbows. Such tactics required less individual skill but many more soldiers. They were in the main conscripted peasants, although these recruits supplemented professional foot soldiers, cavalrymen and chariot-eers. In the large-scale battles they fought there was no scope for courtesy, for the noble conduct that had typified the Spring and Autumn period encounters. No longer would a chariot warrior take care not to offend an enemy of superior rank, prior to an archery duel. War had ceased to be nothing more than a dangerous game as the feudal states now attacked each other without quarter.

Increasing numbers of the common people were drawn to the colours, since military life offered an escape from rural poverty and an opportunity for social advancement. Few successful commanders were of noble birth. There was no place for aristocrats in the deadly serious warfare that came to ravage ancient China, and threw up a new group of professional military leaders who understood strategy, supply and tactics. For them, and not only in Qin, which Shang Yang had virtually placed on a permanent war-footing, success on the battlefield meant social advancement. They did not need to be reminded of Shang Yang's dictum: better to face the enemy than to fall into the hands of the police. Even before the deliberate destruction of the feudal order after Qin defeated all its opponents, the turmoil of the Warring States period had already transformed both Chinese warfare and society. Unremitting inter-state wars swept away much more than the war chariot, for in the remaining feudal courts a similar transformation akin to the one on the battlefield took place. The greater complexity of state affairs gave rise to professional administrators with little sympathy for courtly manners, and none at all for noble claims of precedence. Learning, not birth, was the new path to ministerial power.

Less information is available about the eclipse of the chariot as a war machine in India than China. Chariots were still operational on ancient Indian battlefields when Alexander the Great reached the subcontinent. But at the battle of Hydaspes river, in 326 BC, the chariotry commanded by one of Porus' sons performed badly. Adverse weather conditions stopped its action before any damage could be inflicted upon the Macedonian vanguard as it was making a difficult river-crossing, since the Indian chariots got stuck in mud. The inability of the chariot to cope with heavy rain goes far to account for its eventual replacement in Indian armies by the horseman and the elephant.

But this abandonment of the war chariot was a slow process because of the status accorded to chariot warriors in the ancient Indian epics. Their deeds remained the exemplar of bravery. Utterly familiar were the elaborate rituals involved in duelling on the battlefield: blowing on a conch to challenge a worthy adversary; the sharp exchange of words before the loosing of arrows; a first blow provocatively knocking down an opponent's flagstaff; then the disabling of his horses or charioteer prior to aiming at his person. When the Pandava prince Arjuna shot the entire chariot team of Kripa, in a duel arising from a cattle raid, he stopped firing until his adversary had recovered his balance. For the wounding of the chariot horses sent Kripa reeling. Once Arjuna was certain that he had fully recovered from this setback, the duel continued with great ferocity, not least on Kripa's side. But a victorious Arjuna did nothing to prevent his wounded opponent from being carried away. Honour was satisfied, and there was a chance that Kripa would live to fight another day. Such restraint obviously removed some of the risks from chariot battle, although it proved insufficient to stay the general slaughter on the plain at Kurukshetra, the site of the great battle which forms the climax of the *Mahabharata*. In this epic poem the focus of the battle scenes is always the exploits of the aristocratic chariot warriors. Foot soldiers hardly receive a mention; their death at the hands of chariot warriors is simply regarded as a commonplace event. Yet they were critical to the clash of chariotry, as Kripa's rescue by his followers shows. Like the squad of infantrymen which accompanied each Chinese chariot, their presence was essential for the support of a fighting vehicle so prone to accident and damage.

In India then the chariot continued to play a secondary and comparatively insignificant role in warfare right down to the arrival of

Assyrian chariots struggling over uneven ground

Muslim armies in the eighth century AD. Hide-bound though Indian armies certainly remained, chariotry had fought well alongside cavalry before the Arabs arrived, and indeed before Alexander who preceded them. From the long passage Herodotus devotes in *The Histories* to the description of King Xerxes' army, it can be seen that the Persians valued both Indian horsemen and charioteers. Herodotus places the army review in Thrace, on the plain of Doriscus, where the father of Xerxes, Darius I, had built a palace and left a garrison. On that spot, Xerxes took a census of the expeditionary force which in 480 BC invaded Greece.

> Accordingly the Persian king drove in his chariot past the contingents of all the various nations, asking questions, the answers to which were taken down by scribes, until he had gone from one end of the army to the other, both foot and horse.

Amongst the horse Xerxes inspected an Indian contingent, 'some of whom rode on horseback, others in chariots drawn by either horses or wild asses'. They were accompanied by foot soldiers 'dressed in cotton', who 'carried cane bows and cane arrows tipped with iron'. After the naval reverse at Salamis, the Persian king rushed back to Asia in order to forestall any rebellion that news of military difficulties in Greece might encourage to break out. He left behind as commander his brother-in-law Mardonius, who was given the pick of the expeditionary force. He chose to keep

> first, the Persian regiment known as the Immortals . . . next, the Persian spearmen and the picked cavalry squadron, a thousand strong; and, finally, the Medes, Sacae, Bactrians, and Indians, both horse and foot. These contingents he took over whole; from other nations he picked a few men here and there by their appearance or by their reputation for valour, till he had a total force, including cavalry, of 300,000 men.

This force was soundly beaten at Plataea in central Greece, in the early summer of 479 BC. The Indians, who at the battle faced Greeks from the island of Euboea, may have perished in a rout which Herodotus claims cost 260,000 men their lives on the Persian side. Whatever the fate of the

Chinese cavalryman with halberd

Indian contingent, its selection by Mardonius is witness to the high regard
the Persians had for Indian military prowess.

As early as the *Rig Veda*, India's original text, we find reference to
heroes fighting on horseback as well as from chariots. One of its hymns
beseeches Indra, the god most worshipped by chariot warriors, for victory
on the battlefield: for 'heroes winged with horses' as well as 'warriors in
chariots'. Light cavalry should not be a surprising feature of ancient
Indian armies, considering the esteem in which the Indo-Aryans always
held the horse. After all, the name of the Asvins, the twin horse-headed
gods of India, derives from the notion of horse ownership. Asvin means
owing a horse of one's own. And like Chiron, the wise horse-man in
Greek mythology, the Asvins were renowned doctors, even physicians to
the gods. Doubtless this reputation had something to do with the
veterinary skills necessary for the breeding, training and welfare of horses,
whether used by cavalrymen or charioteers. When in 303 BC Megasthenes was in Pataliputra as the ambassador of Seleucus I to the Mauryan
court, he was deeply impressed by Indian methods for training horses. He
reports how

> it is a practice with them to control their horses with bit and bridle,
> and take them at a measured pace and in a straight line . . .
> Professional trainers break horses in by forcing them to gallop round
> and round in a ring, especially when they show marked signs of
> displeasure. Those who undertake this work need a strong hand as
> well as a thorough understanding of horses.

From other sources we are aware of the extent of veterinary knowledge
at this time, and not just animal diseases and their treatment, but also the
best ways of feeding, grooming and exercising horses. There was
additionally a science of signs, interpreting the auspicious or inauspicious
marks on each animal's body.

Fighting on horseback in ancient armies usually ended as fighting on
foot, however. Without stirrups it was impossible for horsemen to fight
man to man, as both riders would be knocked off their mounts. Cavalry
engagements usually began with a gallop towards the enemy, which
slowed at javelin range so that the missile could be safely hurled. This
might occur several times before riders dismounted and fought like foot
soldiers. When, or how, the toe-stirrup came into use in India is still a

mystery. Only mounted archers had no reason to be anxious about falling off their mounts. Their accuracy of fire, however, was less than an archer on the platform of a chariot. Apart from bouncing around on a horse's back, the mounted archer had to carry his quiver on his shoulder, and twist round whenever he needed another arrow. He also had to let go of the reins when shooting. That is why the Assyrian king Ashurbanipal went hunting on horseback with a squire, whose task was to hand the ruler arrows and keep an eye on the royal mount. When Ashurbanipal rode in a chariot, he could more easily balance himself on its leather platform and steady his aim. Whilst the extra quivers the chariot carried removed any worries about wasting arrows, the vehicle's movement was in the hands of an expert who knew the best approach to the quarry. Where horses were of course better than chariots was in uneven terrain, a shortcoming wheeled vehicles could never overcome, no matter the efforts made by the Assyrians to strengthen the hubs of royal chariots. It was an insoluble technical problem which accounts for the presence of both chariotry and cavalry in so many ancient armies.

Chariots had long disappeared from Greece by the time the Indian contingent of chariotry, cavalry and infantry took part in the battle of Plataea. So complete was the obliteration of chariotry in the Greek consciousness that, as we have noted, Homer was at a loss to explain the function of the chariot on the battlefield. The palace-strongholds of Mycenae and Tiryns were no more than impressive ruins, whose great walls of large boulders and hammer-dressed blocks of stone seemed to later Greeks the work of giants, the one-eyed Cyclops. Given this stark break in the historical tradition, there is no possibility of tracing the relationship in Europe between chariotry and early cavalry. After the catastrophe of the Sea Peoples which engulfed Mycenaean Greece as well as the island of Crete, all that can be said concerns a preference among the succeeding Greek city states for infantry combat. It was this emphasis on the foot soldier which gave the Greeks victory at Plataea. Once it was clear to the Spartan king Pausanias that the Persian infantry had no room for manoeuvre, pressed as it was from behind by a mass of other contingents, he led the Spartan phalanx forward. The fighting at first centred on a hedge of wicker shields. This breached, desperate hand-to-hand combat was the order of the day as Persian infantrymen were reduced to snapping the Spartan spears with their bare hands. Lacking heavy armour, they were no match for the finest infantrymen in Greece, despite showing the courage that had made them masters of a great empire. As the Athenian dramatist Aeschylus remarked, the spear had overcome the bow. In such an engagement there was little room for horsemen, and none at all for chariots.

8

Survivals, Ritual and Racing

As a young man you beat those older, as an old man you defeat the young ones, drivers of victorious four-horse teams. After completing six decades, you received, Porphyrius, a monument for your victories with the approval of the emperor, so that your fame might remain thereafter. If only, just as your fame is deathless, would your body be immortal too.

Greek inscription

The triumph was a procession in which a victorious general entered Rome in a chariot drawn by a team of four horses. Provided the senate accorded this honour to the returning conqueror, he could drive through the city streets at the head of his troops. A lesser honour was a procession on foot, which Marcus Licinius Crassus had to make do with in 71 BC, because the senators deemed his victory over rebellious slaves, no matter that they had terrorised southern Italy for several years, as unworthy of a triumph. The foe could not justify the adulation which a conqueror could expect to receive from the populace. Senatorial sensitivity about the award of a triumph, the highest honour Rome could bestow on a citizen, was understandable in a state preoccupied with war. After a successful campaign in 189 BC against the Galatians there was disagreement over the level of honour the Roman commander deserved. Celts who had settled in Asia Minor in the 270s BC, the Galatians persisted in raiding Rome's ally Pergamum after it was obvious that the recent Roman defeat of the Seleucid king Antiochus III at the battle of Magnesia had irrevocably changed the balance of power in the eastern Mediterranean. An effective method of dealing with the Galatians was found to be stones and sling-shot. During the campaign the Romans used a vast quantity of such missiles, which the historian Livy explains did much to demoralise the naked Galatians, prior to the battle taking place:

'Not one of them dared to run forward from their ranks for fear of exposing his body to shots from all sides; and as they stood immobile, they received all the more wounds for being so closely packed . . . Then in utter confusion, and exhausted from their injuries, the Galatians fled on the first Roman assault.' Some 8,000 of these Celtic warriors fell at this engagement near the Halys river. Two senators, however, objected to the Roman commander being awarded a triumph on the grounds that the enemy had been thrown into panic by missiles rather than the sword. Although stone throwers and slingers often played a decisive role in conflicts both on land and sea, there remained a lingering suspicion that somehow they spoilt the heroic aspect of war. How could one ride in a triumphal chariot after such a banal victory?

The triumphal Roman chariot, drawn by four horses, remains an oddity. There is no record of the Romans ever deploying the war chariot themselves, even though they encountered chariotry on the battlefield. At Magnesia, in early 189 BC, the confusion caused by disabled chariots helped the legionaries to gain a hard-won victory. Scipio Africanus, whose defeat of Hannibal had ended the threat from Carthage, vainly argued that Greece should not be completely evacuated of Roman troops after their victory over pro-Carthaginian Macedon, lest Antiochus III decided to invade it. This monarch already held Thrace and a fugitive Hannibal was urging him to take offensive action. Encouragement from a number of Greek states did lead to a Seleucid invasion, but for the first time a Roman army crossed to Asia in order to deal with Antiochus on his own territory. It was commanded by Scipio Asiaticus, the brother of Scipio Africanus, who came along as a member of his staff. The Scipios could muster no more than 30,000 men against an enemy army of over 70,000. After the defeat of the Macedonians, Antiochus knew the strength of Roman foot soldiers and he set out his battle line so as to exploit his greater variety of combatants, including elephants and chariotry. Despite attempts by pro-Roman historians to gloss over Antiochus' initial success, it would seem that the Seleucid attack routed one Roman legion and came close to outflanking others. Even though the retreating legionaries rallied and returned to the fray, this unprecedented event gave Antiochus confidence in the outcome of the battle, until a chariot charge totally miscarried. As soon as the chariots moved forward they were struck by a barrage of missiles, which crippled the teams of horses before they were able to get up speed. Their confused

The Monteleone de Spoleto chariot

retreat disturbed the ranks of the Seleucid infantry stationed behind them, thereby allowing the Roman cavalry to begin an outflanking movement. Once Antiochus' corps of elephants also collapsed, his army was forced to quit the battlefield and he had to accept defeat.

Once again Rome's well-drilled and well-armed foot soldiers had triumphed. It is almost certain that the Romans were indebted to the Etruscans, their northern neighbours, for the foundation of the legions. From them the Romans learned how to deploy in a phalanx, a solid line of spearmen. This Greek, possibly West Asian, formation was still the core of the Seleucid army at Magnesia: it was equipped with a very long thrusting spear, first developed in Macedon. As long as its members fought in close order, the phalanx was irresistible but, as soon as there was any disorder in its dozen or so ranks, it became a mass of unwieldy spears. Because Roman legionaries prided themselves on flexibility as well as the exploitation of opportunities during a battle, they were able to excel in the hand-to-hand combat into which most ancient battles inevitably degenerated. The battle line of the republican legion was much more open than the phalanx, and the individual soldier had more scope to use offensive weapons, as the Seleucid infantry found to its horror once the main action began. The looser infantry tactics the Romans later came to favour in no way invalidates their ultimate debt to the Etruscans, to whom they owed the triumphal chariot as well. This vehicle was a survival from the era of Rome's Etruscan kings and its ritual implications were occasionally an embarrassment to the religious belief.

The first Roman to have celebrated a triumph was Romulus, the founder of the city of Rome. After a victory over the nearby town of Caenina, Romulus led his soldiers back home laden with plunder. He carried himself the arms of their leader, whom he had killed. Livy recounts how

the victorious army returned, and Romulus divided up the spoils. Magnificent on the battlefield, Romulus was no less eager for popular recognition and applause. He took the armour which he had stripped from the body of the enemy commander, placed on a specially made frame, and carried it in his hands up to the Capitol, where . . . he presented it as an offering to Jupiter. At the same time he chose a site to be consecrated to this god . . . (promising that future spoils would be dedicated there by other victors). Such was the origin of the first temple consecrated in Rome.

Since unlike the Greeks, the Romans shrank from the enemy armour they had captured, dedications on the lines of Romulus' offering were rare. Usual practice was to burn it in the name of Vulcan, the blacksmith god. But the entitlement of Jupiter to a share of the spoils was never overlooked, and they were always offered after the execution of prominent prisoners. Human sacrifice seems to have been a feature of the triumph, especially when persistent enemies of Rome were among the captives. Perseus, the last king of Macedon, was lucky to escape such a fate when he was paraded in the triumph of Lucius Aemilius Paullus Macedonicus, who ended Macedonian independence at the battle of Pydna in 168 BC. He was banished instead to Alba Longa, the birthplace of Romulus' mother. Only when he died was Perseus shown any kindness, as the senate voted him a state funeral to spare the humiliation of a pauper's grave.

Romulus' triumph took place on foot. He did not ride in a chariot. The first to do so were the Etruscan kings, who took over control of Rome in the late seventh century BC. These rulers were not a small dynasty imposing themselves on a subject population. There was evidently such a sizeable infiltration that the Roman and the Etruscan communities merged into a homogeneous whole. After the Etruscan kings were expelled, the Romans retained as the symbol of supreme power the Etruscan device of a double-headed axe encased in a bundle of rods, the fasces, and the custom of victors entering the city in a triumphal chariot, the vehicle which carried the monarch on a victory parade. Etruscan religion also replaced the old, primitive worship of the Romans who had not thought of their gods in anthropomorphic terms or built residences for them, notwithstanding Romulus' supposed consecration of a temple for Jupiter. The new chief deities were Jupiter, Juno and Minerva, for whom a huge temple was built on the Capitoline hill with great statues after the Greek fashion. It was dedicated shortly after the fall of the monarchy in 507 BC.

The word triumph is of obscure origin. The Etruscans passed it to the Romans, but from where they obtained this description of a victory parade is open to argument. They may have got triumph via the Greek language, or it could have been a pre-Greek word which they brought with them when they migrated from Asia Minor. If it is a pre-Greek word taken over by the Etruscan language, quite independent of the Greeks, then certain aspects of the triumphal parade may be more readily understood. For the Etruscan rulers of Rome could be seen as enacting the divine role of West Asian kingship. That a triumph remained a great event, charged with tremendous significance, is evident throughout the period of the Roman republic. The best surviving account of a triumph is that of Aemilius Paullus over Perseus: thanks to this victory Romans never again paid taxes. The splendour of the triumph signalled to the ancient Mediterranean world that Rome had extinguished the homeland of Alexander, until then the model of the universal ruler. The wealth of the eastern Mediterranean was henceforth a Roman preserve. Yet Aemilius Paullus' triumph was opposed by his enemies, who even tried to turn his troops against him because he had not been as generous in the distribution of the spoils as they wished. Before the three-day procession, the inhabitants of Rome erected seating and decorated temples. The first day was given over to a parade of captured statues and paintings, plus a range of enemy arms. On the second day the plunder was on a richer but smaller scale, comprising silver objects used by the Macedonians.

> On the third day, at dawn, trumpeters led the way, sounding out ... such strains as the Romans use to rouse themselves for battle. Behind them followed 120 oxen with gilded horns ... Then came men carrying vessels heaped with gold coins. After these came the bearers of the consecrated bowl, which the triumphant commander had had made of gold and adorned with precious stones ... Then came the chariot of Perseus, which bore his arms ... After a short interval walked the king's children, two boys and a girl, led along as slaves; with them were a group of servants, teachers and tutors, all in tears, stretching out their hands to the spectators and showing the children how to beg for mercy. The children were too young to grasp the fate that had befallen them, and the thought of their future sorrows evoked great pity in the Romans. Perseus followed afterwards almost unnoticed, while the people, moved by compassion, kept their eyes upon the children ...

Not for a moment did the spectators feel any sympathy for the ex-king of Macedon, despite Rome forcing war upon him. At the battle of Pydna

20,000 Macedonians had fallen, the 3,000 men of the royal guard fighting to the last. Later Perseus gave himself up to grace this triumph. To the Romans he was an unworthy prisoner, a man who preferred to live like a slave than die like a king.

> Then Aemilius Paullus appeared in his chariot. He made an impressive figure, his advanced age merely serving to increase the dignity of his bearing. His attire was a purple robe interwoven with gold, and in his right hand he held a spray of laurel. The whole army also carried sprays of laurel . . . first cavalry, then infantry. Some sang comic songs, others hymns of praise for the victor, as was the ancient custom. The general's two sons, along with other distinguished men, followed after the triumphal chariot.

The brandishing of laurel was not especially Roman, since we know that the Spartans associated the plant with victory on the battlefield. It was regarded as a source of energy and strength, the very attribute of a successful soldier or charioteer. Whether in some way it was connected with the fertility role of the triumphal chariot itself is less clear. The chariot was decorated with a phallus, laurel branches, bells and whips. Given the inveterate conservatism of the Romans in matters of religious belief, the exact implication of this bizarre decoration is likely to elude us. In Rome nothing changed in ritual for fear of giving offence to the divine powers. Circumspection was everything. Priests prayed to Jupiter the most great and the most good, adding 'unless you prefer some other name'. And prayers were still recited long after their words had ceased to be intelligible.

In this context it becomes a racing certainty that the triumphal chariot once fulfilled an important religious function for the Etruscan kings. Putting the question of fertility aside, an Etruscan ruler of Rome could have acted the part of Jupiter when on special occasions he rode in a chariot. We know that the impersonation of deities did not give offence in Etruria, where West Asian ideas about the divinity of kings had taken root. When Aemilius Paullus celebrated his triumph his body was not covered in red lead, as the Romans dimly remembered victors once paraded. By then red, the colour associated with Jupiter, had ceased to be used by the triumphant commander for the good reason that the Romans considered it a sacrilege to impersonate the great god, even though he still

Four-horse chariots racing

wore 'Jove's tunic' and a slave held above his head a golden crown borrowed from the Capitoline temple. This change of attitude had occurred by the lifetime of Marcus Furius Camillus, the saviour of Rome after the Gallic sack of 387 BC. The celebrator of four triumphs, Camillus overstepped the mark during the one awarded to him after the capture of Veii, the wealthiest city in Etruria. We are told how

> the return of Camillus drew greater crowds than had ever been seen on such an occasion before, people from all classes pouring out of the city gates to welcome him. And the official celebration of his triumph left in its splendour all previous ones in the shade. But riding into Rome in a chariot drawn by white horses aroused fierce protests, with the result that Camillus was pronounced guilty of anti-republican arrogance, and even of impiety. Might there not be offence, people wondered, in allowing this man such dazzling horses and thus making him the equal of Jupiter as well as Sol, the sun god.

Here we have both strands of the triumph, the sacred and the profane, identified in two offences on the part of Camillus. As only Jupiter and Sol were entitled to a chariot drawn by white horses, he had encroached on the privileges of divinity. Odd as his religious views were, the Severan emperor Elagabalus respected the niceties of Sol's worship at the beginning of the third century AD, when he tried to make this god head of the Roman pantheon. The hereditary priest of the sun god El-Gabal at Emesa, present-day Homs in Syria, Elagabalus celebrated in the streets of Rome the god's festival on midsummer day by running backwards, facing an image of the deity carried in a splendid chariot. In contrast to this imperial abasement, Camillus harnessed four white horses to his triumphal chariot, making it worthy 'of the king and father of the gods', a patently sacrilegious act. The victorious general offended the Romans, too, by reminding them how their former Etruscan kings had driven in a similar fashion through the city. This was interpreted as outright anti-republicanism, a political rather than a religious statement, because the Romans had forgotten how their rulers once impersonated Jupiter publicly. Had they recalled the divine nature of Etruscan kingship, at least on triumphal parades, Christian apologists like Tertullian would have seized on such a pagan excess. Having converted to the new faith, this north African launched a wholesale attack on every aspect of pagan religion and culture. In the late 190s AD Tertullian castigated 'everything to do with shows . . . concerned with idolatry'. Since he chose not to single out the triumph for special criticism, it must mean that the original religious element was lost: the Roman commander might sometimes appear to impersonate an Etruscan king in his chariot, but never a ruler capable of divine impersonation. Even this lesser role was not without its problems in Rome, because Julius Caesar's unlimited dictatorship could never openly be likened to kingship, despite the irony of his own award of divine honours. The Romans were no longer familiar with the Etruscan meaning of the triumph – the god manifesting himself in the figure of the king – but they felt its periodic celebration somehow or other served to preserve the state. It drew upon ancient beliefs about the ruler's ability to ensure prosperity and peace. Behind the shrill sound of the trumpets, an instrument which both the Greeks and the Romans credited the Tyrsenoi with bringing from Lydia, came the peculiarly circular chariot of the triumphant general, the ritual guarantor of continued success on the battlefield. That he rode in a war machine never used in anger by the Romans was of interest to no one.

The numinous quality possessed by the triumphal chariot was still appreciated in early imperial times. Writing during the reign of the second emperor Tiberius (AD 14–37), Valerius Maximus praises a certain Roman citizen who was prepared to put his family at risk in order to assist the Vestal Virgins, the priestesses who tended the sacred fire of Vesta, whose perpetual flame was said to be a guarantee of Rome's survival. He recalls how after the capture of the city by the Gauls, when the Vestals were escaping with the sacred objects . . . L. Albinius, who was taking his wife and children by wagon, saw them, and being more attached to the state religion than to his private affections, ordered his family to dismount from the wagon. Once the Vestals and the sacred objects had been loaded, he abandoned his intended journey and carried them to the town of Caere, where they were received with the utmost veneration . . . How remarkable that a rustic and rather filthy, but conveniently roomy, cart surpassed then the glory of any triumphal chariot, no matter its radiance.

The reason for recounting this memorable deed was Valerius' desire to show the appeal Roman religion had for even the poorest citizen. In doing so he signals the awe with which Romans still regarded the triumphal chariot.

Roman amnesia over the original purpose of the chariot was not matched among the Etruscans, who placed complete vehicles in some of their tombs. This funerary aspect connects with the public spectacle of Roman bereavement, another event of great pomp in which there was an element of mockery, like the triumph itself when soldiers sang ribald songs about their commander. Again we encounter a need to remind the citizens of Rome that honour had to be earned by the individual. The city was in effect full of virtual kings: elected magistrates and senators whose robes were edged with purple, once the colour of Etruscan monarchs. Yet all these men were bound by the laws of the republic and, on their return to Rome from a campaign or a governorship, they had to be on guard. There was no shortage of ambitious young men to drag them through the courts. The funeral of a magistrate was, moreover, a public occasion on which the deceased's achievements could be judged. Wax masks of the faces of former magistrates, made at their death, were worn by actors, if the family of the deceased had such distinguished ancestors. In the funeral procession, these dead men, thus brought back to life, rode on ceremonial chariots in front of the hearse. At the funeral oration their deeds were recalled as well as those of the deceased, so that those present could reach a judgment as to their relative merits. Like the Etruscans, the Romans practised cremation as well as inhumation. According to the elder Pliny, in his *Natural History* which was published before his death in the Vesuvius eruption of AD 79, the burning of

A high official watching chariot racing in Rome

bodies is not an institution of great antiquity at Rome. Originally they were buried. The custom of burning them was started when the Romans realised, during their wars abroad, that tombs were not always sacrosanct. Nonetheless several families preserved the ancient custom. The dictator Sulla was the first of the Cornelii to be burned. He himself had given the order for this because, having disinterred Marius' corpse, he feared retaliation. Rivalry between Marius and Sulla, the so-called 'new man' and the established aristocrat, undermined the late republic because the latter had himself declared dictator by force of arms. As Marius died before Sulla returned, in 83 BC, from campaigning in Greece, the dictator was obliged to take revenge on his corpse. It was a characteristic action, since a retired Sulla later died of a burst internal ulcer through shouting too much when a corrupt official was strangled in front of him.

The mounting of reanimated ancestors on ceremonial chariots points to an Etruscan influence on Roman funerals. For the Etruscans the chariot was as much a status symbol as a vehicle for war and racing. Having fallen out of favour on the battlefield, it came to signify in processions the greatness of the rider, whether nobleman or king. Where chariots have survived in Etruscan tombs their elaborate decoration confirms this social function. One recovered at Populonia, opposite the island of Elba, boasts wheels with eight spokes and iron hoops. Its circular, or U-shaped, box is reminiscent of the rounded one always driven in the Roman triumph. Bronze and iron plaques, originally attached to a leather covering on the outside of the box, show scenes with lines of animals and hunters armed with spears. The tombs at Populonia, once a major seaport, were in use over several generations, and many of the burial chambers were robbed in ancient times. But treasures such as the chariot were missed by robbers because of their placement in side chambers. More fortunate still is the survival of the Monteleone de Spoleto chariot, now in New York's Metropolitan Museum of Art. Found near Perugia, this vehicle has extremely well-preserved, embossed metal panelling all round its box. The subject is the exploits of Achilles, and doubtless is the work of a migrant Greek artist. Its owner would have commissioned the decoration in order to display his high social position and heroic qualities, likening himself to the Homeric heroes. He rode in the chariot before his death and made sure it followed him into the afterlife. The expense of the vehicle is an indication of the esteem in which Etruscans, and their neighbours, held the chariot, as the Monteleone de Spoleto vehicle could have belonged to a Sabine leader, as modern Perugia is located outside Etruscan territory. To be without a chariot in ancient Italy was to be a nobody.

The Roman satirist Juvenal, a violent opponent of social change, was as annoyed at noble extravagance as he was at upstarts, especially if they raced chariots. He blamed the aristocracy for not displaying manners calculated to preserve its proper status. In his *Satires*, which date from the turn of the second century AD, he asks 'when did the purse of greed yawn wider?' Conspicuous consumption had become imperial Rome's curse.

For the rake, who has squandered his family fortune on fast horses, still believes he can enjoy preferment. Watch how he races down the Flaminian Way like Achilles' charioteer, reins grasped in one hand, his mistress shown off with the other, wrapped in his riding-cloak!

Straight enough to show off charioteering skills, the Flaminian Way, which eventually led to Gaul, was the scene of impromptu chariot races, to Juvenal totally unnecessary displays of wealth that only added to aristocratic debt. Fascinating here is his selection of private chariot racing as one of the heights of folly. It was wrong on several counts: false heroism, arrogant display, and unworthy conduct. Roman gentlemen were simply not charioteers, despite Nero's victory at Olympia with a ten-horse team harnessed to his chariot. The emperor had fallen from the vehicle and, although reinstalled, failed to complete the course. He was still declared the winner, a small compensation for what awaited him at Rome: enforced suicide in AD 68. But then Nero was addicted to praise and knew how high passions ran at the circus. As many as 300,000 spectators would cheer on star charioteers in the Circus Maximus, a huge hippodrome shaped like an elongated U, with a low barrier down the centre, dividing it into two runs. Again this event was Etruscan in origin. Just as the Romans retained the chariot of the Etruscan king for the celebration of a triumph, they embraced the chariot race as one of their favourite sports. If they avoided serious injury or death at the races, charioteers in Rome might end their careers with considerable riches – a belated compensation for the lowliness of their social position.

Important though the triumphal chariot remained for the Romans, it was the Indians who raised the vehicle to its ritual apotheosis as a processional car. Temple chariots grew so huge in India that they resembled mobile architecture, multi-storeyed conveyances for deities when their statues were paraded through city streets. Juggernaut is a word we have adopted in recognition of the sheer size of these great vehicles, some of which rolled along on six solid wooden wheels. From present-day temple chariots, the linear descendants of these ancient vehicles, it is obvious how the wheels have always been regarded as the critical component. In diameter often twice the size of a man, they are made from very thick planks, which are bolted crosswise against each other and strengthened with cross bars and iron tyres. The wheels are mounted on heavy iron axles, encased in the massive beams which carry the body of the chariot. The body itself is mounted on the chassis with the help of iron fittings and, in the larger processional cars, may have three or more projecting storeys.

At Srirangam, the southern Indian site of a temple dedicated to the saviour god Vishnu, the largest of the processional cars weighs over 20 tonnes and requires 600 people to pull it. However, the traction of the wheels on the ground and on the axle is so enormous that even this team of pullers is not sufficient to put the vehicle in motion. Essentially a temple town with six enclosing walls, Srirangam's street plan has been specially designed to accommodate the awkward movements of this great vehicle when it emerges once each month from the inner enclosure, for a procession. The number of times the temple chariot gets stuck on its way round the town suggests an almost deliberate device to remind Vishnu's worshippers of the magnitude of the god, who strode through the universe in three steps. 'All creatures dwell in his three wide steps,' his devotees know. 'His three footprints, inexhaustibly full of honey, intoxicate with their own prayer; he alone has supported three-fold the earth, the arching sky, and all creatures.' A further feature of Vishnu's all-pervasiveness was his substitution for Sthanu, the pillar which upheld the cosmos. The great chariot of the god is pulled round Srirangam to the accompaniment of music from a drum and a flute. Whenever there is danger of becoming stuck, the tempo of the music increases to encourage the team pulling the vehicle to greater efforts. At noon, when about three-quarters of the procession is completed, the vehicle is stopped for a break, the two pulling-ropes are put down and the curtains drawn, and the people go home for a rest. During this break all those who cannot take part in pulling the temple chariot, for reasons of health or age, come and touch the ropes lying on the ground, which transforms the occasion into a communal event quite different from the Roman triumph.

So widespread was the ancient appreciation of the chariot in India that it became totally integrated in ritual observance. Not only did it provide the prototype for the processional car, but large stone chariot wheels were also added as architectural decoration so that some temples appeared to be celestial vehicles. The most famous, though now ruined, example of a chariot temple is the one built for the sun god at Konarak, in Orissa. The whole temple is represented as resting on great wheels, being nothing less than a vision of Surya's own celestial chariot. The Indian equivalent of Helios, the Greek solar diety, Surya progressed across the sky in a chariot pulled by seven ruddy horses under the care of his charioteer Aruna, whose name means 'the red one'. That India should have looked upon the dawn as a god, the resplendent Aruna, rather than a goddess like the Greek Eos or the Roman Aurora, reflects a belief in the moral strength of

One of the chariot wheels on the Temple of the Sun at Konarak

light, as the return of the sun's powerful rays at dawn was said to mark the end of demonic influence each night. In the *Rig Veda* there is in addition to Surya's charioteer Aruna the dawn goddess Usas, but she seems to have been a source of anxiety rather than succour. Her dilatoriness could turn her into a menace when she held back the day, with the result that Indra the demon-chaser had to intervene by shattering her chariot and driving her from the sky. The temple of the sun at Konarak is supposedly drawn by horses, although two great elephants stand ready to provide extra strength.

Besides providing a means of transport for the gods, the chariot was used in India as a metaphor for human existence. The indestructible spirit was envisaged as the owner of a chariot, which comprised the body. Awareness was the charioteer, who used the bridle of thought to make sense of the horses of perception. As one commentator wrote: 'He who is devoid of insight and has not fully yoked and tamed his mind . . . will be at the mercy of his senses, like the runaway horses of a charioteer.' Only when the mind is calm and the senses are as disciplined as a good chariot team, we are told, is it possible to complete the journey to enlightenment in Vishnu's paradise, a celestial realm situated high in the sky. Nothing comparable to this elevation of the chariot as a universal metaphor occurred elsewhere. In West Asia there are biblical references to 'a chariot of fire' and 'chariots of iron', but they lack the centrality of the vehicle to Indian religious belief. The prophet Elijah's last ride may well have been in a fiery chariot: his departure from the world, however, was a miraculous happening and not really an exit from the toils of the world to which others might aspire. More mundane is the explanation of an iron chariot, since this seems to be the heavy vehicle developed by the Assyrians, once cavalry took over from the earlier light chariot the tasks of flank attack and pursuit. Assyrian chariot-makers added an iron tyre to its enlarged wooden felloe in order to make driving over rough ground safer. Though the ancient Chinese imagined sky-carriages without wheels, they tended to keep the chariot earthbound. When Huangdi, the legendary yellow emperor, quit the world to rejoin the immortals after an ideal reign, he was carried heavenward on the back of a dragon, along with his wives and his ministers.

In ancient Greece the chariot retained something of a ritual function in the regular cycle of games held at Olympia and other religious centres. No race track has ever been excavated at Olympia but inscriptions mention three kinds of contest: a four-horse chariot race over a distance of seven kilometres, a two-horse chariot race over four kilometres, and a race on horseback over three kilometres. Excavation of Nemea, the site of the youngest pan-hellenic festival, has turned up iron bits and snaffles, plus a bronze plaque which must once have been attached to the statue of a horse dedicated by its victorious owner around 500 BC. He would appear to have been a citizen of neighbouring Sikyon, a city facing the Gulf of Corinth. Prizes for winners at the four great games of the Greeks were rudimentary: they were crowns made of olive at Olympia, laurel at Delphi, wild celery at Nemea, and pine at Isthmia. These four games were distinguished from other, local, festivals, where cash prizes were given to the victors. They stood apart not only for the symbolic nature of their prizes and for the truce imposed on all Greek states during the time they occurred, but also for the pre-eminence of their competitions. Anyone who won at all four games was especially honoured. In equestrian events the winner was the owner, not the jockey or the charioteer, who was usually a slave or a servant. Whilst a few nobles drove themselves, the costs involved in maintaining a stable meant that charioteering was the preserve of the wealthiest families. The Boeotian poet Pindar has immortalised their victories as well as those belonging to a tyrant like Hieron of Syracuse. The advent of tyrants, especially in city states concentrated around the Isthmus, the narrow bridge of land joining the Peloponnese to the rest of the Greek mainland, was a response to the increasing instability which accompanied the decline of aristocratic rule. Except in Sicily, tyranny gave way in the fifth century BC to two forms of government: oligarchy and democracy.

Throughout this period of transition we encounter a concern with the past. Powerful aristocratic families constructed genealogies stretching back to the heroic figures of Greek legend, doubtless to justify their political leadership. They vied with each other in the pursuit of fame, believing that by doing so they emulated the exploits of the heroes celebrated in the *Iliad*. Naturally this competition spilled over to the cycle of great games, and not least into chariot races, the supreme Homeric contest. Yet even the winner of a lesser race could attempt to exploit the fame gained for political purposes. About 640 BC an ambitious noble by the name of Cylon, who had just won a foot race at Olympia, tried to seize power in Athens with the aid of troops lent by his father-in-law, the tyrant of Megara, a small state on Athens' eastern border. No Pelops, the winner of the lethal chariot race against King Oenomaus which had led to the inauguration of the Olympic Games, Cylon still came very close to establishing a tyranny on the strength of his reputation as an athlete. At Rome Cylon's prestige on the running track would have been irrelevant to a candidate seeking public office. There public games were part of a sequence of rituals that brought the military season to a close. They were intended to return the Romans to the ways of peace, to the rule of Jupiter. Second only to Jupiter in the Roman pantheon, the war god Mars had no proper temple in Rome itself. This exclusion is explained by the dangers of his domain, the battlefield. In contrast to the peace of the city, Mars was kept as a sentinel outside the walls, inside which arms should not intrude. As we have noted already, successful generals were permitted to march with their troops through the city streets only on the special days awarded for their triumph.

The Roman games commenced with a procession through the city, from the field of Mars, up to Jupiter's temple on the Capitol, back down to the forum and then across to the Circus Maximus, the venue for racing. Circuses were large buildings used first and foremost for chariot racing, although they doubled as race tracks for ridden horses and athletics, plus stages for gladiatorial combats and other popular entertainments. Gladiators were eventually moved to the Colosseum, a permanent amphitheatre designed to hold 50,000 spectators. Started by Vespasian, the first emperor to be raised to power by his troops in AD 69, the Colosseum was small compared to the Circus Maximus, into which it could fit twelve times. Whereas chariot racing in Greece was often a spontaneous and haphazard affair, in Rome it was highly organised and rigidly controlled. The first chariot race of which we hear, the contest staged at the funeral games of Patroclus near the end of the *Iliad*, was not untypical of many Greek races in that it took place in the open countryside. Nonetheless, many features of later racing are present, such as the use of the lot to determine starting positions, the race down a long straight to a turning-post, and the white stones placed by this sharp corner in order to prevent a chariot's wheel from colliding with the post. Cornering required special attention, as Nestor reminds his eldest son Antilochus before the race.

'There is no real need to instruct you. But expert as you are at cornering round the turning-post, your horses are slow, and so I expect you not to win. Yet even if the other teams are faster, their drivers do not have the judgment that you do. Therefore, my son, rely on your own judgment rather than muscle which distinguishes a good wood-cutter, and judgment which enables a steersman to guide a ship safely across the wine-dark sea during a storm. And it is by means of judgment that one charioteer beats another. The charioteer who leaves too much to his chariot and pair misses the correct line at the turn; his horses wander as he does not keep a tight control. But the clever charioteer, though behind with slower horses, always has his eye on the post and turns closely round it. He knows when to pull on the reins and when to give the team its head, while keeping a careful eye on the charioteer ahead.'

The white stones were in fact reproduced as a low kerb round the bottom of the turning-post in Roman circuses. Arguments over dangerous driving, which to an extent marred the chariot race put on in memory of Patroclus, were kept to a minimum in the Circus Maximus by an umpire, whose responsibility was to ensure that charioteers never interfered with their rivals' teams. To ensure further the fairness of the race for all competitors, the actual start was not left to chance. Starting boxes with gates were built into one end of the circus in such a manner that each charioteer had to travel almost the same distance. At a signal the gates on the boxes were then opened together.

These architectural developments were purely Roman innovations. Having acquired from the Etruscans a passion for chariot racing, the Romans went on to perfect the circus, whose massive structure was reproduced in major cities throughout the empire. During building works in 2003 at Cordoba, the old capital of the Roman province of Baetica in southwestern Spain, the foundations of a hippodrome were discovered. Preliminary study would estimate a seating capacity of nearly 100,000, a very large figure indeed for a provincial city. Its size has led to the suggestion that the audience witnessed more than chariot races in the circus, since the imperial authorities could have taken advantage of the entertainments held there to reinforce loyalty to Rome. Acclamation was a standard method of showing support for the reigning emperor. Every appearance of the emperor in public, whether at a formal ceremony or simply in his travel through the streets, was accompanied by a constant chorus of acclamations listing his titles and identifying him as head of state. On his return to Rome from duties in Italy or elsewhere, there was always a ceremony of welcome from the senate and the people; their acclaim of his safe arrival reaffirmed his authority as emperor, rather like another accession. Since only Roman citizens with regular access to the emperor could show this appreciation, events staged in the great public buildings of the provinces were in all probability occasions for a similar pledge of loyalty. They brought together large numbers of provincials who were reminded about their obligations to Rome. At times of uncertainty either the amphitheatre or the circus, as only the wealthiest cities could afford both, were the scenes of public scrutiny for those accused of disloyalty to the emperor. Thus Polycarp, the Christian bishop of Smyrna, was interrogated in the amphitheatre following his arrest. Nothing except a public denial of his faith could have saved him from death in AD 165, and this action Polycarp refused to make. The crowd called out for Polycarp to be devoured by a lion, but this was ignored by the Roman magistrate on the grounds that the wild-beast season was over, with the result that the bishop was burned alive instead. In the interests of public order, the conservative emperor Antoninus Pius had already attempted to limit the number of occasions on which those who refused to acknowledge the imperial cult could be actively persecuted, possibly because he recognised the potential danger of readily making martyrs, but there was little the provincial authorities could do to curb the enthusiasm for punishment which Polycarp faced in Smyrna. The sheer concentration of numbers in the amphitheatre ruled out anything approaching a judicial inquiry. Even Polycarp's words were drowned by cries of his guilt.

The best-preserved Roman circus, at Lepcis Magna, in modern Libya, has provided answers to most of the outstanding questions about chariot racing. A covering of sand prevented the removal of stone by later builders, so that its excavation was essentially a clearance operation. Apart from revealing the mechanism for opening the starting gates, the layout of the circus shows the care taken by the architect to give each competing charioteer an equal chance of winning. The alignment of the starting boxes is so precise that it reduced the advantage in occupying the one in the middle, closest to the barrier dividing the track into two. This was pole position, as it allowed a charioteer the straightest run on the first lap. In making the turn at each end of the track charioteers aimed to come as close to the turning-post as possible, even to graze the low kerb around it. Too close a turn, however, could mean the chariot striking the stonework and overturning. A plaque in the Vienna Kunsthistorisches Museum depicts the aftermath of such an accident, with attendants on foot struggling to capture and calm the horses. Along the barrier in the centre of the circus there were placed various monuments, including cones. These distinctive, tall pyramids had definite funeral associations: they feature on Roman and Etruscan tombs. Their frequent use as turning-posts seems appropriate, because charioteers were more often than not killed on this part of the track, and thereby dispatched on their way to the underworld. Another feature of the central barrier were lap-counting devices in the form of stone eggs or dolphins. They were

A chariot crash

moved to show how many laps remained in a race. For the Etruscans the egg also had a connection with the dead, although it may have been intended to signify rebirth, or life after death. In tombs the deceased are often shown holding eggs. But this might not be the sole influence in the choice of an egg as a lap-counting device, because the first one at Rome, erected in 174 BC, may have had a connection with a temple dedicated to the Dioscuri, Castor and Pollux. The Greco-Roman equivalent of the horse-headed Asvins in Indian mythology, they were the brothers of Helen, the egg-hatched daughter of Zeus. And they were also renowned as horse tamers and cattle raiders. In the Circus Maximus an attendant used to climb a ladder whenever an egg needed to be lowered. The alternative lap-marker was the dolphin, a creature famous for its speed. It was not introduced till 33 BC at Rome as an additional indicator of the laps run, a date which may be linked with the future emperor Augustus' naval successes against Sextus Pompey, the son of the old rival of Julius Caesar, Pompey the Great.

During the republic there were several stables responsible for charioteering. The Romans called them factions, and they sported different colours – red, white, blue and green – to distinguish the chariots they entered in each race. By the late empire, after Constantine the Great founded in AD 330 a new Christian capital at Constantinople, we hear most about two colours, the Blues and the Greens. The earlier business approach to chariot racing had been superceded by more state control: horses were provided from the imperial stables and fodder from the public granaries. Yet someone still had to supervise and instruct the staff who trained the teams of horses and maintained the chariots in working order, just as someone had to coach the charioteers. Perhaps it was to be

A chariot at the turning-post

expected that this role fell to the senior charioteer in each faction. These latter-day Kikkulis acted as what we would now term player-managers. The greatest of all was Porphyrius Calliopas, who switched factions with amazing ease. By 517 he had won so many races for both the Blues and the Greens that both had put up statues to him. At this stage of his racing career, when he was still in his twenties, it seems unlikely that he was more than a token faction manager, if his changes of allegiance are also taken into account. What set Porphyrius apart from other charioteers was his incredible number of wins. For as one inscription put it:

Fortune has yet to give you rewards worthy of your success, for your victories are greater than the good luck you have had. But may you stay with the faction, your first and best, melting the jealous hearts of your rivals who, when they look upon your ever conquering whip, are forever cursing their stupidity in losing you!

This plea to stay with the Greens is reminiscent of the reaction of present-day football fans when a key player asks to be put on the transfer list, or another club indicates a serious interest in buying him. Porphyrius was simply too good to be lost to the Blues.

In Rome the days on which chariot races occurred had grown from seventeen in the time of Augustus to sixty-six by the fourth century AD. This expansion led to an alteration in the way factions competed, as it became common for charioteers and teams of horses to transfer from one to another. The Roman charioteer usually began his career as a slave; if freed, he was at liberty to leave the faction. Not that this made a great deal of difference to factional loyalty, since Roman spectators were not cheering on the charioteer, but the colour he drove for. A charioteer might change his allegiance, but the faction member would never do so. This pattern survived imperial control of factional finances and in Constantinople meant that even Porphyrius, the outstanding charioteer, had no personal following separate from his colour. It was an attitude to racing which had already been ridiculed by the younger Pliny, when he complained how

thousands upon thousands of grown men behave like children, wanting to look at horses running and men standing on chariots

Charioteer passing the dolphins used to indicate circuits completed

over and over again. If it was the speed of the horses or the skill of
the charioteers that amazed them, there would be some sense in it –
but it is all about colour. That is what they back and that is what
holds their attention . . . Such is the incredible power of one cheap
coloured shirt.

As factions were never more than sporting fraternities, football strip is a
palpable equivalent. They did not champion popular causes or resist the
imperial government, unless it happened to manifest itself in police
action. Then factional unrest totally dwarfed football violence. At the
Nika riot of 532 more than 30,000 people lost their lives.

Church authorities had always been uneasy over public games in all
their forms, but condemnation of them, including chariot races, had less
to do with hooliganism than their long-standing association with pagan
festivals. Charioteers were even refused baptism unless they gave up the

sport and excommunicated if they resumed. A real problem for devout Christians was that everyone enjoyed such events, in particular the extensive calendar of chariot races. They were too popular to be suppressed, although the church managed to persuade the emperor Constantine to prohibit gladiatorial combat in 326. One reason for the clash between the church and the circus was the date of Easter, a controversy that had bothered Christians for well over a century when Constantine called the Council of Nicaea a year before his prohibition of fighting to the death in the amphitheatre. At Nicaea the emperor hoped to settle this matter as well as others dividing the church. A factor in the dispute was a possible clash between the foundation date of Rome and Easter, which caused difficulties in the search of a consensus date for the church's greatest festival. Naturally the bishop of Rome was unhappy if it coincided with the celebration of the city's foundation, for then services in its churches would be in direct competition with the chariot races staged in the Circus Maximus as part of the civic festival. Only after the bishop acquired a higher social standing in Rome was he able to successfully ask for the city's foundation to be celebrated without racing. By that time the seat of imperial power had been transferred from Rome to Constantinople. It was a step as important as Constantine's dethronement of the pagan gods of Rome, and his sequestration of their temple assets to adorn the new capital, and it accompanied the transformation of the imperial house into an eastern Mediterranean monarchy. An imperial diadem of pearls and jewels replaced the bayleaves and simple crown of his predecessors. Because the worship of pagan deities was outlawed in Constantinople, the new Rome, the Hippodrome (to use the Greek word for the circus) built there for the entertainment of the population had no associations offensive to Christianity. What Constantine did was to complete a circus already started by Septimus Severus, who was in 193 proclaimed emperor by his legions stationed on the Danube. Several hippodromes constructed by this emperor were gifts in return for loyalty shown by cities during the civil conflict which surrounded his accession.

It seems that the generosity of Septimus Severus was an effective spur to chariot racing in the eastern Mediterranean, which lagged behind the western provinces in its public commitment to the sport. Not all were pleased by this expansion of charioteering, and one critic denounced 'the wanton dissipation of vast sums of money'. Also deplored was the tendency of people to become 'crazed over a sport' which kept the best horses from the army. Yet the surge of interest in racing among eastern Mediterranean cities may well have been a genuine reaction to a decline in athletics. No longer seen as an essential aspect of civilized living, athletics had been dropped from the student curriculum. Once public sponsorship was not forthcoming for athletic competitions, something else was needed to fill the gap, if only as a spectator sport. The Olympic Games were terminated in 393 by Theodosius I, a strongly anti-pagan emperor. Yet at the same time he erected an obelisk at Constantinople, carved with a representation of the imperial family at the races. Its two inscriptions recall the victories of the emperor had won over rivals in the western Mediterranean. In the first, the obelisk announces that

> formerly I was ordered to obey the serene lords and carry the palm for the extinct tyrants. Reluctantly I did so, but now all yield to Theodosius and his eternal offspring. So conquered and laid low, I was raised again to the lofty sky in three times ten days while Proculus was in office.

Theodosius had held his triumph over the usurpers Victor and Magnus Maximus in Rome, but he ordered the urban prefect Proculus to install the obelisk in the centre of the Hippodrome at Constantinople. It reveals how the race course was always more than a place of entertainment: the site was of importance for political ceremonial as well. And the linking of the obelisk to the power of the ruler, in New Rome as in Egypt, took on a potent significance in the fourth century with the direct association of the emperor with Sol, the sun god. Christian though Theodosius was in outlook, he was also as a ruler assimilated with this cosmic force as the sun emperor. The tradition pre-dates the conversion of Constantine the Great to Christianity. On his coins Christ had had to share that emperor's devotion with Sol, Mars, Jupiter and Hercules for over a decade. Just how great the ritual implications of chariot racing were can be glimpsed in the associations which were acknowledged by the spectators. They knew how the twelve starting boxes represented the twelve months of the year, the seven laps of each race the seven days of the week, the twenty-four races of a meeting the twenty-four hours of the day; also recognised was the symbolism of the factional colours, green for spring, red for summer, blue for autumn and white for winter. With such a heritage it is hardly surprising that Roman-style charioteering caught on in the eastern Mediterranean. Stud farms were established in Asia Minor to provide the horses for chariot teams, and soon the factional rivalries of Rome had found their way to Constantinople and other great eastern cities. Within a century charioteers were being paid salaries direct from public funds.

Imperial patronage had given the chariot a final lease of life. Grumble though ecclesiastics might about the survival of a vehicle once admired as the conveyance of the pagan gods, there was no denying the excitement that races in the Hippodrome brought to Constantinople. A compromise

Part of the base of Theodosius I's obelisk

of sorts was reached in the ceremony at the beginning of each day's races. Compared with the tradition of singing a hymn before the Cup Final, it appears an odd mixture of the sacred and the profane. We are told that

the master of ceremonies said in a loud voice, 'Holy, thrice Holy One,' and everyone responded with either 'Victory to the Greens!' or 'Victory to the Blues!' Then the master of ceremonies added, 'O Lady, Mother of God,' and again the response was 'Victory to the Greens!' and 'Victory to the Blues!' Then the master of ceremonies said, 'The power of the Cross,' and this utterance was also met with 'Victory to the Greens!' and 'Victory to the Blues!'

Such rowdiness was not an entirely new phenomenon among spectators, but at Constantinople the level of violent behaviour reached heights not seen elsewhere. There was even contact between factions there and in other cities. We hear, for instance, of the Blues of Constantinople avenging a wrong done to the Blues of Tarsus, the birthplace of St Paul. It was by imperial decree that seating was reorganised in the Hippodrome at Constantinople so that the Greens should sit to the left of the imperial box and the Blues opposite. Apparently this new arrangement was observed in all the cities of the empire. The public disturbances, which made the factions notorious, began soon afterwards. In his account of the Sasanian siege and sack of Antioch, the empire's military stronghold in Syria, the historian Procopius refers to the Blues and the Greens who helped in the city's defence as 'those who used to fight each other in the hippodrome'. The fall of Antioch in 540 to King Khusrau I was a serious setback for the emperor Justinian, who had nearly abdicated during the Nika riots in Constantinople. His wars of reconquest in the western Mediterranean, against the Vandals in north Africa, the Goths in Italy and Spain, were accomplished at a high price: the neglect of the Balkan and Asian provinces. The Sasanian king used the vast spoils taken from Antioch to build a new city near his own capital called 'Khusrau's greater Antioch', and he populated it entirely with war captives. The best that Justinian could achieve on the eastern frontier was an uneasy truce with the Sasanians.

Justinian's reign was marked by tensions in a number of cities, and not least the capital, but it would be incorrect to suppose this was an exceptional situation. The culmination of factional rivalry had become the urban riot, instances of which are recorded in eastern cities in 491, 493, 498, 507, 532, 548, 560 and 561. The common issue in the two disturbances at Constantinople, which occurred in 507 and 532, was the release of prisoners. Stones were thrown at the emperor Anastasius, in 507, while he sat in the imperial box, which was entered directly from the palace, and fires were lit in the centre of the city. The vandalism destroyed many buildings before order was restored. Setting fire to buildings was a feature of factional disturbances, as indicated in the chant:

'Burn here, burn there, not a Blue anywhere!' But Procopius tells us that much of the disorder was simply mindless.

> They fight against their opponents without knowing the reason for endangering themselves. But they know that, even if they beat the enemy in the fight, the conclusion of the matter for them will be imprisonment. Yet they still fight. Their hatred towards their neighbours is quite irrational, but it persists without apparent end. For it overrides the bonds of kinship, disregards the ties of friendship, even if those who quarrel about the colours are brothers or friends. They care for nothing human or divine except victory in a chariot race.

Urban riots were not, however, always started in the Hippodrome, where rivalry between the Blues and the Greens was most intense. In 507 rioting began in the Forum of Constantine, where statues were overturned amid calls for a new emperor. The ostensible cause of the disturbance was the addition of a few words to the liturgy. In desperation, Anastasius took his seat at the Hippodrome without wearing the imperial diadem. There the eighty-year-old emperor beseeched the rioters to refrain from further violence, which they did after asking him to put on the diadem again.

Urban disturbances were certainly a concern for Justinian, several of whose laws sought to guard against the inhabitants of cities fighting each other. They singularly failed in 532 when Constantinople was convulsed by the Nika riot. The trouble began with a confrontation in the Hipppodrome between the Greens and Justinian in the early days of January. The damp wintry weather had put everyone's nerves on edge, so that a protest about the arbitrary action of a certain official included an insult directed at the emperor. 'Would that Sabbatius have never been born, to have a son who is a murderer,' cried the Greens. Sabbatius was Justinian's father. 'You are the only murderers here,' replied the Blues and the protest turned into the usual slanging match between the two factions. But on this occasion the level of insult was raised by the suspicion of the Greens that Justinian had had a part in the actual death of one of their number. The emperor's habitual support of the Blues only served to embitter the Greens, who left the Hippodrome chanting: 'Farewell justice! No one cares about justice any more. Let us convert and become Jews! It is better to be a pagan than a Blue, God knows!'

During the next few days there were incidents in the streets and a number of people were arrested. Several were condemned to death from both factions, and when on the day appointed for their execution the gallows broke, two of the condemned men, a Green and a Blue, fell to the ground. The crowd shouted 'To the church, the church,' and some monks from a nearby monastery hurried them to the church of St Lawrence for asylum. Learning of this, the city prefect set a guard on the church, while demonstrators in the streets loudly demanded their release. 'Have they not already been reprieved by their escape from hanging?' was the question asked.

Three days later, at the next race meeting in the Hippodrome, there were slogans chanted calling for their release. When the authorities refused to budge, the Greens and the Blues united against the imperial government. Their rivalry forgotten, they adopted as a watchword 'nika', meaning 'conquer', and surged into the streets of Constantinople bent on destruction. A genuine sense of injustice seems to have inspired the rioters, who included women as well as men, even though women never attended chariot races. Continued refusal to pardon the two asylum seekers led to an attack on the prefect's headquarters. Once these were alight, the rioters fired other public buildings, the flames spreading closer to the palace. The emperor tried to ease the tension with more racing, evidently in the hope that the factions would resume their mutual antagonism. But Justinian was disappointed. The Greens and the Blues remained united and, sensing their power, they demanded the dismissal of three senior officials, including the city prefect. Although the emperor agreed to this demand, the rioters were not appeased; fires raged all over the city and the imperial palace itself was besieged. By now they were thinking of the replacement of Justinian as emperor. To head off such an event, Justinian went to his box in the Hippodrome and, like Anastasius earlier, swore on the gospels to the assembled crowd that he would take no reprisals. While some acclaimed him, others uttered curses, perhaps encouraged by his political enemies who saw an advantage in getting rid of him. The clergy also tried in vain to bring the rioters to their senses, but they had already chosen a reluctant general by the name of Hypatius as Justinian's successor. In the Forum of Constantine he appeared in a white robe with a gold collar, the dress worn by emperors prior to their coronation. From there, Hypatius was conducted to the Hippodrome, where a coronation of sorts took place.

Word of Justinian's loss of nerve seems to have enboldened Hypatius. According to Procopius, who may have been inside the palace during the riot, the emperor was resolved to flee in a fast galley waiting at the private harbour of the palace. Then the empress Theodora, who had listened in silence to the arguments for and against flight, rose to her feet and said:

'Whether or not a woman should tell men how to be brave is unimportant. At a moment of danger one must do what one can. I consider flight, even if it saves our lives, as foolish. Everyone who is born is bound to die. But that a man who has been an emperor should endure exile I cannot bear. May I never be without the purple I wear, nor live to see a day when I am not addressed as "Your Majesty". If you prize safety above all else, my Lord, then take to the sea along with your treasure. Consider though that on reaching safety you might wish to exchange your safety for death. As for me, I prefer the old saying, that there is no nobler shroud than the purple.'

Stunned by her intervention, the court fell silent, until two of Justinian's best generals, Belisarius and Mundus, began discussing the military option. Fortunately for the emperor, these commanders had just arrived in the capital with their battle-hardened troops, whose loyalty was not in question, unlike the city's regular garrison. The time for action had come, no matter the casualties. Secretly Belisarius and Mundus left the palace, and by separate routes brought their troops to the gates of the Hippodrome, where Hypatius' supporters were celebrating his accession to the throne. Imperial agents had already been infiltrated into the event so as to stir up trouble. Shouts of 'Long live Justinian' restarted fighting between the factions, when the troops of Belisarius and Mundus burst through the gates and fell on the crowd. These German soldiers cared nothing for the Greens or the Blues, but slaughtered every civilian in reach. Outside, Narses, the commander of the eunuch guard, ordered his men to cut down any fugitives who escaped. A massacre ensued. The next day Hypatius and his brother were put to death and their bodies thrown in the sea. Empress Theodora had had her way.

It was only the presence of the two generals, Mundus and Belisarius, that saved Justinian's throne. The former, a barbarian leader who had incorporated his followers in the imperial army, was on a visit from his command in the Balkans, while the latter had been recalled from Syria, the key to the defence of the eastern Mediterranean. Other than the eunuch guard under Narses, who was a capable soldier, there were no effective troops in Constantinople except the contingents travelling with Mundus and Belisarius. Their surprise attack on the Hippodrome returned the initiative to Justinian, once Theodora had galvanised him into taking action. The suppression of the rioters additionally helped Belisarius to retrieve his reputation, as his recall followed a heavy defeat which the Sasanians inflicted on him at Callinicum. In 533 Belisarius was sent to Africa in order to reconquer the provinces lost there to the Vandals. His swift victory, plus the seizure of the vast treasure accumulated by the Vandal kings from the sack of Rome in 455 and subsequent raids on cities in the western Mediterranean, impressed Justinian enough to grant Belisarius on his return to Constantinople a triumph, the only one celebrated by a non-member of the imperial house since the reign of the first Roman emperor Augustus, half a millennium earlier.

The scale of the Nika riot took contemporaries by surprise, and in seeking to account for it they blamed the usual culprits – conspiring nobles, the senseless mob, demonic activity. Later its devastation was viewed as an opportunity which Justinian grasped to embellish the capital with new buildings, not least of which was the remodelled cathedral church of the Holy Wisdom. Its great dome was a miracle of engineering, despite a collapse in 558. Splendid as refurbished Constantinople was, the Nika riot could never be forgotten: too many people had died for that. An eyewitness like Procopius came to see Justinian and Theodora as demons in human form. In his *Secret Histories* he calls them 'blood-thirsty demons' who wrought havoc by means of 'some very different power'. Discounting Procopius' schizoid attitude to the imperial couple, in his public as well as private writings, the fact remains that the Hippodrome was the scene of unprecedented bloodshed, a strange by-product of charioteering. It was against this backdrop of violence that charioteers like Porphyrius raced. And we should note how in 507 this charioteer played a leading role himself in the Green uprising at Antioch, which involved pitched battles with the Blues and imperial troops. It seems that little happened to Porphyrius as a result, because he was soon back in Constantinople having statues raised to him. Not for nothing did Justinian offer rioters more races instead of political concessions.

Chariots racing round a barrier decorated with monuments

507 is one of the firm dates in Porphyrius' career. An inscription tells us that a certain Calliopas, a charioteer from Constantinople, took over the stable of the Greens at Antioch in the summer of that year. Calliopas was the other name of Porphyrius, who had been sent by the Greens of the capital in order to improve the performance of the Antioch Greens in the local hippodrome. His impact on the city was immediate. Having ended the run of bad luck for the Greens at the races, Porphyrius' victories inspired his factional supporters to assault the Blues. The charioteer did not have to do more than dominate the hippodrome for the Greens to go on the rampage, although there is no question that Porphyrius willingly participated in the fighting as well. At Antioch tension between Christians and Jews was one of the causes of rioting, as a synogogue was burned to the ground. But accounts of the disturbance give no impression that the rioters possessed any clear objectives other than inflicting injury on their factional opponents. Like most urban riots in the ancient eastern Mediterranean, it arose from an apparently inconsequential event, in this instance Porphyrius' success, and mush-roomed into wholesale rebellion as well as an attack on property. The Greens battled not just against the Blues, or even the Jews, but the city guards and detachments of imperial troops drafted into Antioch at the height of the riot. Factional disturbances were always triggered by fans excited at the outcome of the races. A not dissimilar riot had occurred in

412 at Alexandria over a dispute about the pantomine, another bone of contention in city life. Anti-Semitism was again a consequence rather than the cause of the trouble. 'The people rioted,' a commentator wrote, 'for no important reason, but because of that obstinate evil in all cities, enthusiasm for dancing.' One of the largest Jewish communities was at Alexandria, Alexander the Great's Egyptian foundation. In this city a translation of the Hebrew bible into Greek was made. Into the pantomine dispute the Greens and the Blues were drawn, as they were 200 years afterwards at the time of the Arab invasion. Then two generals defending the city quarrelled over theology. It is no surprise that one was supported by the Greens and the other by the Blues.

In 515 Porphyrius was back in Constantinople fighting for Anastasius against the would-be usurper Vitalian. This general had led the troops under his command against the capital in 513, in 514, and again in 515, but was repulsed. We know that Porphyrius sided with the octogenarian emperor against Vitalian from an inscription on a base for one of his statues in the Hippodrome. It reads:

> Not only in the stadium did Lady Victory crown you, but in war too she proved you a victor, at the time the emperor with the Greens in his service fought a furiously raging foe of the royal house, and the dreaded usurper fell when Constantinople was then weak. It was the day liberty came for its citizens. For that reason the emperor granted the Greens a statue of you, Porphyrius, like others before celebrating your skill.

After beginning with the Blues, Porphyrius seems to have switched to the Greens, whom the emperor Anastasius supported, and then back again to the Blues after the accession in 518 of Justin I who, like his successor Justinian, supported the Blues. Quite likely he switched factions more frequently than this pattern of allegiance suggests from surviving inscriptions. Porphyrius started racing in his late teens, like a modern jockey, but he was still winning chariot races in his sixties. As one supporter succinctly put it, 'neither strength nor swift horses know how to win, but the brains of the charioteer'. There is evidence that chariot racing, like many other occupations at this period, was a family calling, passed from father to son. Though we have little detail of Porphyrius' family, he hailed from Libya, a region not without fame in charioteering.

The terrain there lent itself to the use of the chariot and at the great city of Cyrene it remained in service as military transport long after it had been abandoned elsewhere. According to Porphyrius, both his father and his grandfather had been charioteers, while his mother was a dancer. Actors, dancers and charioteers were the stars of the entertainment industry in the ancient Mediterranean world, much to the annoyance of the church authorities. Congregations were challenged to explain how they could benefit from hearing the gospels, if they continued to watch the antics of Satan in pantomines and chariot races. Christians were exhorted to ponder religious truth, and the state of their souls, not gossip about the deeds of infamous entertainers. Salvianus, a presbyter at Marseilles until his death in 470, railed against public entertainment, but at the same time admitted that in most cities it had ceased to exist. Visigothic kings in Spain and Frankish kings in Gaul might occasionally organise chariot races and other spectacles, echoing the patronage of the Hippodrome by the eastern Roman emperors, but the general decline of the western city meant that there was no need to pander to the taste of a large urban population. There were no western equivalents of Antioch and Alexandria, and nor was Rome in the same league as populous Constantinople. At Rome, however, gladiatorial games continued until the reign of the western emperor Honorius (395–423), when the hermit Telemachus sacrificed his life to stop them, leaping into the arena and throwing himself on one of the contestant's weapons. Here that other star of late Mediterranean antiquity, the Christian ascetic, closed down the last vestiges of pagan funeral celebration.

In eastern cities there was less direct action against public entertainments, notwithstanding the disdain of holy men. Chariot races were still held under Heraclius, the emperor who witnessed the loss of Syria and Egypt to the Arabs. His usurpation of the throne in 610 was assisted by the Greens, whose leader, the charioteer Calliopas, had a grudge against Phocas, the emperor whom Heraclius overthrew. The Greens also rescued his mother and his fiancée, then imperial hostages. This was factional violence, but with a serious political dimension. Phocas' own violent seizure of power, when the reigning emperor Maurice and his family were put to death, set the scene for 610.

Stark naked, Phocas was brought to Heraclius, who ordered that his right arm be removed from the shoulder, as well as his head, and that his hand be impaled on a sword. Thus dismembered was Phocas paraded through the city, starting from the Forum of Constantine.

On the same day Heraclius was crowned emperor. Next day in the Hippodrome the flag of the Blues was burned together with a picture of Phocas. Once again the chariot's subtle spell cast its influence over ancient men's minds. Even though Heraclius was keen to receive the blessings of contemporary saints, he chose to present his son to the senate and the people in the Hippodrome, where the Blues and the Greens both hailed the young prince. Had the Arab conquest not swept them away, Green support for the accession of Heraclius might have politicised the factions, given their empire-wide contacts. As it was, the factions survived at Constantinople to perform a ceremonial role in the public display so dear to emperors. The days of the chariot race, and factional strife, were gone for good.

Afterword

Modern Myths

The monster approached slowly, hobbling, moving from side to side, rocking and pitching, but it came closer. Nothing obstructed it; a supernatural force seemed to drive it onwards. Someone in the trenches cried 'the devil comes' . . . Then sense returned . . . and toughness and defiance as the waves of English infantry surged up behind the devil's chariot.

German newspaper report

This dispatch from a correspondent of the *Düsseldorfer GeneralAnzeiger* entitled 'The Devil's Chariots' preserves the sense of shock felt by German infantrymen when tanks were first deployed at the close of the Somme offensive. Continued British and French attacks during October and November 1916 failed to achieve a decisive breakthrough on a battlefield which heavy raids had turned into a sea of mud. By the time the Allied assault was called off, the furthest advance lay only ten kilometres forward from the front attacked in July. Losses were appalling on both sides: the Germans suffered 500,000 killed and wounded, the French and British together an even greater number. Nowhere had the Allies succeeded in ending the stalemate of trench warfare, except where tanks had permitted British infantry to advance 3,000 metres with hardly any casualties at all. A Royal Flying Corps observer noted a 'tank followed by cheering multitude marching through Flers'. The appearance of the armoured vehicle terrified the German soldiers defending this village and, temporarily unnerved, they fled from their prepared positions. The British press made the most of this small success with headlines like 'Battle Cars That Charge the Trenches' and 'His Majesty's Land Navy'.

In the excitement both German and British newspapers recalled the chariot in trying to explain the impact of this new weapon to their readers. Overlooked were the considerable differences between these two revolutionary war machines. Also missed was the vulnerability of both the chariot and the tank. Almost all of the thirty-six British tanks which had crossed the start line on the Somme were disabled. Engine failure accounted for some, damaged wheels and tracks others. German stick bombs and machine-gun fire had little effect on a tank's armoured hull, but an artillery shell was something else, particularly if the tank received a direct hit. Battle conditions were truly dreadful for tank crews. When the first tanks were fully closed up, vision was limited to the commander's periscope, whose glass prisms were soon damaged. Added to the excruciating noise of an uncovered engine was the sound of the tank's own guns, plus that of enemy fire striking the armour. Even though a crewman might consider himself fortunate in not being outside with the infantry accompanying the tank, he found it difficult not to succumb to a feeling of isolation within the dim interior lit by a few lamps. At the height of chariot battle neither a charioteer nor a chariot warrior suffered such psychological problems, although their war machine was subject to sudden breakdown too. At the battle of Magnesia, in 189 BC, the chariotry of the Seleucid king Antiochus III had been totally disrupted by Roman auxiliaries, when a shower of arrows and stones crippled the teams of chariot horses. The result of this failed chariot charge was the unhinging of the Seleucid battle line, an opportunity which the Roman legionaries exploited to the full.

Nervous collapse does not seem to have overcome chariot crews. At Kadesh the charioteer of Ramesses II blanched when he saw how hemmed in the pharaoh's chariot was by the Hittite chariotry, but he could clearly observe how other Egyptian chariots were actively taking part in the pharaoh's counter-attacks. Exposed though they were to enemy fire in a manner inconceivable within an armoured vehicle, a chariot crew was able to watch the twists and turns of each fast-moving engagement, and adjust tactics accordingly. Not so in an early tank, whose better protection hardly compensated for a patent lack of vision. As a British officer commented on the use of tanks in 1917 against the Hindenburg line, the experience 'was bloody awful. One of our tanks that did come back shined like hell from bullets but the bloke inside was mad.' That the nerves of First World War tank crews were stretched had much to do with the frequency of breakdown. Shortages of spares meant that few tanks were in perfect order at the start of an action. It was indeed knocking engines which crews feared most, because this signalled imminent engine failure. Recovering stranded tanks overnight became a regular occurrence on the Western Front. The French had no better luck with their early armoured vehicles. The large Saint-Chamond tank, which sported a 75 mm cannon and four machine-guns, had a hull too long for its chassis and tracks so narrow that it struggled over uneven ground. Produced in a hurry, this tank was unreliable, breaking down frequently. The small Schneider tank was the first armoured vehicle to be used by the French army, but in 1917 it achieved little at Verdun, despite the heroic effort of the crews, many of whom were sailors. From their experience of British tank attacks on the Somme the Germans had learned to utilise their front-line trenches as anti-tank ditches. The Germans were slow to develop a tank of their own, so that during the final offensive they launched in August 1918 the German tank force depended on 170 tanks captured from the French and the British.

Captured chariots were also reused in ancient times, but chariot teams were not so easily taken over. The close relationship between a charioteer and his team of horses came from the familiarity which arose through a programme of training. Kikkuli's famous training manual reveals just how intensive this preparation was for chariot battle in West Asia, a necessity for success understood by Chinese charioteers. At the battle of Han in 645 BC, the ruler of the Chinese state of Qin chose to ignore the advice of an oracle to ride with his usual charioteer, because this man had dared to criticise his tactics in a previous engagement. He rode instead with another charioteer and a team of horses presented by an ally. The stubborn ruler would not heed the warning about the importance of the bond between a charioteer and a chariot team. It almost led to his capture. As tanks gradually improved in design, crews came to view them with greater confidence, but even in the Second World War there still remained the shut-in atmosphere to master. As the English poet Keith Douglas wrote shortly after the battle of Alamein,

the view from a moving tank is like that in a camera obscura or a silent film – in that the engine drowns all other noises, except explosions, the whole world moves silently.

The openness of a speeding chariot was of course utterly different. Only dust thrown up by hooves and wheels obscured the view. And though the chariot was unable to match the mature tank in the terrain it could traverse, being especially vulnerable over muddy or rocky ground, its performance was remarkable wherever conditions allowed a free run. The *Mahabharata* records only a fraction of the archery duels once fought on the north Indian plain, a venue eminently suited to massed chariot engagements in the dry season.

The modern linking of the chariot with the tank is thus unhelpful. Hollywood never made this mistake, despite its lack of understanding of what was involved in a chariot engagement. Its strength has been in making films which feature chariot racing, from the silent *Ben Hur* onwards. For all the drama of the chariot race is readily captured on camera. Whether the actors rely on facial expression as they have to do in a silent film, or there is the advantage of sound in the cheering crowds available in a 'talkie', it is the sheer exhilaration of speeding chariots that moves the cinema audience. Because the danger is so apparent, as competing charioteers literally try to cut corners, we can recall something of the atmosphere of chariot racing in the great cities of Rome and Constantinople.

For this achievement Hollywood studios deserve the highest praise: the universal language of the film communicates an aspect of ancient life as if we were there ourselves. The size of surviving circuses and hippodromes leaves little doubt that they once housed events which foreshadowed the global popularity of football today. Hundreds of thousands of spectators cheered on the Whites, the Blues, the Greens and the Reds. Why these factions became so central to ancient city life in the Mediterranean still remains an enigma. The Blues and the Greens were part and parcel of everyday thought, once support for the other two colours fell away. Allegiances were life-long, with some families supporting the same faction generation after generation, as is not uncommon with our own football teams. The adulation that successful charioteers received, again like modern footballers, helps to explain Nero's foray as a charioteer. Possibly the Roman emperor believed a team of ten horses gave his chariot an unbeatable advantage. As his friend Mithridates of Bosporus, a client state in the Crimea, had shown, it was feasible to drive with such a large team, Nero felt impelled to copy Mithridates. When he fell out, we are told, he came very close to being run over. Yet despite this upset, the shaken emperor carried on, his obsession with winning overcoming common sense. Yet he had no need to worry about the result; the

Olympic judges gave him the prize anyway. It is as if a present-day premier was guaranteed to be named man of the match as long as he made a token appearance on the pitch during a football game.

What enticed Nero to enter the competition at Olympia was of course the chariot itself, a vehicle redolent of high drama and heroism. It was indeed the focus of attention in the ancient Mediterranean for nearly 2,000 years after Nestor had advised his son on driving technique in the funeral games staged for Patroclus at the end of the *Iliad*. For the same reason Nero chose to mark his return to Rome, after winning the Olympic chariot race, as nothing less than a military triumph. He drove the triumphal chariot used a century earlier by the first Roman emperor, Augustus, while wearing a general's traditional purple robe as well as the Olympic olive crown. His chariot was preceded not by captive warriors, as was the custom in triumphs, but by attendants carrying his Greek winnings of 1,808 wreaths and crowns, together with banners listing the places of his artistic and sporting victories, whom he had defeated, and the titles of his songs or dramatic roles. Along the way to the Capitol, we are told, 'sacrifices were made, the streets were sprinkled with perfume, birds, ribbons and sweets were showered upon him'.

Yet the Augustan chariot failed to save Nero and he was forced to commit suicide. Riding in such a prestigious vehicle had always marked out the eminence of an individual Roman, ever since the Etruscan kings had instituted the triumph. In contrast, after the battle of An in 589 BC, the commander Shi Hsieh was careful not to lead the triumphant Jin army back into the capital, lest he appear to claim the victory for himself. His own chariot was in fact the last to enter the northern Chinese city. Triumphal entries, however, have remained a part of European culture ever since Roman times, a legacy we owe to the chariot and four horses always used in triumphs. Horse-drawn coaches may have been substituted for present-day monarchs, but the mounted horse has retained its potency for military parades. Just as the cavalryman replaced the charioteer in the ancient world, so in our time the mounted general retains all the charisma of the triumphal Roman commander.

To celebrate his defeat of Hitler in 1945, Stalin wanted to ride at the head of the victory parade. The Soviet leader's ambition was thwarted by the magnificent mount he chose, a difficult white Arab stallion. Having taken a tumble, Stalin asked Zhukov whether he had forgotten how to ride a horse. When the marshal said he had not, Stalin said, 'Good. You will take the salute at the Victory Parade.' Zhukov protested that as supreme commander it was only proper for Stalin to take the salute, but the Soviet leader said: 'I am too old for review parades. You do it, you are younger.' So it was that the great Russian victory over the German army was celebrated in Red Square, with Zhukov riding the Arab charger – the Soviet equivalent of the triumphal chariot.

Notes and References

1. CHARIOT BATTLE

KADESH A Semitic word meaning 'sanctuary', Kadesh was associated with a number of ancient sites, but the battle between the Hittites and the Egyptians took place next to a city of that name built on the banks of the Orontes river in Syria. Today the site is known as Tell Neby Mend. Kadesh remains a popular chariot battle with ancient historians because of the detailed record left by Ramesses II on the walls of temples at Karnak, Luxor, Abydos and Abu Simbel. In front of his own memorial temple, the Ramesseum, there once stood a huge pylon decorated with scenes from his victories, pride of place being reserved for Kadesh. A full account of the engagement is available in *The Kadesh Inscriptions of Ramesses II*, translated by Sir Alan Gardner, Oxford 1960. This can usefully be compared with James Breasted's *The Battle of Kadesh*, Chicago, 1903, which has the advantage of including line-drawings of the battle as carved on temple walls, plus the accompanying texts. A more recent study is *Perspectives on the Battle of Kadesh*, edited by H. Goedicke, Baltimore, 1985. There is no firm agreement about the date of the battle at Kadesh, since it depends on the date Ramesses II is reckoned to have ascended the throne: either 1304 or 1279 BC. We have accepted the latter so that in his fifth year as pharaoh, 1274 BC, he fought against this battle against the Hittites.

The city of Kadesh itself, and its political fortunes, receive treatment in W. J. Murnane's *The Road to Kadesh. A Historical Interpretation of the Battle Reliefs of Sety I at Karnak*, Chicago, 1985. In the mid-fifteenth century BC Kadesh had come to Egypt's notice at the battle of Megiddo when its king had dared to sponsor a coalition of Canaanite rulers against Thutmose III. Even though Egyptian might tended to overawe Kadesh, the city state managed to remain independent for many years by playing off Mitanni against Egypt. The fall of Mitanni and the rise of Hatti, however, totally transformed the political situation in Syria. Ramesses II's father, Sety I, finally brought Kadesh under firm Egyptian control. His capture, or rather recapture, of the city was commemorated in a victory stele set up in Kadesh. Only a fragment of this stone tablet is preserved, but it is enough to show that, though badly weathered, it was never defaced, even after Kadesh passed into Hittite hands. That the ruler of Kadesh did not destroy Sety's tablet, despite switching allegiance to Hatti, only serves to reveal the extent of political uncertainty in both the Hittite and Egyptian spheres of influence. He was not to know that the Egyptians would never return once Ramesses II and Hattusili III made peace in 1259 BC.

MONTU A falcon-headed god worshipped at Thebes, Montu was a particular favourite of Ramesses II. His personal identification became so strong that a cult statue was venerated in the pharaoh's honour during his lifetime.

AMARNA The discovery in 1887 of a remarkable cache of documents at Tell el-Amarna in Egypt, the site of the palace-city of Akhenaten, offered for the first time an opportunity to read the international correspondence of the pharaohs. Though seen now as only part of a much larger picture, the so-called Amarna letters remain of the highest importance in our understanding of ancient diplomacy in the eastern Mediterranean. Written in cuneiform script with a reed stylus, the letters preserved on the clay tablets record messages sent to, and received from, the rulers of Babylon, Assyria, Mitanni, Hatti and Alashiya (the island of Cyprus), besides instructions to lesser ones like Amurru. The word Amurru was the Akkadian name for the ancient Amorites, the inhabitants of Canaan and parts of northern Mesopotamia prior to the Hebrew settlement. An English translation is available in William Moran's *The Amarna Letters*, Baltimore, 1992. Discussion of the letters' place in ancient history can be found in *Amarna Diplomacy. The Beginning of International Relations*, edited by R. Cohen and R. Westbrook, Baltimore, 2000.

EGYPTIAN-HITTITE TREATY The text of this peace treaty is one of the most remarkable documents which has survived. It can be found in *Ancient Records of Egypt, Volume Three, The Nineteenth Dynasty*, translated and edited by J. H. Breasted, Chicago, 1906. The treaty reviews former relations between Hatti and Egypt, declares a new peace pact, forbids further conquests by either side in Syria, reaffirms a former treaty without stating its articles, establishes a defensive alliance between Hatti and Egypt, outlining duties in terms of dealing with fugitives, rebellious Syrian states and mutual defence, and calls down divine blessings on its observer and curses on its violator. Ramesses II regarded the conclusion of his war with the Hittites as a personal triumph. At Abu Simbel he had carved this bold statement, after the treaty was agreed: the pharaoh was the one 'who made the land of Kush as if it never existed; who has caused Hatti to stop its lies . . .' Ramesses obviously believed he had come a long way since the near disaster at Kadesh.

MEGIDDO The conversation between Edmund Allenby and James Breasted took place one evening after dinner in Cairo. In his journal Breasted noted how Allenby delighted in talking about the battle of Megiddo, which had effectively knocked Turkey out of the First World War. While Liman von Sanders was engaged immediately afterwards in the thankless task of rallying his demoralised Turkish troops, the Allied advance made easy progress. The German general had lost two armies in a matter of days, leaving a third isolated in the Jordan valley. Its maddeningly slow withdrawal complicated all attempts to establish a new Turkish defence line. By the time Damascus fell into Allenby's hands on 1 October 1918, twelve days after the start of the action at Megiddo, fewer than 20,000 Turkish soldiers out of the total of 100,000 serving in Palestine and Syria before the final Allied offensive were not prisoners-of-war.

The Seventh and Eighth Turkish Armies had been commanded by General Eric von Falkenhayn until 1 March 1918, when General Otto Liman von Sanders took over from him. The latter had originally headed a military mission of seventy German officers to Constantinople in 1913, when to assist his work in modernising the Turkish army he was given the local rank of field marshal. Following the collapse of the Turks, Liman von Sanders anticipated the inevitable ceasefire at the end of 1918 by handing over his command to General Mustapha Kema, whose last stand north of Aleppo prevented an Allied invasion of Turkey and the further destruction of its army.

The biblical Armageddon, supposedly the last battle of all between the nations of the world, is expected to take place at the site of ancient Megiddo: hence the unwelcome suggestion for Allenby's title. Armageddon is in fact a corruption of the Hebrew 'Har Megiddon', meaning the 'Mount of Megiddo'. In the Book of Revelation, the last cataclysmic engagement here is foretold after a series of disasters – among others, earthquakes, storms, fires, a plague of locusts, genocide, disease, the death of the sea and total darkness. The books mentioned by Allenby, on the other hand, are Breasted's own *Ancient Records of Egypt* and Smith's *Historical Geography of the Holy Land*. Though unmentioned, it is quite possible that Lawrence of Arabia may have talked with Allenby about Thutmose's victory too, before he returned to the desert in order to lead the Arab advance east of the Jordan. Colonel Lawrence was an archaeologist and a historian with a detailed knowledge of Palestine. Field Marshal Wavell's account of the Fourth Cavalry Division's advance at Megiddo is in his *The Palestine Campaigns*, London, 1928.

LANCERS Although there is still not complete agreement on the origin of the foot-stirrup, an essential item of equipment for the lancer, the earliest evidence of its use comes from third-century AD China. Its development there may have been stimulated by news of the Indian toe-stirrup rather than contact with nomad peoples living to the north of the Great Wall, because this was the period in which Buddhism arrived from India. Sculptures at the great Buddhist centre of Sanchi, in central India, show the toe-stirrup was used in the subcontinent by the second century AD. The earliest known use of the foot-stirrup in the West occurs 400 years after this date. Then the Mongolian Avars brought this invention to the notice of the eastern Roman cavalry, which immediately adopted it. In 557 the Avars demanded of Emperor Justinian tribute as well as land in return for peaceful relations. Within thirty years they overran a large area of the Balkans. Whereas Justinian's cavalrymen were equipped with shields, lances and swords, the Avars stuck to the bow, the favourite nomad weapon. Recommended is E. Hildinger's *Warriors of the Steppes*, Cambridge, Massachusetts, 2001.

IRAN The earliest and greatest imperial dynasty ever to be based on Iran, Persia (559–530 BC) was imitated after Alexander the Great's conquest by two other Iranian empires of the Parthians (171 BC–AD 266) and the Sasanians (226–651), both implacable enemies of the Romans. The campaign of the Ten Thousand, arguably an inspiration for Alexander's eastern victories, is related in Xenophon's *The Persian Expedition*, translated by R. Warner, Bristol, 1981. The Roman defeat at Carrhae can be found in the life of Crassus contained in Plutarch's *The Fall of the Roman Republic*, translated by R. Warner, Harmondsworth, 1958. And Roman preoccupation with Alexander the Great's exploits is well explored in Diana Spencer's *The Roman Alexander. Reading a Cultural Myth*, Exeter, 2002. After Crassus' defeat and death, campaigning against eastern powers came to be seen in republican Rome less as a glorious adventure and more as a risk of disgrace. Mark Antony's later failure against the Parthians merely served to underline the military dangers lurking there.

CHINA Accounts of the battles of Chengpu, Bi and Yenling can be found in the *Zuo zhuan*. Burton Watson's excellent translation is published as *The Tso Chuan. Selections from China's Oldest Narrative History*, New York, 1989. Its entries provide a year-by-year chronicle of major events from 722 to 468 BC, essentially the Spring and Autumn period. Apart from its fascinating military details, the chronicle throws light upon the feudal society in which Confucius and his disciples lived and out of which the Confucian school of philosophy evolved. For Sun Zi's *Art of War* there is the translation by S. G. Griffith, Oxford, 1963. Its excellent introduction is worth reading, although the detailed commentary alongside the text and translation made earlier by L. Giles, London, 1910, deserves study for anyone who wishes to fully understand what is the oldest military treatise known in the world.

2. THE RISE OF THE CHARIOTEER

ZANNANZA The Hittite king Suppiluliuma I found great attraction in the prospect of one of his sons becoming a pharaoh. Apart from extending Hittite influence to Egypt, the proposed marriage arrangement would have eliminated friction between Hatti and Egypt in Syria. The murder of Zannanza was a shock to Suppiluliuma, who had no hesitation in blaming the Egyptians for the foul deed. The scene was thus set for a major confrontation between the Hittites and the Egyptians in Syria.

ETRUSCAN DARING The Roman belief that the dangerous practice of steering a chariot with the reins tied round the hips had originated with the Etruscans is confirmed by a number of surviving illustrations. The most dramatic depiction of a fatal accident arising from such disdain for personal safety was found in the cemetery of Monterozzi at Tarquinia in 1958, when Italian archaeologists explored the Tomb of the Olympic Games, so named because the Olympic Games were about to be held in Rome. An account of the tomb's discovery can be found in *Tarquinia. La Tomba delle Olimpiadi*, by R. Bartoccini, C. M. Lerici and M. Moretti, Milan, 1959.

Though the Romans attributed the dangerous fashion of driving a chariot without hands to the Etruscans, they were unsure whether chariot racing was also Etruscan in origin. It was in fact introduced by them. According to Herodotus, the chronicler of the struggle between the Greeks and the Persians, the Etruscans first took up the sport at the suggestion of the Delphic Oracle. Because they had stoned to death a number of Greek prisoners, a terrible affliction struck every living thing that passed the spot where the atrocity had occurred. Wishing to expiate the bloody crime, envoys were sent to Greece, where at Delphi the priestess of Apollo told the Etruscans to begin the custom of honouring the dead men with a grand funeral ceremony and the holding of athletic and equestrian games each year.

HARNESSING The singular ability of Commandant Lefebvre des Noëttes to ask questions which nobody could answer led to the investigation of the ancient harness. His own study, *L'Attelage et le Cheval de Selle à travers les âges*, was published in Paris in 1931. After the Second World War the question of effectiveness was seriously pursued in France by J. Spruytte, who reconstructed ancient chariots in order to understand the problems of traction. Worth reading is the English translation of this prolonged study, which was published as *Early Harness Systems. Experimental Studies*, by J. Spruytte, translated by M. Littauer, London, 1983. It includes both photographs and diagrams relating to the construction of chariots and the use of harnesses.

THE GENESIS OF THE CHARIOT Much ink has been spilled on this subject, and a deal more is likely to be spilled before any final conclusion is reached. Two books pose the different points of view: *Wheeled Vehicles and Ridden Animals in the Ancient Near East*, by M. A. Littauer and J. H. Crouwel, Leiden, 1979, and *The Earliest Wheeled Transport, from the Atlantic Coast to the Caspian Sea*, by S. Piggott, London, 1983. While the former places the evolution of the light, spoked-wheeled, horse-drawn chariot firmly in West Asia itself, the latter surveys the archaeological evidence for its genesis, or at least the critical stages in its development, over a much wider area, although the author concedes how it was in 'the Near East, the Levant, Egypt, Asia Minor, and Mycenaean Greece . . . in highly organised states that social conditions allowed not only the development and maintenance of the vehicles and their horses, but the emergence of a professional chariot-warrior class as a military cadre in disciplined warfare'.

MARI, close to the Iraqi–Syrian border, was excavated by French archaeologists following its discovery in 1933. Under the direction of André Parrot they discovered the great palace of Zimri-Lim, along with its extensive cuneiform archive. Finds from the twenty seasons of excavation at the site are detailed in four volumes comprising the *Mission Archéologique de Mari*, edited by A. Parrot and published in Paris from 1956 until 1967. A more concise treatment is available in Stephanie Dalley's *Mari and Karana. Two Old Babylonian Cities*, London, 1984.

SCYTHED CHARIOTS are first mentioned in West Asia during the disbandment of the Trojan chariotry. Apparently Cyrus the Great (559–529 BC), the founder of the Persian empire, considered the light Trojan war chariot to be outdated, substituting instead a heavier scythed chariot. The latter possessed a longer axle and carried a single occupant, the driver, encased all over in mail and further protected by a turret-like box.

THE BUHEN HORSE is discussed by Juliet Clutton-Brock in the *Journal of Archaeological Science*, I, pages 89–100, London, 1974. Though well known to archaeologists since its discovery in 1958, this was the first detailed description of its skeleton. The horse's remains were found beneath rubble and a new pavement built during the Egyptian reconstruction of the fortress. It seems the horse died during the siege and sack of 1676 BC: workmen simply resurfaced the area afterwards, thus sealing it in the deposit. What Juliet Clutton-Brock's article established beyond doubt was that the Buhen bones belonged neither to an ass nor a zebra, but to a large horse probably imported into Egypt from West Asia, which had been ridden or driven with a bit made from bronze, or possibly bone. This makes the find the earliest material evidence for the use of the bit. It is not surprising that horse remains from Egypt are rare: a horse would have been an expensive import which would be difficult to acclimatise to the hot low-lying Nile valley. Only after the Hyksos occupation, which ended in 1555 BC, did horses become more plentiful.

ARCHERY remains, with one notable exception, a strangely neglected subject, despite the enthusiasm of gifted amateurs. Most impressive is the study of American Indian practice which arose from a chance meeting in 1911 of Saxton T. Hope, an instructor in surgery and research at the University of California medical school, and Ishi, the last of the Yahi tribe. Hope and Ishi became friends, the latter helping Hope to develop his archery skills. Hope's *Bows and Arrows*, Berkeley, California, reprinted 1974, is a detailed account of Yahi archery, plus experiments with replicas of museum exhibits. My discussion of the Turkish composite bow leans heavily upon Sir Ralph Payne-Gallwey's fascinating book entitled *The Crossbow. Medieval and Modern, Military and Sporting*, London, 1903. The author treats this weapon and other oriental bows in an extensive appendix. The arrival of the composite bow in Egypt may well be a result of the Hyksos occupation: these Asiatic warriors were charioteers familiar with its use. It is clear that the Egyptians adopted chariot warfare in order to expel the Hyksos, and so they would have needed to become expert with the composite bow at the same time.

The notable exception as regards the study of the bow, composite and otherwise, is Stephen Selby's *Chinese Archery*, Hong Kong, 2000. It is an example to historians everywhere. Selby worked in Hong Kong for many years and developed there a profound interest in East Asian archery.

TUTANKHAMUN has been the subject of many books. Christine Desroches-Noblecourt's *Tutankhamun, the Life and Death of a Pharaoh*, London, 1963, still remains a good starting point, although more recently there has been a spate of publications on the famous excavation, one of the most readable being *Howard Carter. The Path to Tutankhamun*, by T. G. H. James, London, 1992. This provides an excellent account of the tomb's discovery, excavation and aftermath. Though Carter was delighted to have located the pharaoh's place of burial, he could not hide his initial disappointment at the signs of forced entry into the tomb. Only the resealing of the entrance showed that there had been no further disturbance since ancient times. For detailed treatment of the wonderful things Carter found in the tomb the Griffiths Institute series is by far the best, and especially for warfare there are W. McLeod's *Composite Bows from the Tomb of Tutankhamun*, Oxford, 1970, and *Chariots and Related Equipment from the Tomb of Tutankhamun*, Oxford, 1985.

TUTANKHAMUN'S DEATH was first attributed to a chariot accident by D. S. Forbes, 'A New Hypothesis of Tutankhamen's Early Demise', *KMT*, vol. 3, no. 1, Sebastopol, California, Spring 1992. Well worth reading too is his *Tombs, Treasures, Mummies: Seven Great Discoveries of Egyptian Archaeology*, Sebastopol, California, 1998.

3. WEST ASIA AND EGYPT

KIKKULI was the supreme horse trainer of ancient West Asia. His incomplete manual survives on a series of clay tablets found at Boghazköy, the present-day Turkish name for the site of Hattusha, the Hittite capital in Asia Minor. Although Kikkuli dictated the manual in Hurrian, the tablets found at Boğhazköy are not the original Hurrian text, but translations into Hittite and Akkadian. The first publication of Kikkuli's manual was H. A. Potralz's *Das Pferd in der Frühzeit*, Rostock, 1938. It comprises a transliteration of the original and a German translation.

MITANNI remains a mystery because of the lack of Mitannian records. The location of the capital, Washukanni, is still unknown. And an Indo-Aryan presence amongst the Hurrians is also a continued matter of debate. It has even been suggested that maryannu, meaning 'warriors', is actually a Hurrian word.

Apart from personal names derived from Indo-Aryan deities and technical terms connected with horsemanship (like uartana, meaning 'circuit' or 'course') found in Kikkuli's training manual that are definitely not Hurrian in origin, the main evidence for an Indo-Aryan presence in Mitanni is the specific reference made to gods in peace treaties concluded with both the Hittites and the Assyrians. One such deity is Varuna, the upholder of the moral order for the Indo-Aryans as well as the Iranians. Varuna's association with Mithra-Mitra goes back to a period before the Indo-Aryans and the Iranians split into two distinct peoples. In the *Avesta*, which probably means 'Injunction of the prophet Zoroaster', Varuna is an elevated figure like the supreme Iranian deity Ahura Mazda. Similarly Varuna is described in the *Rig Veda*, the earliest Indo-Aryan text, as 'all-enveloping', the one who is 'seen beyond all things'. One verse tells how speech itself is nourished by Mitra and Varuna, plus Agni and the two

Asvins – all Indo-Aryan gods who appear in Mitannian peace treaties. Most frequently mentioned is Mitra, along with Varuna, the guardian of truth and morality. The later transformation of the Iranian Mithra into Mithras, the war god who fought on the side of the just, and his adoption by the Roman legions, should not obscure Mitra's original function as a guarantor of oaths, and by extension the chief protector of international agreements.

That Mesopotamian and Anatolian gods and goddesses are also invoked in Mitannian treaties does not diminish the importance of Mitra. In some ways it could be said to enhance his authority, for unlike the temple-based deities of West Asia, the Indo-Aryan pantheon was at this stage of its development entirely free of geographical limits. Thus the *Rig Veda* could say of Mitra 'the wide one' that his 'greatness fills heaven, while his glory fills the earth'. Some West Asian deities were then emerging from the multitude of city gods and aspiring to such universal power, but they still lacked the range of Mitra's authority, which was in part a consequence of early Indo-Aryan ignorance of temples and cult images.

Until more information becomes available, it is difficult to draw firm conclusions about Mitannian society other than to recognise the importance it attached to chariot warfare. Two books offer a general introduction to what is known about Mitanni: *Hurrians and Subarians*, by I. J. Gelb, Chicago, 1944, and *The Hurrians*, by G. Wilhelm, translated by J. Barnes, Warminster, 1989.

HATTI Not until the early twentieth century were the Hittites properly located in central Asia Minor, a land they called Hatti. German archaeologists were primarily responsible for taking our knowledge of the Hittites beyond what is contained in the Bible. No longer regarded as a small Canaanite hill tribe, they now stand revealed as one of the great imperial peoples of ancient times. Of mixed ethnic origins – Indo-European, native Hattian, Hurrian and Luwian, a people who lived in southwestern Asia Minor – the Hittites had considerable impact on West Asian history until the early twelfth century BC, when their capital Hattusha went up in flames. Something of Hittite civilisation survived afterwards in Syria, especially at Carchemish, once the seat of a Hittite viceroy, but the days of power were gone, as biblical references suggest nothing more than a mercenary role for men from such post-Hittite states.

Though it is now somewhat out of date, O. R. Gurney's *The Hittites*, Harmondsworth, 1952, is still very readable. It offers an outline of Hittite history, an analysis of the Hittite state and its institutions, a survey of warfare, plus a discussion of Hittite religion. For detailed information, however, two newer publications should be consulted. Both written by Trevor Bryce, they are *The Kingdom of the Hittites*, Oxford, 1998, and *Life and Society in the Hittite World*, Oxford, 2002.

UGARIT Modern Ras Shamra on the Syrian coast, Ugarit was a rich trading kingdom during the later part of the second millennium BC. Discovered by French archaeologists in 1928, the city was largely dug before the start of the Second World War, when finds from its archive threw new light on Canaanite politics, society and religion. Good relations with Egypt were typical before the rise of Hatti. An Amarna letter expresses the loyalty of Ammistramru I, who declares how he falls at the pharaoh's feet 'seven times seven times'. He hopes, too, that the pharaoh, 'my lord, will not turn against me'. Like Hatti, Ugarit suffered massive destruction early in the twelfth century BC at the hands of the Sea Peoples. For reflections on the numerous finds made during the long excavation there is *Ugarit in Retrospect. Fifty Years of Ugarit and Ugaritic*, edited by G. D. Young, Winona Lake, 1981.

THE HYKSOS OCCUPATION, termed the fifteenth dynasty by the historian priest Manetho, was a severe shock for the ancient Egyptians. Even though the previous dynasty was not stable, and its last pharaohs no more than a series of usurpers who each stayed on the throne for only a few years, the seizure of the Nile delta by foreigners was unexpected. Yet a large Asian settlement had already developed there connected with trade and specialist crafts like shipbuilding. Accumulated wealth gave these foreign residents a powerful say in policy-making once central control weakened in Egypt. Prior to the Hyksos domination, a number of petty rulers had already set up their courts in different parts of the Delta, but these rulers were ineffectual compared with the Hyksos dynasty, who took over one small kingdom based on the city of Avaris. A prominent ruler was the third Hyksos pharaoh, Seuserenre Khayon, since large monuments were constructed during his reign and diplomatic ties were established with Knossos on the island of Crete and Hattusha in Asia Minor. But most notable of all was the fifth pharaoh, Aawoserre Apophis (c. 1605–1565 BC), the doughty opponent of Kamose and the slayer of his father Sekenenre Ta'o. His authority was acknowledged as far south as Memphis in the Nile valley and throughout the whole of southern Palestine.

Resistance to the Hyksos pharaohs centred on Thebes, for a while one of their vassals. Sekenenre Ta'o was the first Egyptian leader to raise the standard of revolt, a move which led to his violent death on the battlefield. Ahmose, his youngest son, eventually succeeded in carrying the revolt into the Nile delta. Memphis was the first city to be stormed, followed by many others until Avaris itself surrendered after a long siege. The Hyksos having departed on agreed terms, Ahmose built within the citadel at Avaris a military headquarters for his continued campaigning against Hyksos allies in Palestine. Decoration of his palace there is reminiscent of Aegean painting with Minoan-style scenes of bull-leaping, acrobats and hunting. One explanation may be a very determined effort on Ahmose's part to secure the alliance of the Minoans, whose navy could have aided the expelled Hyksos. Excavation of sites in the northeast of the Delta indicate the survival of a foreign state which could have formed the base for another assault on Egypt, especially if it had given shelter to Hyksos expelled from Avaris. How long this small power lasted is uncertain. It would have soon become isolated by Egyptian pressure on Palestine, a military move intended to protect Egypt from another invasion. Recommended books are J. Van Setters' *The Hyksos. A New Investigation*, New Haven, 1966, and D. B. Redford's *Egypt, Canaan and Israel*, Princeton, 1992.

WRRT, the Egyptian word for chariot, was supplemented during the reign of Amenhotep III (1410–1372 BC) by htry, meaning 'chariotry'. This was the term used for a distinct military unit, a squadron of chariots. Neither wrrt nor htry is Semitic in origin, unlike the word adopted by the Egyptians for horse, ssmt.

WENAMUN travelled abroad to buy wood at a time when Egypt was no longer the power it had been in West Asia. As a result, he was robbed, ignored and overcharged. It seems likely that he only succeeded in accomplishing his mission through enjoying some semi-official status: Wenamun had been sent to obtain timber for the construction of a sacred bark for the Theban god Amun. Just in case there might be political repercussions if he failed in this task, the Byblian harbour-master let him quietly slip away with his cargo. A translation of Wenamun's story can be found in the second volume of Miriam Lichtheim's *Ancient Egyptian Literature*, Berkeley, 1976.

MOSES does not appear in surviving Egyptian records, and attempts to identify him historically remain problematic. Yet no figure casts a greater shadow in the pages of the Old Testament than Moses, and for that reason alone his story deserves to be included in any treatment of Egyptian chariotry. For 'the signs and wonders' that accompanied the struggle to free his people from the pharaoh's clutches ended with the drowning of many Egyptian charioteers, chariot warriors, chariots and chariot horses. The disaster did not of course destroy the Egyptian army. Such a setback, however, would have been enough to let Moses and his followers escape into Sinai, while giving any pharaoh reason to pause for thought. In an age of divine signs, the sudden movement of water could not be safely ignored. A useful discussion of the Moses question is available in J. K. Hoffmeier's *Israel in Egypt. The Evidence for the Authencity of the Exodus Tradition*, Oxford, 1997. Thoroughly readable, too, is *A Pharaoh Triumphant. The Life and Times of Ramesses II*, by K. A. Kitchen, Warminster, 1982.

4. EUROPE

NESTOR is described by Homer, in book four of the *Iliad*, as 'the old man who used the experience he had gained in battles long ago to inspire his troops'. There is no doubt that his instructions to his charioteers are heroic and practical, until he speaks of storming cities. Chariots cannot breach city walls, nor can they prepare on their own the conditions necessary for a successful assault. This always remains the job of infantrymen, who have to secure the area round a city's defences before any breach can be made in them. Nestor's sudden switch from chariot tactics to cities carried by storm at the end of his speech can only reflect the inability of Homer to round it off in a convincing manner. The poet simply knew nothing about battles between opposing chariotries.

THE DENDRA ARMOUR was found in a tholos tomb, a typical Mycenaean burial chamber. These tombs were comparatively easy to build, provided the underlying rock was not too hard. A horizontal passage, open to the sky, always leads to a doorway; the circular underground chamber behind sometimes has pits or shallow shafts sunk into the floor for burials. At Dendra, ancient Midea, the tholos in which the warrior with the bronze suit of armour was interred had largely escaped the attention of robbers. Never a major settlement, Midea was dependent on either Tiryns or Mycenae, while for trade it would have had to rely on Tiryns or Epidauros as a port. But its inhabitants were rich enough to afford grave goods of high quality – swords with golden hilts, armour, and gold and silver cups. The tomb containing the armour had three burials, a prince and his wife in one pit, with another woman, possibly an attendant, in a separate pit. The armour itself is very heavy indeed, so much so that its use in warfare remains baffling.

APOLLO slew the monstrous serpent Python with a bow and took over the famous oracle it guarded at Delphi. Cult associations suggest Asia Minor or the eastern Aegean as places where Apollo was first worshipped. Yet on Delos, long a holy island for the ancient Greeks, the earliest temple was dedicated not to him, but his sister Artemis. Possibly her initial seniority explains Apollo's own excellence with the bow: though not a hunter himself, he may have acquired this divine weapon from the virgin huntress Artemis, in whose rites survived vestiges of human sacrifice. Early on Apollo added to his quiver the plague-infected arrows of a West Asian deity like Reseph, with whom the Greek settlers on Cyprus readily identified him. According to Homer, the prayer of Chryses at the beginning of the *Iliad* was heard by Apollo, who attacked in the Greek camp animals as well as men. 'Day and night,' we are told, 'innumerable fires consumed the dead. For nine days the god's arrows fell on the encampment.'

While *Apollo. Origins and Influence*, edited by J. Solomon, Tucson, 1994, looks at 'the terrible twins', Apollo and Artemis, largely from a Greek viewpoint, M. C. Astour places them in a much wider context through his pioneering *Hellenosemitica. An Ethnic and Cultural Study in West Semitic Impact on Mycenaean Greece*, Leiden, 1967.

THE COMING OF THE GREEKS No consensus exists on the arrival of Indo-Europeans in Greece. Linguistic evidence is enough to show that its earlier inhabitants did not speak Greek, however. What it cannot reveal is the time or the manner of the Indo-European incursion. Fortification of pre-Greek settlements on the mainland and on the Aegean islands, with the notable exception of Crete, already testifies to a growing militarism and the concentration of wealth in the hands of a few families. The culmination of this tendency can be seen in the late second millennium BC in the massive fortress that housed the Mycenaean palace at Tiryns. Only Crete was lacking fortifications: neither the earliest settlements before 2000 BC nor the palaces and mansions after that date reveal traces of any real defences. The apparent peacefulness of Minoan Crete, before the Mycenaean Greek takeover of 1400 BC, cannot be entirely attributed to the development of a powerful navy, though its vessels would have had a salutary influence on the activities of pirates. A quiet sea does not necessarily mean a quiet island. Yet it would seem that the pre-Greek inhabitants were able to devote far fewer resources to defence than their neighbours, and in the process be the first European people to achieve civilisation.

The utterly different situation on the Greek mainland suggests that upheavals there were not uncommon and may have had a connection with migration. It is possible that Indo-European speakers infiltrated gradually, perhaps over a long period of time; the presence of Greek in the Linear B texts of the early fourteenth century BC does not prove that the whole of southern Greece was by then largely inhabited by Greek speakers, but merely that Greek was the language used by dynasts for palace archives. Along with their followers, these new rulers may have arrived by sea, possibly in the wake of earlier Greek speakers. A very good case is made out for a takeover of Greece by a charioteering community which came from lands south of the Caucasus in Robert Drews' *The Coming of the Greeks. Indo-European Conquests in the Aegean and the Near East*, Princeton 1988.

LINEAR B Again there were scholars who did not accept that an early form of Greek appears in Linear B tablets when in 1952 Michael Ventris achieved a decipherment. For it has to be admitted that this first advance failed to lead to an easy understanding of the script, which was found on tablets at Pylos, Knossos, Thebes, Athens, Tiryns and Mycenae. Later decipherment attempts have improved our understanding of these ancient Greek palace records, although they remain little more than lists and records of transactions. As James Hooker put it in *Mycenaean Greece*, London, 1976, they 'are relevant of the outward manifestations of the Aegean cultures: they speak of methods, not of motives'. See M. Ventris and J. Chadwick, *Documents in Mycenaean Greek*, Cambridge, 1956, and J. Chadwick, *The Decipherment of Linear B*, Cambridge, 1958 and 1967.

GREEK CHARIOTS are well described in J. H. Crouwel's *Chariots and Other Means of Land Transport in Bronze Age Greece*, Amsterdam, 1981, although the author cannot accept his limp conclusion that 'chariots must have functioned primarily as military conveyances'. Such a view ignores the greater historical context in which the Mycenaeans lived and fought, for their time was the great age of the charioteer in the eastern Mediterranean. Here again the negative influence of Homer may well be at work in excluding chariot warfare from ancient Europe.

FUNERAL GAMES appear in the earliest works of Greek literature and art. A Mycenaean sarcophagus from Tanagra in central Greece gives us a gruesome glimpse into ancient funeral practice, for it has depictions of a funeral accompanied by armed combat and bull-leaping: the latter was invented by the Minoans, whom the ancient Greeks believed had sacrificed human beings to bulls. The Minotaur myth about a half-man and half-bull fed on Athenian hostages is a dim memory of the bull games held much earlier in Minoan palaces on the island of Crete. Whether or not the Minoans expected their athletes to sacrifice themselves in these sacred events is not the issue. Only honed skills would have ensured survival. Armed duels, on the other hand, must have always presupposed very serious injury, if not death. There are fewer references to them in Greece than Italy, possibly because the Romans took up gladiatorial contests with such enthusiasm from the Oscans and Campanians. Even the Etruscans had had gladiators fight at funerals. In 317 BC, however, it is known that four soldiers fought in two single combats at the funeral of a Greek king and queen. The quotation concerning the origin of gladiatorial contests at Rome comes from a late commentary on Marcus Terentius Varro, the Roman antiquarian who died in 27 BC. Recommended for further detail are *Emperors and Gladiators*, by T. Wiedemann, London, 1992, *Spectacle Entertainments of Early Imperial Rome*, by R. C. Beacham, New Haven, 1999, and *Combat Sports in the Ancient World*, by M. B. Poliakoff, New Haven, 1987.

EPEIUS' VICTORY in 'painful boxing' was a singular triumph, as this Greek hero admitted how on the battlefield he was 'not so good at fighting'. But Epeius said that in boxing he was without equal. 'I am going to tear a fellow's flesh to ribbons,' he told would-be challengers, 'and then smash his bones. I recommend him to have mourners standing by.' It was perhaps fortunate for Euryalus, his challenger, that he was soon felled by a mighty blow when for a second he took his eye off Epeius. Those listening to the *Iliad* would of course be aware that the champion boxer had a key role to play in the fall of Troy. In the *Odyssey* he is identified as the craftsman who made the Wooden Horse.

HEPHAESTION'S DEATH caused Alexander a paroxysm of grief and for two days he was unable to eat or see anyone. The funerary games were on an unprecedented scale with 3,000 artists and athletes, as was the pyre built for Hephaestion's cremation which rose five storeys high. It was decorated with gilded eagles and ships' prows, lions, bulls and centaurs. According to Diodorus Siculus, who wrote a history of the world during the reign of the Roman emperor Augustus, on the top of the pyre 'stood sirens, hollowed out and able to conceal within them the persons who sang a lament in mourning of the dead'. The funeral cost well over 10,000 talents, while the tomb Alexander commissioned afterwards added more to the colossal bill. This expenditure would only have been exceeded by a proposal of the artist Stasicrates, who was renowned for 'magnificence, boldness and ostentation'. But Alexander turned down his idea for a Mount Rushmore-like monument to himself carved from Mount Athos in northern Greece.

PELOPS, like the Theban founder-hero Cadmus in central Greece, came from abroad, and gave his name to the Peloponnese. Either Lydian or Phrygian in origin, Pelops' father was believed to have been the arrogant Tantalus, son of the Titaness Pluto and Zeus, head of the Greek pantheon. The Pelopid family is rich in mythology. The white birthmarks its members displayed on their shoulders were but a pale continuation of the ivory insert required after the corn goddess Demeter chewed Pelops' shoulder. For some unknown reason, Tantalus chose to serve his son to the gods in a stew. So preoccupied was Demeter at the disappearance of her own daughter Persephone that she absentmindedly ate a piece of this gruesome dish. When the gods restored Pelops to life, they had to patch the damaged shoulder with a piece of ivory. Curiously, the cannibalistic feast is repeated in the Peloponnese as a result of Myrtilus' curse. A quarrel between Atreus and Thyestes saw the latter eat parts of three of his sons in another stew. Afterwards he was shown their hands and feet. Atreus himself was then slain by Aegisthus, Thyestes' fourth son, who also helped Clytemnestra dispose of Agamemnon on his return from Troy. Agamemnon and his brother Menelaus, king of Sparta, were Pelops' grandsons. Clytemnestra could not forgive Agamemnon for sacrificing Iphigenia in order to obtain for the becalmed Greek expeditionary force 'a fair wind to Troy'. The final unravelling of the curse occurred at Orestes' acquittal of matricide in Athens. This son of Agamemnon avenged his father by slaying Aegisthus as well as Clytemnestra. Of Pelops' end we know nothing at all.

NERO'S VICTORY AT OLYMPIA was an extension of his charioteering exploits in Rome. Suetonius writes how 'Nero set his heart on driving a chariot himself, in a regular race, and after a preliminary trial in the palace gardens before an audience of slaves and hangers-on, he made a public appearance . . .' It is worth recalling that Augustus had had to reprimand and restrain Nero's grandfather, Lucius Domitius, who was an avid promoter of unusually cruel combat-shows and a renowned charioteer in his youth. For an account of the reigns of Caligula and Nero there is Suetonius, *The Twelve Caesars*, translated by R. Graves, Harmondsworth, 1957. Worth reading, too, is E. Champlin's *Nero*, Cambridge, Massachusetts, 2003, since it covers the emperor's triumphant tour of Greece.

CELTIC CHARIOTS are discussed in a number of articles and books. An excellent starting point is *The Celtic World*, edited by M. J. Green, London, 1995. More accessible are R. L. Jiménez's *Caesar against the Celts*, Staplehurst, 1996, and P. B. Ellis' *Celt and Greek. Celts in the Hellenic World*, London, 1997. And the narrative of the Gallic campaigns is available in *Caesar. The Battle for Gaul*, translated by Anne and Peter Wiseman, Boston, 1980.

SELEUCID USE OF CHARIOTS, scythed and unscythed, is discussed in B. Bar-Kochva's *The Seleucid Army. Organisation and Tactics in the Great Campaigns*, Cambridge, 1976. The Seleucid dynasty was one of the beneficiaries of the collapse of Alexander's eastern empire. At its height the Seleucid kingdom stretched from Asia Minor to Bactria, present-day Afghanistan. Eventually it was squeezed out of existence by the Romans and the Parthians. In 64 BC the Roman general Pompey ended the dynasty, by this time ruling a petty Syrian state. He bluntly told the last Seleucid king that he did not deserve a throne as he was unable to defend himself: he had been acclaimed by no more than the people of Antioch. So Syria became another Roman province.

5. INDIA

ALEXANDER'S EXPLOITS have received extensive treatment, but the works of Nicholas Hammond are by far the best and most reliable. Recommended are his *The Genius of Alexander the Great*, London, 1997, and *Alexander the Great. King, Commander and Statesman*, London, 1980. For original sources there are

Plutarch, *The Age of Alexander*, translated by Ian Scott-Kilvert, Harmondsworth, 1973, and Arrian, *The Campaigns of Alexander*, translated by Aubrey de Sélincourt, Harmondsworth, 1958. Once again an excellent study of the materials these two ancient historians used can be found in *Sources for Alexander the Great. An Analysis of Plutarch's 'Life' and Arrian's 'Anabasis Alexandrou'*, by N. G. L. Hammond, Cambridge, 1993.

THE ARTHASASTRA of Kautilya is an extensive work on political economy. Its authorship was not attributed to Candragupta's mentor until a later period, while the present form of the text is the work of Vishnugupta in the third century AD. Though the presence of peoples and places unknown in Mauryan times makes it impossible now to credit Kautilya solely with its authorship, the *Arthasastra* may preserve the original thoughts of this great minister, not least because the theoretical treatise is a pointer to what were once regarded as the essential issues of governance. See *The Arthasastra*, translated by R. Shamasastry, Mysore, 1956, and S. Konow, *Kautalya Studies*, Oslo, 1945.

CELESTIAL WEAPONRY Besides the thunderbolt wielded by Indra, the supreme deity of the Indo-Aryans on their invasion of India, other gods possessed celestial artillery of their own. Of these deities the most powerful weapons were owned by Shiva and Vishnu, rivals for supremacy after the demotion of Indra, which involved the humiliation of his castration. In the *Ramayana*, Indra is punished with this drastic loss by the sage Gotama for seducing his wife. In an unimaginable happening in the Greco-Roman pantheon, the Indian gods tore out the testicles of a ram and gave them to Indra as a replacement. And from that time onwards, they only feasted on the flesh of castrated rams. The diminished status of Indra is obvious in the world-shaking arms belonging to Shiva and Vishnu. Apart from his celestial bow, which fired arrows stored in a thousand quivers, Shiva appropriated Indra's thunderbolt and possibly his fiery discus, which the sage Visvamitra gave to Rama for his battle against Ravana. Among other celestial weapons Visvamitra provided were Shiva's spear, the noose belonging to Varuna, the upholder of the moral order, thunderbolts, spears, and a sword. Rama was instructed to 'accept these weapons at once, for they are very powerful. They can assume any form at will and will bring you all that you desire.'

THE EPICS have long been recognised for their centrality to Indian culture. Like the *Iliad* and the *Odyssey* in the Greco-Roman world, the *Ramayana* and the *Mahabharata* set the epic standard for the Indian subcontinent.

Yet they did more than this for ancient India, because their heroic narratives were not so detached from the heavenly powers as Homer's retelling of the

Greek epics. In the *Ramayana*, where the protagonist Rama is an incarnation of Vishnu, and the *Mahabharata*, where the same great god acts as Arjuna's charioteer, there is a potent element of divinity. Charioteer Krishna does more than stiffen the resolve of Arjuna to fight on the Kurukshetra plain; he expounds in his sermon, the so-called *Bhagavadgita*, a whole philosophy of the world. It could be said to contain the essence of the Upanishads, early mystical texts which dealt, among other things, with reincarnation: the idea of an almost unending passage from death to rebirth and death again. Even when punctuated by periods of residence in the heavens, the prospect of rebirth after rebirth in a vale of tears was a heavy psychological burden to carry. Through self-realisation alone, Krishna tells Arjuna, can the individual learn to cope with this apparently endless round of lives, and even escape from its thrall. 'He who understands God and Nature, whatever be his condition in life, he comes not again to earth.'

The bardic origins of the Indian epics, however, were no different from the traditions to which Homer gave their final shape in the *Iliad* and the *Odyssey*. It is known that Indian bards accompanied their masters into battle or the hunt as charioteers, enabling them to base their descriptions of hunting or chariot battle on their own first-hand experience. But over the centuries, the epics gathered to their narratives strong religious elements, which, like Krishna's encouragement of Arjuna, could stand on their own as a separate didactic work. In the *Harivamsa*, a supplement to the *Mahabharata*, we have an entire poem devoted to Krishna, whose worship as a deity was on the increase during the third and fourth centuries AD, the period of the *Harivamsa's* composition. Earlier stories about Krishna's exploits as well as his passionate love for Radha had already persuaded Greek settlers in northwestern India, whose kingdoms flourished during the second century BC, to identify him with the hero Herakles. Unlike the Greek hero, the divinity of Krishna was never in doubt. Vishnu plucked two of his own hairs, one white and one black. These two hairs entered the wombs of two women; the white hair became Balarama, and the black Krishna, whose name means 'black'. Their reputed father was Vasudeva, the brother-in-law of Pandu. Full discussion of the *Ramayana*, the *Mahabharata* and the *Harivamsa* can be found in John Brockington's excellent study, *The Sanskrit Epics*, Leiden, 1998. For the poems themselves there are *The Ramayana of Valmiki*, translated and annotated by R. P. and S. J. Goldman, Princeton, 1984 onwards, and *The Mahabharata*, translated by J. A. B. van Buitenen, Chicago, 1973 onwards.

DEMONS are supposed to have sprung from Brahma's foot. Their chief, Rama's enemy Ravana, had increased his own strength by his devotion to this great god, whose own meditation was sufficient to bring creatures into existence. But Ravana also adopted the austerities of the ancient Indian sages in order to prepare for his fight with Rama, the incarnate Vishnu. Implicit in the eternal rivalry between the gods and the demons is a recognition of the necessity of evil. The gods find evil necessary for their own existence; they tolerate demons in order that they may thrive as gods. Thus Vishnu becomes incarnate to prevent the demons from destroying mankind, but never to annihilate the demons, for this preserver god accepts the need to maintain a balance between the forces of good and evil. The absolute necessity for worship is apparent in a rare intervention of Brahma. 'In a former time,' we are told, 'anarchy arose which worried Brahma, for without men the gods are not able to sustain the world, since the gods live upon the nourishment from sacrificial gifts and prayers. So a king was chosen to bring order on earth. This he did until the demons in envy chose to do him harm.'

INDIAN KINGSHIP was edged round with divinity, although kings were never regarded as gods in the manner of the Egyptian pharaohs. Only in South-east Asia, where Indian religious ideas were transplanted in the fifth and sixth centuries AD, was it believed that in a monarch an incarnate deity actually resided. In Cambodia the 'god king' was usually identified with Shiva. Hence there were no abdications on religious grounds by Cambodian rulers: none felt the urge of a Candragupta to quit the throne for a contemplative life. In India the origin of kingship was associated with the breakdown of natural order. At first there was no need of kings and royal punishments, since people behaved in such a way that no harm came to anyone. Then evil began to disrupt this idyllic existence, and the gods, fearing total chaos, appealed to the creator god Brahma as well as the saviour god Vishnu, who arranged for the first king to appear. He was Prithu, an ideal ruler who made some kind of social contract with the gods and the sages on behalf of mankind.

Not seen as a divinity himself, Prithu was said to embody divine qualities which set him apart from other people. According to the fourth-century AD *Laws of Manu*, the seminal work of what we term Hinduism today, the king was a warrior formed by mixing together 'eternal particles of Indra, whose weapon is the mighty thunderbolt, of the wind god Yayu, the very breath of life, of Yama, king of the dead, of the sun god Surya, whose ruddy horses pull his chariot across the sky, of Agni, god of fire and sacrifice, of Varuna, upholder of the moral order, and of Kubera, god of wealth. Because a king has been made from particles belonging to these gods, he surpasses all other created beings and, like the sun, he scorches eyes and hearts, so that none may look upon him.' Different though this is from the single incarnation thought to be present in a Cambodian ruler, the divine inheritance of Indian kings following Prithu's reign could hardly be denied. Thus the monarch was the focus of an ancient Indian state, the essential ingredient which ensured its survival in troubled times. Hence the anger of the Pandavas at their exclusion by the Kauravas from Hastinapura, the capital from which they expected to rule. They had been denied their birth-right as Pandu's sons, and the proper exercise of the divine talents all Indian kings had inherited from Prithu.

THE INDUS CIVILIZATION was discovered in the 1920s when excavation of mounds in the Indus valley uncovered two large ruined cities of which there was no mention in ancient records. These major sites – upwards of five kilometres in circumference during their heyday – were Mohenjodaro in Sind and Harappa in the western Punjab. They were both situated on old river courses and contained many-storeyed, palatial, solidly built houses, which were supplied with good wells, drains, bathrooms and toilets. In 1931 another city at Chanhudaro, closer to the mouth of the Indus river, was dug and the existence of an Indian civilisation prior to the Indo-Aryan invasion was firmly established. Knowledge of the so-called Indus civilisation is still far from complete. Over a hundred sites have been found of which five were obviously cities, but to date there is no convincing decipherment of the Indus script, which appears on seals, pots and copper pieces. Mesopotamia and Egypt had long emerged into a civilized way of living when the Indus people built their remarkable cities shortly after 2400 BC.

Like other ancient civilizations, the Indus one relied on agriculture, the majority of the people living in villages clustered around the cities. With the aid of silt-bearing floods and irrigation the farmers cultivated wheat, barley, vegetables, fruit, and sesame as well as mustard for oil. In the vicinity of Lothol, at the head of the bay of Cambay, rice cultivation had been mastered, a crop of untold significance in the later history of India. Moreover, cotton was grown in the Indus valley several centuries before it was in Egypt. Farmers most probably handed over to the public granaries located in the cities a large part of their crops. The vagaries of river courses, flooding of which could cause famine instead of a bumper crop, were offset by this storage of cereals. Yet the cutting down of trees for fuel and timber, and the increased grazing of grass, could have exacerbated natural conditions. Mohenjodaro was repaired nine times after flooding.

Little is understood about the rest of Indus valley society other than the presence of a priestly class. Of warfare there is nothing to point to the organisation for forces, besides finds of arrow-heads and axes. No proof survives of the chariot's use, before the arrival of the Indo-Aryans. These incoming cattle-keeping people would have had little sympathy with the crop-growing inhabitants of the Indus valley. A clash of cultures was inevitable. Whether they came to India by land or sea, the Indo-Aryans would have soon become aware of the extensive sea-borne trade conducted by Indus valley merchants. Lothol had a dock which merchant ships could enter at high tide through a specially designed channel. On the quay stood warehouses ready to discharge export items and store imported goods. From this port high-prowed vessels sailed to the island of Bahrein, where a walled trading port exchanged articles from West Asia and India. Some of the ships sailed farther west and traded direct with Mesopotamia. 'Meluhha' may well refer to an Indian trading settlement there. First mentioned in the late third millennium BC, Meluhhan ships were a not uncommon sight at Mesopotamian ports until the end of the Indus civilisation, which occurred around 1700 BC. Degeneration was in progress at most sites after 1900 BC. Underlying the decline of the Indus valley city was a deterioration of the surrounding landscape. Into this depressed economy poured the Indo-Aryans, who would have been more interested in grazing land than inundated fields for crops.

For more information about the Indus civilisation there are B. and R. Alluchin's *The Rise of Civilization in India and Pakistan*, Cambridge, 1982, W. A. Fairservis' *The Roots of Ancient India*, London, 1971, Sir Mortimer Wheeler's *The Indus Civilization*, Cambridge, 1968, which is a supplement to the *Cambridge History of India*, and S. R. Rao's *Lothal and the Indus Civilization*, London, 1972.

THE RIG VEDA documents the Indo-Aryan settlement of northwestern India, which was called Aryavarta, 'the land where the Aryans live'. Though the language of the *Rig Veda* belongs to the Indo-European family of languages, Sanskrit or Old Indo-Aryan is most closely related to the Iranian group of languages, in particular Old Persian and Avestan. This linguistic relationship is so close that these two peoples, the Indo-Aryans and the Iranians, must in remote times have constituted a single nation. Their split brought into existence two distinct religious traditions: Vedic in India, Zoroastrian in Iran. Whereas the Indo-Aryans recorded their earliest thoughts about the gods in the hymns of the *Rig Veda*, the Iranians (later to be known as the Persians, Parthians and Sasanians) expressed their beliefs in the *Gathas*. It was the religious reforms of the prophet Zoroaster some time before 1000 BC which really made the Iranian faith so different, as he insisted upon a scheme of redemption that was to be achieved by means of Ahura Mazda's final victory over the spirit of evil, Angra Mainyu, twelve millenniums after creation. In this redemptive process mankind was to be helped by three 'saviours'. For the Indo-Aryans, however, there was no real sense of an end to time, let alone a grand sorting out of good from evil in some last judgment. Possibly because the idea of continuous rebirth took the sting out of death, they lacked any anxiety over cosmic change. Even Indra found it hard to grasp the idea of an endless cycle of emanation, fruition, dissolution and re-emanation, when on one occasion Shiva and Vishnu told him that there already existed an army of Indras. These deities recurred in each slowly moving cycle to repeat their mythological actions. Such a view of course postdates the *Rig Veda*

and incorporates religious notions the Indo-Aryans absorbed from the indigenous Indus civilisation. That is why the Indian epics can develop such complex
plots, since they reached their final stages during a period enriched by the divine
exploits of Vishnu, the Indian equivalent of the Zoroastrian saviour.

A really accessible edition of the *Rig Veda* is Wendy Doniger O'Flaherty's
translation, Harmondsworth, 1981. Also recommended is *Chariots in the Veda*, by
M. Sparreboom, Leiden, 1985.

HORSE-SACRIFICE was a widespread rite among Indo-European peoples. It
is discussed along with other common traits in Jan Puhvel's *Comparative
Mythology*, Baltimore, 1987, a fascinating treatment of Indian, Iranian, Greek,
Roman, Celtic, Germanic, Baltic and Slavic myths. How far the Ulster ritual
found in Gerald of Cambrai was garbled in the retelling it is now impossible to
determine. That a horse was somehow involved in the assertion of sovereignty
cannot be ignored, given the animal's significance to Indo-European kings. A
recent treatment of cattle in India is *The Myth of the Holy Cow*, by D. N. Jha,
London, 2002, which touches upon the ancient practice of horse-sacrifice. The
abolition of animal sacrifice in later times, whether horses or cows, meant that
the non-violent teachings of the Buddha won the day.

6. CHINA

THE SPRING AND AUTUMN PERIOD took its name from the title of the
chronicles of the state of Lu, the *Spring and Autumn Annals*, which cover the
years 722–481 BC. Chinese feudalism was already in decline prior to its start,
although the emergence of fully independent states occurred well after the Zhou
kings took up residence at Luoyang, to which they had fled in 770 BC. The focus
of both military and political action during the Spring and Autumn period was
the Yellow river valley, the Shandong peninsula, and to the south, the Huai river
valley. It eventually expanded to include present-day Shaanxi, Shanxi and Hebei
provinces in the north and the Yangzi river valley in the south. Even though 200
feudal territories are known to have been in existence at the start of the seventh
century BC, by 500 BC that number had dropped to fewer than twenty. The
major states were Qi, Qing, Jin, Chu, Lu, Song, Chen, Yan and Wu. It was
Huai, the duke of Qi (684–642 BC), who first strove to establish some kind of
order among these rival powers. As hegemon, he claimed to act on behalf of the
Zhou king, now restricted to a ceremonial role on an impoverished domain at
Luoyang.

Even though the Spring and Autumn period takes its name from the annals of
the state of Lu, the most important source is the *Zuo zhuan*, or 'Zuo's tradition'.

A partial translation is available in Burton Watson's *The Tso Chuan. Selections from China's Oldest Narrative History*, New York, 1989. For the Warring States period there is a full translation of the *Zhanguo ce*, or *Strategems of the Warring States*, by J. I. Crump, entitled *Chan-Kuo Ts'e*, Oxford, 1970.

THE WARRING STATES PERIOD, which followed on from the Spring and Autumn one, witnessed a complete transformation of ancient China. Between 481 and 221 BC a number of large states arose under the control of powerful rulers, who mobilised the peasantry in order to increase the size of their armed forces. This acceleration of conflict not unnaturally caused the emergence of specialists, like Sun Zi, the author of the *Art of War*, who were masters of the theories and techniques of warfare. Chariotry continued to play a role on the battlefield throughout the Warring States period, notwithstanding the invention of the crossbow, the most destructive hand-held weapon to be used in ancient times. For an account of the development of the chariot in China there are the appropriate sections of Joseph Needham's *Science and Civilisation in China, Volume Four, Physics and Physical Technology, Part Two, Mechanical Engineering*, Cambridge, 1965, and for the crossbow Joseph Needham and Robin Yates' *Science and Civilisation in China, Volume Five, Chemistry and Chemical Technology, Part Four, Missiles and Sieges*, Cambridge, 1994. A difficulty in coming to an understanding of ancient Chinese warfare is the general absence of translations of relevant studies written by specialists in the Chinese language. Current excavations of chariots are discussed at length in two journals, *Wenwu* (*Cultural Relics*) and *Kaogu* (*Archaeology*), while a good survey of ancient arms is available in *Zhongguo Gu Bingqu Lun Cong* (*A Discourse on Ancient Chinese Weaponry*), Yang Hong, Beijing, 1985.

THE SCHOOL OF LAW, for which Shang Yang spoke, was one of four main philosophies that competed for attention during the Warring States period. The other three were Daoism, Moism and Confucianism. Though Daoism and Confucianism were to have lasting importance in Chinese history, the most heatedly debated philosophies before the Qin unification of China in 221 BC were Legalism and Moism. It has been said that traditionally the Chinese were Daoist in private and Confucianist in public, but it might be added that those who entered the imperial civil service always felt the lingering influence of the administrative concepts of Legalism. Only the doctrines of Mo Zi (479–438 BC) vanished from the Chinese mind after the first emperor burned the books in 213 BC, so as to 'make the people ignorant' and to prevent the 'use of the past to discredit the present'. Shang Yang (390–338 BC) and Han Fei Zi (280–233 BC), Legalism's other leading thinker, looked forward to the totalitarianism of the centralised Qin empire. 'In the state of an enlightened ruler,' wrote Han Fei Zi, 'there are no books; law supplies the only instruction. There are no sermons on kings of old; the officials serve as the only teachers.' The Legalist attempt to stupefy the mind of China failed miserably. In reaction to the repression and violence of Qin rule, which lasted from 221 to 206 BC, the second imperial dynasty, the Han, turned to Confucianism as a means of holding together what were recently independent feudal states. By promoting scholars of the Confucian persuasion, the Han emperors paved the way for the ultimate Confucianisation of a bureaucratic empire. The transformation was a slow one because there was need for political compromise after the terrible years of Qin. Some feudal houses were restored and fiefs granted to imperial relatives, but these diminished holdings were intertwined with districts controlled by imperial officials. Once it was decreed that inherited land had to be divided between all sons in a family, the end was in sight for large estates. Emperor Han Wu Di (140–87 BC) completed the dispossession of the old feudal aristocracy.

An overview of political thought in general, including the use of coercive power, is provided in *A Political History of Chinese Thought: From the Beginnings to the Sixth Century AD*, by Hsiao Kung-chuan, translated by F. W. Mote, Princeton, 1979. Books on individual philosophers are *Confucius and the Chinese Way*, by H. G. Creel, New York, 1960, *The Book of Lord Shang: A Classic of Chinese Law*, by J. J. L. Duyvendak, London, 1928, and *Motse. The Neglected Rival of Confucius*, by Yi-Pao Mei, London, 1934.

SHANG ruled much of the Yellow river valley and its tributaries from around 1650 to 1027 BC. The core of the Shang kingdom was that part of Henan province where the higher ground declines into the flood-plain of the Yellow river. Not all of the sites used by Shang kings as capitals have been located, which makes the final one at Anyang so valuable for archaeology. Recommended are *Anyang*, by Li Chi, Seattle, 1977, *The Cradle of the East. An Inquiry into the Indigenous Origins of Techniques and Ideas of Neolithic and Early Historic China, 5000–1000 BC*, by Ping-ti Ho, Hong Kong, 1975, and *Shang Civilization*, by Kwang-Chih Chang, New Haven, 1980.

TOCHARIANS In the absence of written material actually associated with the Tarim graves, it is still possible to query the identity of the mummified bodies on display in Urumchi museum. Yet in *The Tarim Mummies*, London, 2000, J. P. Malory and V. H. Mair make a convincing case for them being Tocharians. It does seem more than likely that the Tocharian-speaking inhabitants of the oases on the north side of the Tarim basin, where Urumchi is situated, were there long before the Tocharian manuscripts were produced in the sixth century AD. These texts are primarily translations of Buddhist works, but there are also monastery records, caravan travel passes and other commercial documents. Their discovery points to the possible speech of the mummies, while the preserved features of the mummified bodies themselves underline a definite non-Central Asian ethnicity.

THE CROSSBOW caused consternation in Europe because of its effectiveness against armour. It had claimed many knightly and even royal victims before the Second Lateran Council condemned the weapon, along with the self bow. What this prohibition tried to do was outlaw all missile weapons: churchmen's views on the conduct of medieval warfare were of course ignored by military leaders impressed with the accuracy of crossbow-fire. The English king Richard I was an excellent shot himself, but at the castle of Chaluz Chabrol, which was taken by storm in 1199, he received a shoulder wound from a crossbow bolt, which turned gangrenous and killed him. Invaluable though archers and crossbowmen were on the battlefield, a knightly unease over the use of missiles often manifested itself in their execution when captured. Lords who had crossbowmen and archers in their pay would order such reprisals, almost as if they resented being vulnerable themselves to weapons that were handled by common folk. See Matthew Strickland's *War and Chivalry. The Conduct and Perception of War in England and Normandy, 1066–1217*, Oxford, 1996.

7. THE END OF THE WAR CHARIOT

THE SEA PEOPLES were the perpetrators of widespread destruction in the eastern Mediterranean in the late thirteenth and early twelfth centuries BC. That they contributed to the collapse of the Hittite empire there can be no doubt: their subsequent depredations in Syria and Palestine are equally clear. What is not so easily explained is the sudden collapse of Hittite power, notwithstanding the real possibility of mercenaries in the employ of King Suppiluliuma II throwing in their lot with the invading Sea Peoples. Internal division in Hatti seems to have played a role in weakening Suppiluliuma's position in the same way that dissent among the nobility later undermined the authority of Assyrian kings. But the few surviving texts from the last years of Hittite power show no lack of confidence: the account of successful land campaigns in Tarhuntassa and sea operations from its port of Ura reads like previous royal records. The end must have come, therefore, quite suddenly.

The Sea Peoples were well known as mercenaries in Egypt before, in 1182 BC, they were halted on its borders by Ramesses III. In a previous assault on the Nile delta in 1218 BC some of them had served alongside Libyan tribesmen. Even though the Egyptians, unlike the Hittites, weathered the storm of the Sea Peoples, the days of their greatness were coming to an end. Before Ramesses III died, there was unrest in the village on the west bank at Thebes occupied by the workmen engaged on the royal tomb, and the pharaoh himself was the subject of an abortive assassination attempt hatched in the royal harem. It would seem that the movement of the Sea Peoples happened to coincide with a moment of weakness for two great powers, Hatti and Egypt. The latter appears to have been more fortunate in retaining the loyalty of the mercenaries in its employ. The Shardana, long bodyguards of the pharaohs, stood firm, as did other Sea Peoples in the Egyptian army. Ramesses III was sufficiently confident to decide against a full call-up of Egyptians, a remarkably relaxed attitude considering the extent of the damage already caused by the Sea Peoples beyond Egypt's borders.

In Egyptian inscriptions the names of the Sea Peoples are listed as the Lukka, Sherden, Denyen or Danuna, Tjeker, Peleset, Teresh, Skekelesh, Weshesh, Ekwesh and Shardana. There was no grand conspiracy among these disparate peoples, whatever the Egyptians liked to believe, but rather a common need to overcome one of the periodic breakdowns which afflicted ancient political systems. The movement of the Sea Peoples could thus be seen as a by-product of growing economic problems caused by an over-extension of the Hittite empire. Strained resources, especially if aggravated by poor crop yields, could have given impetus to their trek east and south. Ramesses III's account of the land battle he won, carved on the walls of his memorial temple at Medinet Habu, portrays the invaders on foot and in chariots, their ox-carts loaded with women and children. This was a migration, not a raid. The Sea Peoples were hoping to settle as well as conquer, which was something the Peleset actually achieved when they became the biblical Philistines.

The best survey of the phenomenon of the Sea Peoples is still N. K. Sanders' *The Sea Peoples: Warriors of the Ancient Mediterranean*, London, 1978. The Medinet Habu inscriptions can be found in *Ancient Records of Egypt, Volume Four, The Twentieth through to the Twenty-sixth Dynasties*, translated and edited by J. H. Breasted, Chicago, 1906. It also contains details of the trial of the harem conspirators, who were led by Tiy, one of Ramesses III's queens. She wished to give the crown to her son Pentaweret instead of the legitimate heir. About forty people were put to death, while Pentaweret was forced to commit suicide. The conspiracy and the trial, which involved the arrest of five of the twelve judges drawn from the highest ranks of civil and military officials, revealed an ominous division between the dynasty and the governing class. As none of Ramesses III's eight successors achieved anything memorable, he is regarded as the last significant pharaoh, lucky though he was to avoid a violent death in his own palace.

MILETOS, possibly the Hittite Millawanda, was believed by the Greeks to have been a city which acquired great wealth through the virtue and industry of its inhabitants, who then became enslaved by pleasure and luxury, so that the city went into steep decline. Hence the ancient saying: 'Once, long ago, the Milesians were mighty men.' Behind this legend is the fact of Miletos' prosperity as an early trading port. Its site was continuously occupied from the sixteenth century BC onwards. During the heyday of the Hittite empire Miletos seems to have carefully preserved its independence by keeping out of quarrels between Hittite kings and their western subjects in Asia Minor. The rebel Piyamaradu may not have been handed over to the Hittites, but nor was he allowed to remain a resident of the city. Post-Hittite Miletos depended for its recovery on migration, the so-called Ionian one, from mainland Greece. The changes which then overtook the Aegean, and indeed the mainland itself, are well treated in *Citadel to City-State. The Transformation of Greece, 1200–700 BC*, by C. G. Thomas and C. Conant, Bloomington, Indiana, 1999.

THE PHILISTINES were such a serious threat to Israel that the Old Testament portrays a complete collapse of self-confidence prior to the elevation of Samuel as its first king. So dominant were the Philistines that even metalwork was restricted, presumably to exercise control over the supply of weapons. The relevant passage runs, 'Now there was no smith found throughout all the land of Israel: for the Philistines said, Lest the Hebrews make them swords or spears: but all the Israelites went down to the Philistines, to sharpen every man his share, and his coulter, and his axe, and his mattock.' The downfall of Samson, the strong man of Israel, was the climax of the ascendancy which the Philistines briefly enjoyed. Once Delilah had discovered the secret of Samson's strength there was no warrior brave enough to face the Philistines. The famous duel between David and Goliath, the youth and the giant, was a true reflection of Israel's weakness on the battlefield, while its outcome was a miraculous event, a precursor of the future strength of Israel under David and his son, Solomon. For further information on the struggle between the Philistines, formerly the Peleset, and the Israelites there is *Battles of the Bible*, by C. Herzog and M. Cichon, London, 1978. The whole issue of warfare is, however, discussed in Susan Niditch's fascinating study entitled *War in the Hebrew Bible*, Oxford, 1993.

THE REVOLT OF THE RUNNERS, as a factor in the success of the Sea Peoples, cannot readily be discounted. Robert Drews makes the case in *The End of the Bronze Age. Changes in Warfare and the Catastrophe ca. 1200*, Princeton, 1993. In this important analysis of ancient warfare he shows how vulnerable chariotry was to determined infantrymen attacking in strength. Although the chariot did not succumb to the equivalent of the 'runners' in ancient China, there were occasions on which something similar occurred, usually when hillsmen moved down to the plains on raiding expeditions. They provide distant confirmation of Drews' original thesis.

NUBIA enjoyed a great upsurge of power in the eighth century BC based on the city of Napata, modern Gebel Barkal near the fourth cataract of the Nile. How this obscure settlement rose to become the capital of an Egyptian-style state remains little understood. But it is a wonderful irony that Pianky, a Nubian ruler whose ancestors were once depicted by Egyptian artists as trodden beneath the feet of triumphant pharaohs, should then be portrayed as a pharaoh himself, a brother king to Thutmose III and Ramesses II. During his rule in Egypt and Nubia Pianky adopted and used their titles as the mood took him. Known to the ancient Egyptians as the Kushite dynasty, the Nubian house remained a force until 663 BC, when the Assyrians sacked Thebes and drove it back to Napata. After losing control of Egypt, an Egyptianised dynasty survived in Nubia for a millennium, until its rule was ended by Muslim armies. Recommended are *Nubia, Corridor to Africa*, by W. Y. Adams, London, 1977, and *The Kingdom of Kush. The Napatan and Meroitic Empires*, London, 1996.

THE BRONZE SNAFFLE-BIT, Robert Drews argues in his *Early Riders: The Beginnings of Mounted Warfare in Asia and Europe*, London, 2004, was the crucial innovation for the development of cavalry, at the end of the second and the beginning of the first millennium BC.

THE ASSYRIAN CHARIOT, with an eight-spoked wheel, became notably heavier once larger horses were available to pull it. The most striking feature of this vehicle, the biggest ever to appear on an ancient battlefield, was the thickness of the felloes. Obviously enlarged to provide the chariot with a safer passage over rough ground, these huge felloes, which were strengthened with iron, made late Assyrian wheels seem grossly out of proportion to the passenger box, as indeed they were in comparison with those fitted on earlier chariots. By the seventh century BC though, chariotry was waning as a main battle force, not least because the larger horses imported from Urartu and Nubia permitted the full development of cavalry. The heavy chariot first appears in the reign of Tiglath-pileser III (744–727 BC) and it easily accommodated a crew of four. One of the reasons for the chariot team being able to pull the greater weight, besides the larger build of the horses themselves, was a more efficient harnessing arrangement. It did not match the ancient Chinese breast-harness, but there was some relief of the pressure placed on the horses' necks. It would appear that the inner rim, or felloe, of the chariot wheel was separate from the outer one, to which it was attached by metal plates. The ends of the spokes fitting into the inner felloe were sheathed in metal as well. Corrugated iron tyres also assisted the wheels in gripping the ground.

FORT SHALMANESER, a military complex at ancient Kalhu, was excavated between 1957 and 1963. An arsenal rather than a fortress, it was built by Shalmaneser III (858–824 BC), the son of Ashurnasirpal II, who sought to enhance his father's new imperial foundation. No reason was ever given by Ashurnasirpal for the removal of the Assyrian capital from Ashur to Kalhu, modern Nimrud. Why he overlooked Nineveh, the later capital, also remains unexplained. But his son Shalmaneser, on ascending the throne, lost no time in commissioning a major building programme, of which Fort Shalmaneser was a key part. A number of building projects were also undertaken at his command in Ashur, then still important as a religious and commercial centre. What Fort Shalmaneser appears to have been is the headquarters of the Assyrian army, its high command, arsenal and training centre. Records survive of men, horses and arms. A large open space nearby could have been used as a parade ground, on which infantrymen mustered and horsemen trained alongside charioteers. An insight into the military records found there is available in *The Tablets from Fort Shalmaneser*, by S. Dalley and J. N. Postgate, published by the British School of Archaeology in Iraq, 1984, while Ashurnasirpal II's inscriptions are translated and explained in A. K. Grayson's *Assyrian Rulers of the Early First Millennium BC, Volume One (1114–859 BC)*, Toronto, 1991. For an overall account of Kalhu there is Joan and David Oates' detailed study of the city, entitled *Nimrud. An Assyrian Imperial City Revealed*, also published by the British School of Archaeology in Iraq, 2001.

ROYAL HUNTS were a favourite subject of Assyrian sculptors. Ashurbanipal's exploits in the British Museum still attract wondering onlookers today. They show the king hunting in a chariot, on horseback, and on foot. In nearly every case his weapon is a composite bow. The best photographs of these exhibits are to be found in a remarkable publication entitled *Assyrian Sculpture in the British Museum*, by R. D. Barnett and A. Lorenzini, Toronto, 1975. For Napoleon's sudden discomfiture see *Napoleon and Wellington*, by A. Roberts, London, 2001.

MEGASTHENES was an Ionian Greek who served on several embassies to the court of the first Maurya king, Candragupta. Following the treaty between Seleucus I and Candragupta in 302 BC, Megasthenes paid a number of visits to India, and the book he wrote about what he saw there was popular, since it appeared not long after Alexander the Great's eastern campaigns. 'It is a remarkable thing,' he wrote, 'that all Indians are free, and no Indian at all is a slave.' The reason for this surprising situation, according to Megasthenes, was the teaching of the Indian sages, who held 'that those who have learned neither to domineer over others nor to subject themselves to others will enjoy a manner of life best suited to all circumstances'. The very different notions of wisdom prevalent in India had already been noted by the Greeks, and contributed to the shaping of sceptical thought. Pyrrhon of Elis (365–270 BC), the founder of Greek scepticism, had travelled to India as part of Alexander's train. Just how unlike Europe things could be in India is seen in the Jain tradition of Candragupta's end as a recluse at Sravana Belgola, now in the southern state of Karnataka. A famine persuaded the king not only of his own unworthiness to rule but more of the pointlessness of all human aspiration.

8. SURVIVALS, RITUAL AND RACING

MAGNESIA was a turning point in the politics of the eastern Mediterranean because it established Rome as the dominant power there. Antiochus III seems to have been trying out new tactics against the Roman legions, after their defeat of Macedon at the battle of Cynoscephalae in 197 BC. Then the Macedonian phalanx was overcome through a mixture of rashness and circumspection, the impetuous character of King Philip V of Macedon and the calm generalship of the Roman commander, Titus Quinctius Flamininus. Chance was certainly a factor in the Roman victory, something Antiochus was concerned to minimise at Magnesia. So he decided to charge both wings of the Roman army at the same time and, once they were in disarray, advance with his main force of infantry intact. Whereas his plan worked on one wing, it failed on the other, as his chariotry succumbed to missile fire and a counter-attack by cavalry. A good discussion of the battle, and indeed others fought by Seleucid kings is available in B. Bar-Kochva's *The Seleucid Army. Organization and Tactics in the Great Campaigns*, Cambridge, 1976.

THE SCIPIOS were typical of the narrowness of the Roman ruling class in the middle period of the republic, approximately 300 to 150 BC. The family held no fewer than twenty-three consulships, the highest public office. The oldest tomb in the family cemetery at Rome belongs to Lucius Cornelius Scipio Barbatus, consul in 298 BC; its inscription records his military exploits against the Samnites, who in 321 BC had inflicted a major defeat on the Romans at the battle of the Caudine Forks. The most famous member of the family was Scipio Barbatus' great-grandson, Publius Cornelius Scipio Africanus Major, the victor over the Carthaginian general Hannibal in 202 BC at Zama, in present-day Tunisia. His younger brother, Lucius Cornelius Scipio Asiaticus, was accused of corruption after beating Antiochus at Magnesia. An inquiry was set up to discover the whereabouts of the war indemnity paid by the Seleucid monarch. It seemed outrageous to the elder Cato, the scourge of luxury, that Scipio Asiaticus brought back from Asia Minor the first bronze couches, bedcovers, ornate tables and singing girls to be seen in Rome. And Cato's moral condemnation prevailed, for not long afterwards, political enemies of the Scipios drove both brothers out of public life. Yet their careers marked a significant change in Roman politics: they were not like the previously anonymous consuls who with little fuss defeated Rome's enemies. Instead, the elder brother was the first general to be known by the name of the country he had overcome, Africanus, just as his greedy younger brother was called Asiaticus. Much to the annoyance of Cato neither Scipio was afraid to take personal pleasure in display, a un-Roman habit that he blamed on their fascination for all things Greek. For the background to this alteration in the outlook of Roman aristocrats there is *Scipio Africanus: Soldier and Politician*, by H. H. Scullard, London, 1970.

GAINING A TRIUMPH at Rome was by no means easy because seven conditions had to be met before senators would agree to one. The first ensured that only senior magistrates could celebrate a triumph, while the second insisted it should occur during their period of office. Only they could be awarded a triumph, no matter that their subordinates may have been responsible for a victory, which the fourth condition said should account for at least 5,000 enemy dead. Also the war had to be legitimate, according to the fifth, in that civil conflicts did not count. Territory needed to be added, too, and not lost areas simply regained. And last but not least, peace had to prevail after conquest and the withdrawal of troops. If the senate found these conditions were met, a triumph was granted and funds voted towards defraying the costs involved. Spectacular events like triumphs were very expensive. Accounts exist in the books of most Roman historians, the description of Aemilius Paullus' one of 167 BC being derived from several sources. The best treatment of the whole subject is *Triumphus. An Inquiry into the Origin, Development and Meaning of the Roman Triumph*, by H. S. Versnel, Leiden, 1970.

The circumstances of Camillus' triumphal entry are difficult to understand. Why did he risk provoking such a reaction? A possible explanation is the removal of Juno's cult statue from Veii to Rome. In all probability it was the Veian double of the goddess which was carried in the triumphal procession. The Etruscan city was stormed after a prolonged siege in 396 BC. The religious commentator, Valerius Maximus, writing in the first century AD, states that on the order of the Roman commander the statue of Juno was removed to Rome. 'When as a joke,' he tells us, 'the goddess was asked by a soldier if she wanted to move, she replied that she did. On hearing her speak, the joking turned to amazement and, believing now that they were carrying not a statue but Juno herself, they joyfully installed her at Rome.' Most likely the imported goddess was Uni, Juno's Etruscan counterpart. We know the practice of removal was very old, since Tertullian wrote: 'The Romans have committed as many sacrileges as they have trophies, they have triumphed over as many gods as they have over nations. No more proof is needed than the host of captive statues.' It is not, therefore, impossible that Camillus was deliberately recalling Jupiter when he harnessed white horses to the triumphal chariot; thus he could properly announce the arrival of his divine consort, Juno.

VESTAL VIRGINS attended the sacred flame of the goddess Vesta. Her ever-burning hearth was looked upon as a guarantee of continued occupation of Rome; hence the concern of L. Albinius at the sight of the Vestals' flight. Only they could ensure the reoccupation of the city, with their 'sacred objects', once the Gallic invaders had withdrawn. Valerius Maximus' *Memorable Deeds and Sayings* has been translated, with an introduction and commentary, by D. Wardle, Oxford, 1998. See also Hans-Friedrich Mueller's *Roman Religion in Valerius Maximus*, London, 2002.

JUVENAL targets amateur charioteers because of the amount of money wasted in such display. These enthusiasts served to confirm what he feared most, a Rome dominated by wealth rather than birth. After the quotation from his first satire, which appears in the text, he heaps disdain on a forger, carried about in a litter by six porters. 'A will, a mere scrap of paper, a counterfeit seal – with these he acquired wealth and honour.' Still a very good translation of the satires is Peter Green's revised *Juvenal. The Sixteen Satires*, Harmondsworth, 1998.

KONARAK, in Orissa, contains the famous temple dedicated to the sun god Surya, which was built in the thirteenth century AD. It is sometimes called the Black Pagoda. For more details, including photographs, there are the two volumes of Heinrich Zimmer's monumental study entitled *The Art of Indian Asia. Its Mythology and Transformations*, Princeton, 1960.

RACING TRACKS are discussed at length in *Roman Circuses. Arenas for Chariot Racing*, by J. H. Humphrey, London, 1986. This thorough survey is well worth reading for its technical detail alone. The author believes that chariot racing spread to Britain, despite the fact of no circus having ever been identified. He thinks it is quite possible that one existed in London, near St Paul's.

LATE CHARIOTEERING is the subject of two books by Alan Cameron: *Porphyrius the Charioteer*, Oxford, 1973, and *Circus Factions. Blues and Greens at Rome and Byzantium*, Oxford, 1976. Quotations in the text about Porphyrius have been translated from the original inscriptions reproduced in the former. Commemorative statuary seems to have originated in ancient Greece, as an honour to Olympic victors. In Rome both the senators and the people could erect statues to particular individuals, but the emperors took an interest in these honorific dedications and, when they felt it appropriate to do so, they would veto statues. They also cleared them away whenever public places became too full. However, in Constantinople the statues recalling Porphyrius' victories were specifically approved by the imperial government.

CHRISTIAN DISLIKE FOR THE GAMES is best explained as a recognition of their pagan origin. At the beginning of every show there was a religious ceremony, a dedication of the event to one deity or another. Often in processions preceding shows given as part of religious festivals, statues of gods were actually carried from their temples to the circus where they were positioned to witness the races. Later, statues of deified Roman emperors were placed in the circus as well. And not lost on Christian critics was the significance of the monuments placed on the central barrier of the circus, recalling the old ritual of funeral games. In Rome the rites attending the deaths of prominent citizens were often transformed into spectacular shows not only through the gladiatorial entertainments associated with them, but even more by the public nature of the funeral procession, enhanced as it often was by the parade of distinguished ancestors. The absence of impressive tombs, at least until the emperor Augustus built his own mausoleum, only encouraged an emphasis on display in funeral rites: a herald would even announce a funeral and invite the public to attend. The advent of Christianity changed all this, putting the clergy in an unchallengeable role where death was concerned. It is worth remembering that Constantinople was a city filled with great churches, in the chief of which, the Holy Apostles, the emperor Constantine was laid to rest. With this new ecclesiastical strength, the eastern bishops in particular could take a more relaxed attitude to chariot races, provided they were not held on church feast days. They could be sure, too, that after the abortive attempt of the emperor Julian to revive pre-Christian beliefs in 361–363, there would be no further challenge to their faith. See A. H. M. Jones, *The Later Roman Empire*, Oxford, 1964.

MAGNUS MAXIMUS was proclaimed by the Roman legions stationed in Britain. With them he crossed to the continent and advanced as far as the Alps. The policy of Theodosius was initially peaceful coexistence, but in 387 he responded to Magnus Maximus' invasion of Italy with force. Two defeats ended in the execution of the usurper and his son, Victor.

JUSTINIAN more than any other eastern Roman emperor was responsible for shaping what we call today Byzantium, the Christian Greek civilisation centred on Constantinople which survived through the Middle Ages. For he was an empire-builder, a law-giver, and a commissioner of great buildings such as the Church of the Holy Wisdom. But he was also the author, at Theodora's prompting, of the great slaughter at the end of the Nika riot. In his *Secret History*, Procopius relates how the extravagance of Justinian's schemes undermined the strength of the empire. Within fifty years of his death in 565, all that remained was Asia Minor, Syria, Africa, with scraps of Thrace, Greece and Italy. Nothing of course like the collapse Heraclius later faced with the rise of Islam, but it was a major reduction of territory nevertheless. Procopius is best approached via Averil Cameron's *Procopius and the Sixth Century*, London, 1985. His *Secret History* is translated by G. A. Williamson, Harmondsworth, 1966.

AFTERWORD: MODERN MYTHS

THE TANK was compared with the chariot because of its novelty. The idea was not wholly new: H. G. Wells had anticipated the tank in his short story 'The Land Ironclads', published in 1903. But it was Winston Churchill's enthusiastic support as First Lord of the Admiralty that ensured the British produced the first operational armoured vehicles. The French soon copied the idea, but not the Germans, who were slow to appreciate the future role that a tank would perform. At Cambrai in 1917 the British deployed 300 tanks in a dense formation and broke the German defences. Only a swift counter-attack prevented the British from exploiting the breakthrough. John Glanfield's *The Devil's Chariots. The Birth and Secret Battles of the First Tanks*, Thrupp, 2001, places the new weapon's development in context. He charts with skill the political, military and technological difficulties which had to be surmounted in the formation of the first armoured corps. In Keith Douglas' memoir, *Alamein to Zem Zem*, London, 1947, we encounter at first hand the experience of tank crews.

Of the British success at Cambrai Major-General Heinz Guderian wrote in *Achtung-Panzer!*, published in Germany shortly before the Second World War, how 'as a weapon the tanks had fulfilled their missions magnificently'. But he pointed out 'that the defence of Flesquières shows that infantry are perfectly capable of holding a great variety of locations against armoured attack, provided that those places are properly evaluated and exploited; conversely unsupported armour cannot always be guaranteed to wipe out defending infantry'. German infantrymen were able to hold out because of the protection afforded by the solidly built houses in the village of Flesquières: they also used their deep cellars. In a similar way, chariots would have been unable to disperse foot soldiers stationed behind natural or artificial defences. When Guderian adds that 'it is no good sending armour into an attack over ground where it can have no hope of making progress', he could well have been referring to the problems faced by ancient charioteers, when confronted by large stones or mud.

List of Illustrations

Most of the illustrations have been based on images that date from the era of the chariot. Where ancient ones could not be found, however, care has been taken to draw diagrams as true to the original vehicle, armour or weapon as possible. The age and provenance of each illustration are provided as far as details allow.

the gods. The famous earthskater Poseidon unyoked his horses, put his chariot on its stand and covered it with a cloth.'

Index